Paul Daley is a Canberra author, columnist and multi-award-winning journalist. He has worked extensively overseas—including in conflict zones—and has covered national affairs for major Australian publications including *The Age*, *The Sunday Age* and *The Bulletin*. He is the author, most recently, of *Armageddon: Two men on an Anzac trail*. He is married to political journalist Lenore Taylor and they have three children. He is now writing a novel.

BEERSHEBA

A JOURNEY THROUGH AUSTRALIA'S FORGOTTEN WAR

PAUL DALEY

VICTORY BOOKS

Imperial to metric conversions

1 inch .... 2.54 centimetres   1 mile ....1.6 kilometres
1 foot .... 30.5 centimetres   1 gallon .... 4.5 litres
1 yard................. 0.9 metre   32°F (Farenheit).....0°C (Celcius)

VICTORY BOOKS
An imprint of Melbourne University Publishing Limited
187 Grattan Street, Carlton, Victoria 3053, Australia
mup-info@unimelb.edu.au
www.mup.com.au

First published 2009
Reprinted 2009 (twice), 2010
This edition published 2011
Text © Paul Daley, 2011
Design and typography © Melbourne University Publishing Limited, 2011

Designed by Phil Campbell
Typeset by TypeSkill
Printed by Griffin Press, South Australia

National Library of Australia Cataloguing-in-Publication entry:
Daley, Paul.

Beersheba: a journey through Australia's forgotten war /
Paul Daley.

9780522857962 (pbk.)

Includes index.
Bibliography.

Australia. Army. Light Horse Regiment, 4th.
World War, 1914–1918—Campaigns—Middle East.
World War, 1914–1918—Campaigns—Palestine.
World War, 1914–1918—Cavalry operations, Australian.
Beersheba (Israel) —History, Military.

940.41294

FSC
www.fsc.org
MIX
Paper from
responsible sources
FSC® C009448

Cover photographs
Front: Trooper Jim Gallagher of the 1st Light Horse Regiment at Khalasa two days before the movement on Beersheba. (State Library of Victoria)
Back: Australian troops feeding and tending to their horses in Palestine, 1917–18. (Ernest Pauls)

Frontispiece
Susan McMinn, *Night Duty*, encaustic, charcoal and pastel on hardboard, 19 × 25 cm, 2008.

For Eugenia, Joseph and Claudia

FOREWORD

Beersheba shimmers at the far reaches of the Australian consciousness; a mirage in the desert.

The world's last great charge of the light horse was witnessed by no war correspondent and thus did not wedge itself into the national mythology like Gallipoli or the Somme. It is curious, for the events that led to Beersheba and beyond constitute a truly thrilling story of almost unimaginable resilience and derring-do: a long, travelling series of victories quite unlike the nine-month hopelessness of the Gallipoli campaign or the bogged-down horror of the Western Front. How many Australians know now that their home-grown Sir Harry Chauvel led through the Holy Lands the world's greatest mounted column since Alexander the Great?

Paul Daley has granted this old story new life and contemporary significance. Taking the trouble to walk in the steps of the Australian light horse, the desert sand sucking at his boots just as it swallowed the hooves of the Walers and the Middle Eastern sun teaching him the lessons of thirst that tormented the men of the saddle and dominated every strategy of the mounted military, Daley has blended the past with the present to build a powerful narrative.

He has pored through letters penned by exhausted hands, revived the gripping words of the warrior-bard of the light horse Ion Idriess, rediscovered forgotten interviews by those who were there and woven the history into conversations with the living who remain obsessed with what happened at Beersheba and the desert campaign that led to that climactic event. He finds Christians who see the hand of God in the struggle of the horsemen and listens in on those who believe modern Israel can trace its beginnings to the advance of laconic antipodean bushmen and those who deny any such thing. And he stands at the graves of young men who never made it out of the desert, reconstructs their parts in the legend and reminds us of the anguish of their mothers.

Daley also finds, quite against his wishes, a terrible secret. A forgotten Bedouin village; men from another world turned savage by years of blood and hardship; a mad and bad explosion of retribution. Here Daley is the journalist intent on peeling away the layers of almost a century of official cover-up. His awkward discovery grants new, gritty dimension to a myth, and explains why many men of the light horse were denied the formal honours they so deserved.

Here is a full-bodied, human telling of the deeds of the Australian light-horsemen who traversed the wastes of Egypt, Palestine and Syria during World War I and who created a legend that merits much more of our attention than shimmering as a mirage, just beyond the Australian consciousness. It is as much part of the Australian story as Gallipoli, Kokoda or Glenrowan. Paul Daley has granted us the ability to restore Beersheba to its rightful place in our national history.

Tony Wright

CONTENTS

CONTENTS

COMPOSITION OF THE IMPERIAL MOUNTED TROOPS

Desert Column
(Formed in Sinai,
February 1917)
Anzac Mounted Division
- 1st ALH Brigade
- 2nd ALH Brigade
- NZ Mounted Rifles
  Brigade

*Imperial Mounted
Division*
- 3rd ALH Brigade
- 4th ALH Brigade
- 5th (British)
  Yeomanry Brigade
- 6th (British)
  Yeomanry Brigade

Desert Mounted Corps
(The Desert Column
prior to Allenby's
reorganisation, August
1917)

Anzac Mounted Division
- 1st ALH Brigade
- 2nd ALH Brigade
- NZ Mounted Rifles
  Brigade

*Australian Mounted
Division*
(Formerly the Imperial
Mounted Division)
- 3rd ALH Brigade
- 4th ALH Brigade
(In Palestine in 1918,
this Division expanded
to include the 5th ALH
brigade.)

*Imperial Camel Corps
Brigade*
- 1st (Australian)
  Battalion
- 2nd (British)
  Battalion
- 3rd (Australian)
  Battalion
- 4th (Anzac) Battalion

*Yeomanry Mounted
Division (British)*

MAP OF THE CHARGE OF BEERSHEBA

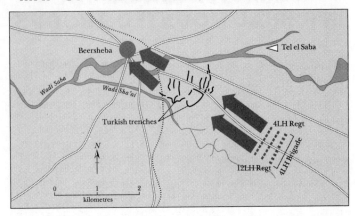

Beersheba

Tel el Saba

Wadi Saba

Wadi Sha'ai

Turkish trenches

4LH Regt

12LH Regt

4LH Brigade

N

0   1   2
kilometres

MAP OF THE LIGHT HORSE BATTLEFIELDS

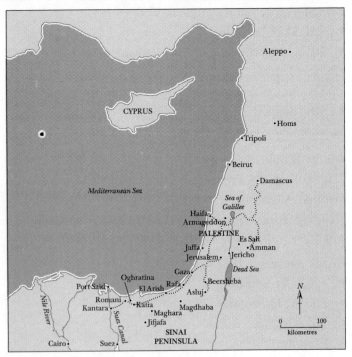

Aleppo

CYPRUS

Homs

Tripoli

Beirut

Damascus

Mediterranean Sea

Sea of
Galilee

Haifa
Armageddon
PALESTINE

Es Salt
Amman

Jaffa
Jerusalem
Jericho

Gaza
Dead Sea

Oghratina
Beersheba

Port Said
El Arish
Rafa

Asluj

Romani
Katia
Magdhaba

Kantara
Maghara

Nile River

Suez Canal

Jifjafa

N

SINAI
PENINSULA

0   100
kilometres

Cairo
Suez

XII

PROLOGUE

Beersheba.

The name meant nothing to me when I first heard it half a lifetime ago. I was working on a suburban newspaper west of Melbourne, and the cranky late middle-aged newsman who was then my editor dispatched me to a nearby town called Bacchus Marsh. A new movie, *The Light Horsemen*, was about to hit the cinemas and, my editor said, 'There's an old bloke in the Marsh who was part of the Charge of Beersheba ... Go and get him to tell you what it was *really* like.'

I had no idea what he was talking about. Horsemen? Charge? Beersheba?

I went to the local library but couldn't find out anything about it. So I rang my father, who told me what little he knew: the Australian troops, mounted on horses, had stormed a Turkish town in Palestine during World War I. It marked the beginning of the end of the Ottoman Empire.

I then used the resources of the *Age*, which owned the little throwaway paper for which I worked, to piece together what had happened. Only then did I visit the old digger in Bacchus Marsh.

~

The Charge of Beersheba happened at 4.30 in the afternoon of 31 October 1917. About eight hundred mostly young men (although a few were well into middle age) of the 4th Australian Light Horse Brigade, furiously waving bayonets that glinted in the dying light, careered across 6 kilometres of open, unprotected ground on the gently sloping plain that led to the Turkish trenches on the outskirts of Beersheba.

Back then Beersheba was little more than a small camel station in what was Turkish-occupied Palestine. Today the modern city that has enveloped Beersheba is Be'er Sheva, in Israel.

The men charged as shells burst around them and bullets whirred by. Blinded by the setting sun and terrible dust from thousands of hooves and a long day of artillery strikes, the Australians swore and cursed as they raced towards the Turks waiting in the trenches before them. Their horses hadn't drunk for at least a day, and they could smell the water in the wells, at least one of which is said to have been dug by Abraham, the ancient Hebrew prophet. The Turkish trenches were the final line of defence for a town that held the key to the rest of the Middle East campaign of World War I: water. Failure meant a long march back and almost certain death for some horses, if not the men. They had to succeed.

After leaping the first line of trenches, some of the horsemen bolted straight into town to try to stop the enemy blowing up the booby-trapped wells and the railway station, to capture the Turkish and German guns and take scores of prisoners. Many others dismounted and literally threw themselves into the redoubts with bayonets in hand. The fighting was vicious and hand-to-hand. Hundreds of Turks, thinking they'd been overrun by devils on horseback, threw down their weapons and surrendered immediately.

But many others fought to the death. Hundreds and hundreds of Turkish soldiers were killed and countless more were injured. Just thirty-one Australians died in the charge itself.

On paper, at least, the charge seemed doomed to failure. Although it is still regarded as one of the last great cavalry charges in history, the Australians who took part were not, in the traditional sense, cavalrymen. They were 'mounted infantry', men who customarily travelled to the battle on horseback before dismounting to fight with rifles and bayonets. And they were a volunteer army of Australian men (and even a few boys) from the bush and the city. They did not carry the cavalryman's sabre. Instead they charged into the Turkish guns, their rifles slung over their backs, in most cases armed with nothing more than bayonets and the colourful obscenities they spat at the enemy from parched mouths.

There had been bitter fighting all around Beersheba—a strategic enemy stronghold in Palestine—all day. Since dawn hundreds of English, Scottish, Welsh, New Zealanders and Australians had died in a series of pitched battles against the resilient Turks. The charge was a last-ditch effort to crush the Turks and break the line of an enemy that the British and imperial forces had pursued for almost two years across Egypt's Sinai and Palestine's Negev deserts.

Guided through the dusk and the dust by the town's only mosque, its minaret reflecting the last of the dying sun, they made it. Some of the Australians threw themselves into the Turkish trenches and ripped into the terrified enemy with their bayonets. Others, carried away by frenzied, uncontrollable horses that could smell nothing but the water, roared straight up the main street, past the mosque and directly to the wells. There is, perhaps, no more salient military metaphor than Beersheba when it comes to Australian doggedness, perseverance and courage in the face of adversity.

It was also the turning point in the British campaign against the Turks. The Armistice took effect a year later to the day, after the Desert Column—the largest force of men and beasts mounted since Alexander the Great traversed the same desert sands—had pushed the Turks to defeat and mass surrender at Damascus and Aleppo in bordering Syria to end four hundred years of Ottoman rule in Palestine.

~

As it transpired, the old veteran I was sent to interview in Bacchus Marsh, Lionel Simpson, had fought at both Gallipoli and Beersheba.

Then 98 years old, Simpson gave me a candid account of what happened when his regiment was first deployed to Gallipoli in May 1915, before returning to Egypt to take on the Turks in Sinai and in Palestine. At Gallipoli Simpson participated in one of the most tragic and ill-conceived movements of the Dardanelles campaign: the Battle of the Nek on 7 August 1915.

This harrowing event was vividly portrayed in Peter Weir's 1981 movie, *Gallipoli*. Young Australian men mostly under British command were ordered to scramble from their trenches at the sound of a whistle and charge on foot, straight into the Turkish machine-guns, across a small patch of open ground barely the size of a tennis court. Some hardly managed to stand before being mowed down. Hundreds of bodies piled up. Other men, like Simpson, managed a few desperate yards before being felled by machine-gun fire.

'I just lay there for a moment ... Everybody around me was dead. I knew if I lay there too long they'd finish me off ... there was a lull in firing,' he told me. He hobbled back to his trench, fully expecting a bullet in the back of the head. 'Johnny Turk could see me. He had his sights on me but for some reason, he spared me.'

A little over two years later, Simpson's regiment fought in the day-long battle for Beersheba that culminated in the charge.

'We'd been waiting in the desert outside Beersheba for the right moment to charge,' he explained. 'We'd given the horses the last of our water so if we didn't win Beersheba we'd die of thirst. We were sitting ducks because we had to charge ... over open ground to get to the Turks.'

~

Why, I wondered back then, do I know about Gallipoli, with all its horrors that ended ultimately in defeat, and not the victory at Beersheba?

Many years later I determined to find out. I would visit the sites where the light-horsemen fought and died in and around Beersheba and would stop at the very wells where they watered their horses before the long, thirsty night ride to the outskirts of the town. I would pore over the letters and diaries of the horsemen to see whether Beersheba continues to resonate through their bloodlines. I would also meet Australian and Israeli Jews, Arabs, Christians and historians for whom Beersheba all held a special—although, in all cases, different—significance. Everyone I met told a similar story: Beersheba should be known in both Australia and Israel as more—much more—than a mere footnote to the Gallipoli-centric Anzac story.

Most had a view about why Australians had become more familiar with Gallipoli than Beersheba. Some said it was simply a matter of historical chronology, because the Egypt and Palestine campaign, and the Charge of Beersheba, came two years after Gallipoli. Others said it was because Beersheba was overshadowed by the horror and unthinkable human carnage at Gallipoli and the Western Front. Still others suggested it was because, unlike Gallipoli and the Western Front, the Middle East was not covered by an official correspondent-cum-historian; Gallipoli and the Western Front had CEW Bean and Keith Murdoch. But only at the war's end did Palestine have the official historian and former newspaper correspondent, Henry Gullett.

Nearly everyone with a view will also tell you that the actions of the Australian light horse across Egypt and Palestine from early 1915 until the end of 1918 received scant coverage back home because the British largely claimed credit for them in official dispatches. And it is true: the British troops, especially the English officers, were disproportionately rewarded with medals and citations while the actions of the Australians were left comparatively unacknowledged. But this view doesn't explain why the government and the then Australian Prime Minister Billy Hughes didn't push Great Britain for a greater official recognition of the light horse's actions, and for a re-evaluation of the medals and citations awarded to them.

~

The ninetieth anniversary of the Charge of Beersheba could not have been worse timed when it came to winning Australian media attention and captivating public imagination as the Gallipoli landings have done. It fell on 31 October 2007 in the middle of a momentous political battle that would oust, after eleven and a half years, John Howard—a 'khaki' prime minister if ever there was one. Howard was never more comfortable than when promoting the Anzac legend, especially Gallipoli and the Western Front, where both his father and his grandfather had fought, and cementing its ties to the Australian character.

There was a well-attended Beersheba ceremony in Canberra in 2007 when the Reserve Forces Day Council commemorated the battle with a parade featuring ninety horses and the standards flown by the fifteen light horse regiments that participated in World War I. Unlike Anzac Day, which was first commemorated in 1916, the anniversary of Beersheba has been an official day of commemoration only since 1992, an acknowledgement won only after a concerted lobbying effort by descendants of the light-horsemen.

In October 2007 the main commemoration happened right in Beersheba—Be'er Sheva—itself when about eighty riders, including descendants of the original horsemen, re-enacted the charge. Thousands of Be'er Sheva's residents watched and cheered. Splendid photographs and footage of the riders, dressed in original regalia—down to the light-horsemen's distinctive slouch hat with emu plume—graced front pages and headlined television news across the Middle East and Europe. But in the middle of such an extraordinary election campaign, it was largely an inside-page story in Australia where it should have mattered most.

Despite the emotional resonance for those involved in the re-enactment, public acknowledgement paled in comparison to the ninetieth anniversary, in 2005, of the Gallipoli landings. Howard attended the dawn ceremony along with thousands of other Australians, in Gallipoli.

Again in 2008, record crowds of Australians descended on Turkey for the commemoration service.

The *Australian* newspaper summed up the significance of the ninetieth anniversary of the Beersheba charge thus:

> Ninety years ago ... the Australian Light Horse Brigade charged into history, glory and, sadly for most Australians, into oblivion. Virtually every Australian knows about our heroic defeat by the Turks at Gallipoli but few are aware of the sunset charge by 800 Anzacs, mounted on horses, that defeated 4000 Turks, captured Beersheba and led to the liberation of Jerusalem and the fall of the Ottoman Empire.
>
> Without knowledge of our history it is impossible for Australians to celebrate our achievements or have a sense of our contributions to shaping the modern world ... Australian casualties were low at Beersheba ... but the strategic significance of the battle was great.[1]

~

Twenty-one years after I met Lionel Simpson I went to see Chanan Reich, an Israeli academic who specialises in relations between his country and Australia.

He opens the door to his neat, early twentieth-century rented bungalow in benign Australian suburbia, while a blue heeler growls and prowls in the dusty out-reaches of the yard—an archetypically Aussie dog look-ing out for its Israeli owner. Reich, a solid man with a great shock of white hair, stoops in the doorway. Each hand extends across his upper body, clinging to its oppo-site bicep in an acknowledgement of—or a futile attempt to ward off—the early autumn chill.

'Come in, come in, welcome,' says Reich, looking me over. 'What is troubling you today?'

We've never met. I wonder if my sadness is really that palpable.

It has been a terrible month. My father died and, just a few weeks earlier, the corporate buccaneers of private equity erased my job in the process of killing off the *Bulletin*, the 128-year-old cultural institution for which I wrote. My life has suddenly lost much of its customary ballast.

We talk for a while about Beersheba, then he asks me, 'Do you know about the massacre by the Australians?'

With that question, Reich set my story on a differ-ent course.

~

I had originally embarked on an odyssey to discover more about the Australian men who took part in the last great cavalry charge and the battles in and around Beersheba.

I wanted to know who they were and where they came from, who commanded them and, not least, what they felt about their achievements at Beersheba. I wanted to know about their commanders and what their fellow Australians—and, indeed, their British masters—thought about their actions. I went looking for the Beersheba that was the setting for an amazing Australian military action. Along the way I'd be diverted by stories about another town that once stood in Palestine. Its name is Surafend and, while it no longer stands, it is linked to Beersheba by the men of the Australian light horse—soldiers who, in many ways due to their resilience and self-sufficiency in extreme circumstances, could be compared with today's elite Australian special forces troops, the Special Air Service.

Beersheba was the scene of great heroism and daring. Conversely, Surafend was the setting for an act of extreme cowardice and premeditated violence so shameful that it sits starkly—almost irreconcilably—at odds with the incredible achievements and, just as importantly, the myth and the legend, of the Australian light horse.

I

TOWARDS BEERSHEBA

1

HEBRON ROAD

It is the beginning of Passover. For weeks Jewish friends and acquaintances have been warning me that this is probably the worst time to travel within Israel. There would be no public transport, they warned, car-hire companies would be closed and only Arab taxis would be on the roads.

But accommodation arrangements have all been made. Owing to the influx of foreign Jews for Passover, all hotel rooms—even in Arab East Jerusalem—are booked. But a room awaits me at Be'er Sheva's main hotel. There is, however, a problem—it's 80 kilometres away from where I'm staying in Jerusalem.

For the past week 'Rasheed', a middle-aged, portly Palestinian with a permanent five o'clock shadow and a beautiful late-model European car, has been driving me mad as he drove me about Jerusalem. In a former life

Rasheed was probably a poker-player or a medicine man, such are his powers of persuasion and his capacity for empathy. I've tried hard to fight the urge to laugh while in his company, for laughter only encourages his jokes and proselytising about domestic violence, Jews, Christians and Muslims, the Palestinian leadership, George Bush and Tony Blair. But I just can't help laughing. I have been living in a cloud of post-bereavement melancholy and anxiety about my new post-*Bulletin* life. I haven't laughed properly for a long, long time. And I find this guy side-splittingly funny, with his politically incorrect quips and risqué jokes about Israeli public figures and Iraqis and Afghanis as we wind our way through the Old City or crawl along the main street of the German Colony in peak hour.

The first time he drives me out of Jerusalem to the town of Ramleh, where we visit a Commonwealth war cemetery containing many Australian graves from World War I, a small satellite navigation unit on the dashboard calls out directions in a weirdly disconcerting Israeli–American hybrid voice. Every second sentence warns the driver: '*Caution, Caution—Danger.*'

I haven't seen (or, at any rate, noticed) one of these things before. 'What do they call it?' I ask.

'They call this a fucking annoying machine,' he says. Then, in a single swoop of an arm, he tears the unit from the dash and throws it, wires dangling from the back, into the rear seat. He shrieks raucously.

But Rasheed's jokes come at a price. I know that he is a merciless carpetbagger who has seen me coming from miles away. Each fare costs a good few shekels more than a standard taxi. Not that you'd ever talk shekels with Rasheed. For him it's strictly greenbacks, more of which I am, by week's end, determinedly reluctant to provide him with—jokes or no jokes. In the end I have no choice.

'Can you take me to Be'er Sheva?'

'Yes, Mr Paul. Right away.'

'How much?'

'One million dollars. American.' Hysterical laughter.

'How much?'

'Seriously, Mr Paul, I can do it almost for free because you are my friend and I love you so very, very much … two hundred American dollars.'

'One fifty.'

'Okay, Mr Paul—last offer. Two fifty.'

'Hang on, Rasheed, we're going backwards here …'

And so it goes, all punctuated by his cackles.

~

The blistering day renders the road before us a hazy black blur. Imaginary pools of water appear, from nowhere, on the bitumen out front, then vaporise in a shimmering haze as the limo screams towards them.

We are heading out of Jerusalem towards the Negev, tracing on our left the huge concrete and wire security fence that divides the Arab West Bank from the predominantly Jewish east. The fence has made life a nightmare for ordinary Palestinians who live—and are now virtually imprisoned—behind it, for they now require permits to move through the checkpoints. But most of Israel's Jews have welcomed the fence because of the undeniably positive influence it has had on security. Suicide bombings, common after the second intifada, have become rare since the fence went up.

'Mr Paul, why are you going to Be'er Sheva? There is nothing to look at in Be'er Sheva besides sand. Do you like the desert, Mr Paul?'

I explain the Australian connection: the Charge of Beersheba coincided with the Balfour Declaration by the British War Cabinet to support the establishment of a Jewish state in Palestine. I tell Rasheed that the Australian involvement in the operation to oust the Turks from Palestine—and especially the fall of Beersheba—helped pave the way for the establishment of Israel in 1948.

It seems to be the first he has heard of Australia's involvement in the Palestine conflict of World War I, the military machination that so coincidentally or— depending who you listen to—fatefully, aligned with Balfour. And he's not a bit impressed. Like most Palestinians and Jews, Rasheed has firm views on the politics and history of his land and has his own particular take on it all.

'So, Mr Paul, you are telling me that Australia helped to establish Israel? And you think this is a *good* thing?'

I don't want to talk politics with Rasheed or any other Palestinian, just as I do not want to talk politics with any Israeli Jew. For someone like me who's spent every day of the past fifteen years talking and writing about politics, it feels like a cop-out. But I am determined to focus only on past events in and around Beersheba; I do not want to talk about the many wrongs, on both sides, of the Israel–Palestine conflict. But Rasheed is determined too. And it doesn't take long for me to realise that he is anything but an island; throughout Israel and the Palestinian territories, the past constantly collides with the present and, perhaps more than anywhere else in the world, goes on to determine the future.

The Charge of Beersheba was the most critical act—even, perhaps, the turning point—in a long military campaign that ended more than four hundred years of Turkish rule in what was then Palestine. Success at Beersheba was also, arguably, a critical step in the re-establishment of the Jewish state of Israel sixty years ago. As fate or (again, depending which stakeholder in this story gets to you first) divine providence, would have it, the charge occurred on the very day the War Cabinet formulated the Balfour Declaration. This document formalised and foreshadowed Britain's intent to oust the Turks from Palestine and restore the Jewish homeland there.

Although the War Cabinet must have known that its declaration would roughly coincide with the fight for Beersheba, it could not have known the battle would culminate in the dramatic charge by the 4th Australian Light Horse Brigade. That would have been a coincidence. Nevertheless it could be argued, as many do, that Australian and, consequently, British, success at Beersheba played some part in the birth of the state of modern Israel in 1948.

I say: 'I'm not saying it's a good thing or a bad thing—it's just a thing. It just is … it's just a fact.'

Suddenly he is silent at the wheel. Then I realise that we are driving through Hebron, a West Bank city that is home to 160,000 Palestinians. A small number of Jews have also sought to make Hebron home. These so-called settlers are among the most provocative in the West Bank because their existence—on the very edge of security and, depending who you believe, the law—is hugely disruptive for ordinary Palestinians. Almost anywhere the settlers build, the Israeli security apparatus follows. And so, to protect the Jewish settlers of Hebron, there's an elaborate network of Israeli-only roads, guard posts and check-points. In some cases the Israeli roads dissect Palestinian lanes and thoroughfares. In other cases the Israeli security fences literally cut some big properties in half, preventing Palestinian farmers from entering parts of their land or walking into neighbouring fields.

He has driven me this way for a reason. He wants a conversation about Israel's defence policies and the wall, about suicide bombings and settlers. But I will not be baited.

'So, Mr Paul, what do you think?' he asks.

'What do you mean?' I say.

'You see what the Israeli roads do to the Palestinians? They are making life unbearable for them. They are deliberately trying to drive them crazy.'

'Maybe so,' I say.

'Mr Paul, the problem is not the Israelis. The problem is not the Palestinians. No—the problem is the Palestinian and the Israeli politicians—all of them,' he says. Politics. Always politics.

On the outskirts of Hebron, market gardens have been laboriously chipped out of the rocky, rich black soil. There are cucumbers and tomatoes, capsicums and chillies. As we head further into the desert, grape vines, pregnant with purple fruit, cling improbably to the rocky earth.

I open my window. But a blast of scalding air prompts me to shut it again immediately. The further we head towards Be'er Sheva, the hotter it gets. The thermometer on the instrument panel now reads 38°C. I stare straight ahead through the windscreen. Israeli settlements, comprising—in stark contrast to the white concrete and flat-roofed Palestinian homes—modern brick and timber houses that wouldn't look out of place in western Melbourne or Sydney, punctuate what has become a flat sandy, scrubby landscape. The horizon is now a washed-out hazy grey-green blur, courtesy of the blazing sun and a hot wind laden with fine dusty sand.

Of the drive from Jerusalem to Beersheba, Australia's official war historian Henry Gullett wrote: 'and the mountain road would be followed down through Hebron, where the patriarchs are buried, and where the fanatical Moslem natives have fortunately kept the tourist at bay and so have remained relatively independent and uncorrupted. The brief journey would be completed at the bare, straggling little modern town of Beersheba.'[1]

We are following the Hebron road. Ninety-one years ago it was the intended escape route for Ottoman troops fleeing the combined British Empire forces, including the Australian light horse, during the invasion of Beersheba. Imperial forces skirmished with the retreating Turkish units earlier on the day of the charge, when they blocked their retreat towards Hebron. Today it remains the main route from Beersheba to Jerusalem via Hebron. It is marked, in parts, with Israeli flags. Some Palestinian roads have effectively been blockaded with massive stone bollards at the points at which they intersect with the highway. Some of the Israeli roads leading to the settlements are, conversely, lined with tall cyclone-wire fences, their entries marked with military guard towers.

There's a flock of scrawny sheep. The shepherd, dressed in flowing white robes and checked headscarf, guides them. He holds a staff in one hand. The other hand hides in its opposite sleeve. This is a picture straight from my primary-school Bible.

'Bedouin,' says Rasheed contemptuously. 'They are everywhere. Bedouin are a menace here—everyone hates the Bedouin.'

We drive in silence. Kilometre after kilometre of desert is punctuated by little but rock and saltbush. Then, as we approach Be'er Sheva, orange orchards, courtesy of elaborate Israeli irrigation, and rows of prickly pear, break the skyline. Summer has come early. There's not a blade of grass. Suddenly there's a set of traffic lights and a McDonald's, a hardware barn and a farm equipment showroom. A pall of dust hangs in the air. The thermometer says 40°C. There's little traffic on this first Sunday of Passover. Jewish families are at home inside, celebrating the festival together. It's as quiet as the main street of Mudgee on Christmas Day.

'How many days do you live in Beersheba?' Rasheed asks.

A week or maybe two, I tell him. Perhaps longer.

'Two weeks! Mr Paul, two weeks is too long in Beersheba.'

'Really?'

'Tell me, Mr Paul, do you like Russian Jews?'

'I don't know.'

'After one day I will ring you up and ask you.'

Be'er Sheva, known in Israel as the 'desert capital', has a large population of Russian and Ethiopian Jews. But it is also home to thousands of Bedouin, some of whom live in purpose-built housing estates and others in camps of corrugated iron, plastic sheeting and canvas—some of which have been in the same place for a hundred or more years—that line the road into Beersheba, way beyond the town's semi-industrial fringes. I'm reminded of ramshackle Aboriginal camps, clinging to the edges of rural centres back home, that I've seen over the years.

There are really three towns. The first is Abraham's ancient village of Tel el Saba, today an archaeological mound on the outskirts of Be'er Sheva, which from 1948 became an Israeli town that consumed the Turkish town of Beersheba. Beersheba, meanwhile, was established by the Turkish army at the turn of the twentieth century.

We arrive at the hotel. Rasheed counts the number of big red stars above the entrance. He roars laughing.

'It says it has five stars, Mr Paul. I don't think so.' *Cackle, cackle.*

'We'll see,' I say. 'It looks fine.'

'And *I* will see *you* tomorrow, Mr Paul … Call me and I come straightaway and take you back to Jerusalem.'

~

The hotel is bustling with Jewish families getting together for Passover. I feel like the only gentile in town. I probably am. The kids are running wild. A soccer game is being played outside my room, on the carpeted hallway into which dozens of matzo crackers have been ground.

It's getting dark. I stand in front of my fifth-floor south-facing window and stare into the inky haze of dust and smoke from the Bedouin fires. Be'er Sheva is in the middle of a natural saucer that slopes gently up to a rim of barely discernible hills, a series of little lumps and bumps in this falling darkness. One of those highpoints became known in 1917 as 'Chauvel's Hill', the natural vantage point from which Australia's Lieutenant General Harry Chauvel directed thousands of imperial troops, including the Australian Light Horse, in the battle for Beersheba. Chauvel's Hill is there before me in the semi-darkness above the rooftops of multistorey apartment blocks and shopping malls.

From here Chauvel, in a hasty and tense meeting with his various commanders late in the afternoon of 31 October 1917, uttered the words that have become famous in military folklore: 'Put Grant straight at it.' This was the order for Victorian-born Brigadier General William Grant, commander of the 4th Light Horse Brigade, to lead his men in the charge on the Turkish trenches. From where I stand at the window there's an almost perfect view of the gently sloping plain over which the Australians galloped into the Turkish guns at precisely this time of day more than ninety years ago.

~

Trooper Ernest Pauls, a member of the New South Wales–raised 12th Light Horse Regiment, together with the 4th Regiment, charged across that plain. Born in 1891 near the beautiful New South Wales hinterland town of Dorrigo to a farming family from Germany, just two months before his twenty-fourth birthday Pauls travelled down to Sydney to join up. Barely five months later, he left Australia for Egypt, and from there he was among the many light-horsemen who were deployed to Gallipoli without their horses to serve as regular infantry.

He survived the horrors of Gallipoli and, after a protracted illness, rejoined the 12th Regiment in Egypt in mid-1916. Trooper Pauls was not well educated. But like so many members of the Australian Imperial Force who fought in Europe and the Middle East, he kept a diary in which he recorded his experiences of war in detail and with great emotion: the terrible sickness and the hardships, the battles, the endless search for water, the legion of lost mates and, even more sadly, in his case a brother, too. Pauls was also a keen amateur photographer who was forever training his lens on the machines of war, the horses, the Bedouin, the Turkish prisoners and the stark aftermath of battle. His record of the war, retrieved from a box in the garden shed after his death in 1967, is enormously moving.

Like so many, Ernest Pauls returned to Australia after the war and never travelled again. On his return he was not yet 30 but aged, by experience and by the unspeakable cruelty and inhumanity of war, well beyond his years. He married, farmed for a while back at Dorrigo, moved to work in a sawmill and, together with his wife and five children, led a modest life into old age that revolved around hard work and family. He liked to help out in the local Catholic parish, and he always marched on Anzac Day. He never spoke about the war. Never, except perhaps with his mates at the RSL.

Did they, I wonder, ever contemplate the part they played in the Charge of Beersheba? Did they ever toss around their experiences about the frenzied horses, the shells exploding overhead, the Turkish shrapnel buzzing about their ears and the vicious, elemental bayonet fights in those first Turkish trenches? Or did the excitement of it all, even among mates who'd experienced the same thing, ultimately succumb to melancholy thoughts about the horsemen who didn't grow old with them?

~

Until the war, Ottoman-occupied Palestine—within whose borders sixty-year-old Israel sits—and Egypt to the south, together with the lands to the north that harbour today's modern states of Lebanon, Jordan and Syria, were not generally part of Australia's collective consciousness. Not, at any rate, in any immediate geopolitical sense. Most Australians who'd heard of them would have done so through the Bible, with its stories of Moses and the Holy Land, the Hebrews and Abraham, the Holy City of Jerusalem, Bethlehem and, of course, Jesus King of the Jews. It was not just a world away but also another world.

Almost fourteen years after Federation, Australia's population was just five million. Yet, despite the absence of conscription for all but home service militias and a bitter, divisive community and political debate about the merits of contributing young lives to the service of the British Empire, 416,809 men enlisted for service with the Australian Imperial Force. Almost 332,000 of them saw service in Gallipoli, the Western Front or the Middle East.

Those who saw active service included about twenty thousand Australian light-horsemen drawn from fifteen regiments, most raised from specific areas of each state. Other regiments were the direct descendants of colonial and citizen-soldier militias, some of which fought in the Boer War from 1899 to 1902. They were young men from a new country, who, in the opening chapters of their lives, took part in a war that included one of history's most extraordinary military manoeuvres. Certainly some of the men, including Ernest Pauls, who participated in the charge, were fully aware that they had just ridden into history. Others, however—perhaps inured to the nature of their achievement by the long series of bloody battles against the Turks that preceded the charge, and all that would follow—didn't see anything remotely extraordinary about Beersheba.

They came home from the war and resumed work as barmen, as suburban solicitors, as teachers and book-keepers, as dairy farmers and grocery store owners, as wool classers, horse breakers, shearers and doctors. They had children and grandchildren. Most spoke little of their experiences. But they marched, like Ernest Pauls, on Anzac Day with mates who understood. They retired. They raked the leaves, and they went to bowls. Some of those fortunate enough to die as civilians, not soldiers, wept alone and cried out in the night during their final years, at the thought of it all.

The photographs of men of the light horse tell much of their story. Some have crooked teeth and imperfect features. Some are tall, some are short and some are fat. Some have unruly mops of black hair, and some are balding. Some have movie star looks. Women wouldn't notice others in the street. They are ubiquitous Australian men. It was their achievements at Beersheba, in the battles leading to it and beyond, that encapsulate the capacity of ordinary people to do extraordinary things in extreme circumstances. And no circumstance is more extreme than war.

~

As the children scream and cheer while their soccer game continues outside my hotel door, I go to the window again.

It's hard to equate the wild ride of the light horse across the gently sloping plain that led to what was then a dusty, unwelcoming camel-trading town with the neon-lit urban vista that fills my window tonight. Besides Chauvel's Hill, I can see nothing of the town that was taken from the Turks by the charge. Be'er Sheva has swallowed Beersheba. But I am wrong. So much has changed. But so much has not.

2

BUSHMEN OF THE EMPIRE

Australia's mounted soldiers were known by British officers as the 'Imperial Bushmen' in the Boer War, in which many of them served with distinction. In some ways they would always be known to the Brits as the wild colonial men from the bush.

In the Boer War the bushmen operated, for the most part, with a deep contempt for British discipline and military mores, especially relating to uniform. In stark contrast with British cavalrymen, with their fine uniforms and sabres, and their lucrative commissions, the bushmen were a direct product of the land—men who, out of necessity, could ride and shoot, stalk and hunt and live off their natural surroundings.

Horsemanship was second nature. An intimate affinity with the immediate environment—that is, an ability to contemplate its contour and its terrain, to anticipate its weather, to seek out its shelter and water, and a capacity to live independently off its resources—distinguished the Australian soldier from his English ally. The Australian was fiercely independent. Yet he could work cooperatively in the troop, the squadron or the regiment.

Often only a bandolier, a military-issue rifle and his sturdy horse would distinguish the Australian mounted soldier from the Boer mounted guerrilla whom the colonial had crossed the ocean to take on. Before long the Australian mounted rifleman won a formidable reputation with the Boer, who regarded him as more than a worthy adversary and, yes, a notable 'bushman', too. British officers also rated the rag-tag Australians highly and continued, for the duration of the Boer War, to request more and more mounted men from the colonies.

Although a few of the earliest Australian soldiers came from the cities, the mounted soldiers of Australia's colonial militias were mostly drawn from the land. They were the sons of immigrants or were immigrants themselves. Some were descended from convict stock. Others had fled what they saw as the tyranny of British rule in Ireland—only to fight, somewhat ironically, under the British in Africa and again, after the declaration of war against Germany, in the Middle East and Europe. Some had already been in the British Army and, having come to Australia for the opportunity (and adventures) offered by the colonies, joined up promptly when Australia answered the call to send troops to South Africa.

The reputations of the great Australian military men of the Middle East operations in World War I— among them such names as Chauvel and Ryrie, Royston and Maygar—were forged in Africa. Chauvel, of course, would go on to play a seminal role in the war against the Turks in Palestine when, as General Harry Chauvel—knighted on the battlefield—he became commander of the largest force of men and animals to traverse the Holy Land since Alexander the Great. The others would, during the Great War, enhance their reputations as heroic and inspirational leaders of men, as fearless and at times almost super-human, if not completely foolhardy, mounted soldiers.

As a young soldier Edmund Allenby—who, as a knighted general himself, would later command the imperial war effort in Egypt and Palestine—was briefly in charge of a squadron of New South Wales Lancers during the Boer War. Allenby, a great disciplinarian, arrived for the first time at the Lancers' camp very late at night, according to the poet and *Bulletin* writer AB 'Banjo' Paterson. Just as Allenby rode in, the deeply tired and emotional men were somewhat flippantly drinking to the health of their new leader. 'I heard you. But that's no excuse for keeping the whole camp awake. You tell them to be in bed with all the lights out in five minutes, or I'll have to do something about it,' Allenby snapped at Paterson.[1] That was Allenby's introduction to the Australians.

His parting with the Australians almost twenty years later, after the sorry events at Surafend, would be just as inglorious.

~

The citizen militias and the battles of the Boer War, meanwhile, laid the groundwork for the establishment of the Australian light horse regiments.

In 1909 Australia introduced compulsory military training. The scheme aimed to raise a fighting force capable of defending the newly federated nation. But it was strictly for self-defence; Australia would remain bitterly divided about conscripting its young men to fight overseas under the imperial umbrella. Any troops who fought overseas would, therefore, be volunteers. Compulsory training, however, led to the rapid rise of the light horse throughout the states so that, by the time Britain declared war on Germany in 1914, twenty-three regiments had been formed.[2]

The prime minister of the day, Andrew Fisher, promised England that Australia would contribute—and finally commit—twenty thousand troops to the fight against the Germans and the Turks. That number would include more than two thousand light-horsemen, most of whom would fight in Egypt and Palestine, although some, like Lionel Simpson would go to Gallipoli without their horses, and others would also go to the Western Front.

In August 1914, when Australia followed Britain into World War I, the conflict presented our young soldiers not only with an opportunity to serve their new country. For many it was also, without doubt, an opportunity for adventure and to see distant lands. Recruiting drives at the time certainly emphasised that volunteering would give young men an opportunity to experience the world.

The men who enlisted quite often knew other men in the same regiment; school mates and work friends, brothers and even sons and fathers were in the same units. The bonds of family and friendship were strong. According to Gullett, the Australian volunteers represented the pinnacle of Australian manhood. But even more than that, he depicted them as absolutely exemplary and beaming examples of mankind. While the light horse regiments included men from the cities, most came from the land. Gullett wrote of them in glowing— if not purple—terms:

> They represented every phase of Australia's diverse rural industries: dairymen and small cultivators from the long rich coastal belt between the Dividing Range and the sea; orchardists from the foot-hills; timber-getters from the sparkling forests on the ranges; men from the larger farms of the long wheat-belt, on the inside slope of the mountains; and men whose lives had been spent on sheep and cattle stations of the vast inland plains … Every worn road and grass-grown track carried its eager, excited volunteers, some riding singly, some in twos and threes. Squatters and stockmen

and shearers, farmers and labourers and prospec-
tors, they paced the same road in that spirit of true
democracy, which, as the war went on, became
perhaps the most beautiful and valuable of all the
great qualities that in this war shone out of the
Australian soldier.

... For these men were the very flower of their
race. All were pioneers, or the children of pioneers.[3]

Doubtless few would have viewed themselves quite so.
But the broad point Gullett was making is right: they
were men who, in many ways, represented the backbone
and the future of the new Commonwealth of Australia.
And there is no doubt that, as a volunteer force, the light-
horsemen offered their commanders an enviable wealth
of raw talent.

They were men like Ernest Pauls, a son of German
immigrants to Australia who felt such a connection
with his birthplace that he was willing to enlist in a war
against his parents' former countrymen (he later changed
his middle name from Heinrich to Henry). Pauls' horsemanship was evident throughout his life; his daughter,
Patricia, would later recall to her children her father
stitching up her pony Dinks after it ran through a
barbed-wire fence.

The official historian elaborated:

All were horsemen of various degrees of excel-
lence; not mere riders of educated horses, but men
who had from their school-days undertaken, as a

matter of honour and pride or of necessity, the breaking and backing of bush-bred colts and the riding of any horse that came their way. Their horsemanship came next to, if not sometimes before, their religion.

These young Australians were by their daily occupation expert observers and judges of their country. They possessed a highly trained sense of distance and direction; accustomed to riding the country roads and tracks by night almost as frequently as by day, they were at home in the dark.[4]

~

Lionel Simpson, born in the Victorian high plains town of Corryong—the home also of Paterson's semi-fictitious Man from Snowy River—left his job at the outbreak of war and travelled to Melbourne to join the 8th Light Horse Regiment.

In 1987, aged 96, Simpson told me: 'In those days every bush kid rode a horse and every kid with a horse wanted to join the light-horsemen. But in those days the Army had tough restrictions; they only took the fittest and best riders and horses.'[5]

Most of the light horse recruits were in their twenties. But many were, by the time they returned to their horses in Egypt in early 1916, old before their time. The horrors of protracted trench warfare saw to that.

The warrior-writer, Ion Idriess, who served as a sniper with the Queensland-based 5th Light Horse

Regiment, explained in his book *The Desert Column* how the light horse regiments functioned and fought. In so doing, the importance of absolute trust among small groups of men becomes apparent.

The term 'mateship', as a defining characteristic of Australian performance, especially on the battlefield or the sporting arena, is often so thoughtlessly applied that it undermines the true value of a human commodity that was, quite literally in some circumstances, critical to survival among the light-horsemen. Idriess's take on the importance of mateship to men in the light horse regiments belies the notion that the regiment, the squadron or even the troop were all comprised of mates. True mates, it seems, found each other and sought each other out, by necessity, in small groups. Mateship, then, was not just a by-product of circumstances that forced men to spend time together in the closest of circumstances. They could not possibly all have been friends or acquaintances, let alone mates; many, perhaps, would not even have liked each other. But there can be little doubt that special bonds, based on absolute trust, became almost a prerequisite for survival:

> We are all concentrated in sections. A section is four men. A section lives together, eats together, sleeps together, fights together and when a shell lands on it, dies together. A full troop of men has eight sections. There are four troops to a squadron, three squadrons to a regiment. I'm not going further than the regiment. Our big world is the

regiment and even then most of us don't know intimately the men out of our own squadron. Our life is just concentrated in the section.

We growl together, we swear together, we take one another's blasted horses to water, we conspire against the damned troop sergeant together, we growl against the war and we damn the officers up hill and down dale together; we do everything together—in fact, this whole blasted war is being fought in sections. The fate of all the east at least, depends entirely upon the section.[6]

One of the four men in each section was the 'horse handler'. It was his job, when the light-horsemen dismounted to attack the enemy on foot, to hold the horses and lead them away to a safe position beyond gunfire, then return them to the fighting men when it was time to extract them from the fight.

~

The deprivations and horrors of war have always brought out the best and worst in men. In the case of the Australian light horse in Gallipoli, Egypt and Palestine from 1915 to 1918, the good includes the prolific writings of average soldiers, be it in journals or letters to loved ones back home or in later, more formal, published accounts. From the prosaic (the lousy 'tucker', the extreme weather, the dirt, the lice and the constant dust) to the profoundly psychological (the loss of mates, the constant smell of death and the black, greasy blowflies grown corpulent on human flesh) the light-horsemen, writing from the battlefields, bequeathed a wealth of written material chronicling the impact of war on men.

Idriess enlisted in the Queensland-drawn 5th Light Horse Regiment at the outbreak of war in 1914. He served as a sniper in Gallipoli, Egypt and Palestine, where he witnessed the charge at Beersheba from the hills overlooking the town. He was, it seems, a born adventurer. For after the war Idriess chased gold in New Guinea, shot buffaloes in the Northern Territory and explored Cape York.

Idriess's writing was, however, his greatest gift. It's true that he was no stylist, but there can be no doubting his capacity to tell a story with the 'listen to me' magnetism of a bush poet. He held a journalist's pen and a reporter's eye where trained journalists, like official historian Henry Gullett, were absent. He also had a novelist's sense of drama and timing. There is something of the travelogue in Idriess's writing also, a naive quality laden with observation of people and places—some of it extremely disturbing—to which no value judgment is applied. Perhaps that's not surprising; he, and countless other men who had joined up partly out of a spirit of adventure, considered themselves tourists of sorts as well as soldiers. The spirit of their adventure resonates strongly with the young Australian backpacker pilgrims who retrace their steps across Gallipoli if not yet in great numbers across Israel and Palestine.

Not least, however, Idriess's writing about Gallipoli, Egypt and Palestine was extraordinary because he put himself in the box seat: he chose a life that exposed him to the raw material that invariably made him the envy of both journalists and historians. Put simply, he found the yarns.

By the time of his death, aged 90, in 1979 Idriess had written forty-seven books, including perhaps, his most famous, *The Desert Column*, published in 1931. Based on excerpts from his World War I diaries, the immediacy of Idriess's writing, his utter absence of pretence and his profound honesty, make *The Desert Column* one of the best, professionally published, first-person accounts by an Australian of what it means to be a man at war.

I began the diary as we crowded the decks off Gallipoli and watched the first shells crash into Turkish soil [he writes]. Gradually it grew to be a mania: I would whip out the little book and note, immediately, anything exciting that was happening. As the years dragged on, my haversack became full of little notebooks ...

The diary was a very young soldier's idea. He thought that if he survived shot and shell and sickness, he would like, when he came to be an old man, to be able to read exactly what his feelings were when 'things were happening'. Have a private picture show all his own, as it were, to refresh his memory.[7]

Idriess, wounded at Gallipoli, was evacuated aboard a hospital ship before the British forces, including Australians and New Zealanders, withdrew from the Dardanelles in December 1915. Along with most of the other light horse units that had been dispatched from their base in Egypt, without horses, to fight as infantry at Gallipoli in early 1915, Idriess returned to his unit in Cairo in early 1916.

The unpublished sections of Idriess's diaries, held at the Australian War Memorial, are even less compromising. Much of this material, doubtless, was excluded from *The Desert Column* to save sensibilities, including, perhaps, Chauvel's. For example, in one entry in July 1916, Idriess refers to his mate Stan being in trouble again. 'A cold footed, lying bastard of a corporal is the cause. May he die in the desert,' Idriess writes.[8]

More surprising is his sense of wonder at the sights, sounds, smells and horrors of war: of columns of horses marching on the long night rides while sleeping; water boiled by the desert sun so that it burns' the men's throats as it leaves their canteens; the unmistakable sound of a Turkish bullet striking a horse's stomach; the woeful food and the vermin. And the Bedouin— always the hated and mercenary Bedouin, who raked over the battlefields like hyenas and finished off the injured, dug up and stole from the dead, and spied for the Turks.

~

The Australian light horse were more than their official description as 'mounted infantry' suggested.

For the mounted infantryman the horse is intended to be merely a means of transport to and from the battlefield and not (in the jargon of today's modern military) a 'war fighting platform'. Many of the early colonial regiments in Australia were familiar with the cavalry charge and, indeed, some of the light horse units drilled such tactics in Egypt in 1915 and, intermittently, throughout the war in Palestine.

Beersheba was not the only battle in which the Australian light horse employed a charge rather than dismounting, handing the reins to the horse handler in their section and attacking the enemy on foot. One of the final acts of the light horse in the desert campaign was another daring charge. Emboldened, no doubt, by success at Beersheba, this time they charged in darkness, at Semakh in September 1918.

Those who successfully sought entry to the light horse regiments could apply to take their own animals to war with them. If the animal was deemed young and healthy enough, the authorities purchased it; a strong emotional attachment would remain between man and horse, but the War Office now owned the animal. Most of the light horsemen, however, rode remounts, horses purchased from breeders in Australia.

More than a hundred and sixty thousand Australian horses were sent to the war in Egypt and Palestine, the Western Front and Gallipoli. It is said that only one returned: Sandy, who belonged to Major General Sir

William Bridges, Commander in Chief of the Australian Imperial Force, who died at Gallipoli.

About eleven thousand were sold at the end of the war in Palestine. Perhaps two thousand were destroyed because they were deemed to be too old, while some of the light-horsemen, unable to bear the thought of their horses going to new owners, also shot their animals. Apocryphal stories abound of the light-horsemen being forced by the unsentimental British to shoot all their animals when perhaps two hundred Australians killed their horses out of choice to prevent them being sold. Mobile veterinary units shot about two thousand horses that were deemed too old—that is, over 12 years of age—to sell. There are stories that some men did exaggerate the age of their horses so that the authorities would shoot rather than sell them.

Barry Rodgers, a member of the Australian Light Horse Association and a collaborative organiser of a re-enactment of the Charge of Beersheba in 2007, breeds heritage horses, including some descended from Midnight, an animal that died in the charge.

'Well, basically the horse was your mate,' Barry says. 'When you travel on horse and the horse carries you through very, very difficult circumstances, and when you share a common march into danger with man or beast, it does bring about a relationship that is very significant. There was an old light-horseman who died only about eleven years ago, and right up until the week before he died he was still pining for the horse he'd had to leave behind in the Middle East.'[9]

Most horses were Walers, sturdy stock animals that had long been exported from Australia for use by the British cavalry. In colonial Australia the Hunter Valley became a prime breeding district for stock horses from English and Irish thoroughbred lines. The mounted soldiers of England and India referred to the horses by their origin from New South Wales as simply 'Walers'.

The Waler, although not a specific breed, is defined as having a sturdy, thick body, a vast chest cavity to allow for his great heart and lung capacity, a low-set head at the end of a graceful and strong neck of the type favoured by cavalrymen for the cover it offered from on-coming rifle fire. The Waler was renowned as fast and courageous, and his genesis of draught, coach, pony and riding horse adapted him for arduous work over long distances and a capacity to march on little water.

Gullett noted that the animals of the Australian light horse regiments 'were not uniform. They included every kind of animal; large sturdy ponies, crossbreds from draught Clydesdale mares, three-quarter thoroughbreds, and many qualified for the racing stud-books. As a consequence of such mixed breeding, they frequently offended the horse-lover's eye by their faulty parts.'[10] By 'horse lovers', no doubt, Gullett was referring to English cavalry officers.

The bond between the light-horseman and his mount was absolute. The men fretted over the welfare of their horses, especially when water was scarce. Indeed, on the long rides across the deserts of Egypt and Palestine, the men frequently shared—contrary to orders—their spartan water ration with their horses, which were capable of riding for fifty, sixty or even seventy hours without a drink. On the night rides, meanwhile, the men would sleep in the saddle while their animals followed the path to the next camp or battle. In the blazing sun, the horse provided shade for his master, who could lie on the sand beneath him and sleep.

The light-horsemen set little store by military spit and polish. They often wore individual variations of the Australian uniform, and each regiment had its own distinctive colour patch, worn on the sleeve. The standard uniform included sturdy leather riding boots and leather leggings, riding pants, a khaki shirt customarily rolled up above the elbows and, of course, the distinctive broad-brimmed Digger's hat. When the light-horseman rode, his rifle would be slung across his back, and at least one bandolier filled with ammunition would be curled across his chest.

Most of the light-horsemen in Egypt wore the distinctive emu plume—a patch of emu leather with the flowing feathers still attached—in their hats. The tradition of wearing the emu feathers began with the Queenslanders, whose mounted infantry adopted it as a battle honour after their work in the shearers' strike of 1891.[11]

The men of the Australian light horse might have looked like an unruly rabble on their untidy, solid animals. But they were perfectly suited to the long desert war that they were about to fight.

3

SIDESHOW IN SINAI

In January 1916, when the British general Sir Archibald Murray became commander of what would soon become known as the Egypt Expeditionary Force, the British imperial forces were losing on each front of World War I. The retreat before Christmas 1915 of British forces from Gallipoli released thousands of Turkish troops from what had become an intractable trench warfare stalemate in the hills and dugouts over-looking the Dardanelles.

Turkish forces, commanded by the German colonel Kress von Kressenstein and comprising mainly Arab units from Damascus, first invaded Egypt from its south-ern border with Palestine in early 1915. They crossed the unforgiving Sinai Desert from the Palestine border and attacked the Suez Canal, the waterway that was com-pleted in 1869 in order to link the Mediterranean Sea at

Port Said with the Egyptian city of Suez on the Red Sea. Having already closed the Dardanelles and the Bosphorus to shipping and thereby isolating Russia, the early Turkish move on the Suez Canal represented an unacceptable threat to the world's other most commercially important shipping route.

Before the canal opened, ships travelling from Europe to Asia had either to make the long circumnavigation of Africa or offload their cargo at Port Said so that it could be moved 163 kilometres overland and reloaded onto other vessels for the continuation of the sea voyage at Suez. Britain had moved in to protect the canal during a civil war in Egypt in 1882. The waterway was then declared a neutral territory under official British control under the 1888 Convention of Constantinople.

British, Indian and New Zealand troops easily resisted the first Turkish attack on Suez in 1915, when a few Turks managed to cross the canal on pontoons. But the Turkish attack on the canal preceded the Anzac landing at Gallipoli by just two months. Therefore the British and Anzac invasion created a much more pressing military priority—and a hefty diversion—for the Turks, on the Dardanelles. Ottoman designs on Suez were, temporarily at least, held in abeyance. But with the completion of the Gallipoli retreat on 20 December 1915, the Turks had the resources to refocus on Suez, which they did in early 1916 by advancing across the desert slowly towards the canal and in the general direction of Kantara, at the Mediterranean end of the great waterway.

Their advance began the best part of a three-year campaign by the British imperial forces, including at almost every critical point the Australian light horse, to push the Turks on a massive northern retreat across the Sinai, back through Palestine, up the Jordan Valley and finally through to defeat at Damascus in Syria on 30 October 1918. As it transpired, the only troops to fight in every major action from Romani to Damascus were the 1st, 2nd and 3rd Australian Light Horse Brigades.[1] Exactly a year before the Armistice took effect, the Australian light horse played a critical role in the turning point of the Palestine campaign: the capture of Beersheba.

Water was the key to success in the Sinai. If an army was sufficiently disciplined to march through the stifling desert with very limited water rations, it could be assured of reaching a series of oases (in use since ancient times) that harboured springs or barely concealed bores. The coastal route, stretching from El Arish, just over the Egyptian border with Palestine, to Romani and Katia along the Mediterranean flank of Egypt, had always been the preferred route of invaders. From El Arish an army would have to trek about eighty kilometres without water, until it reached the legendary oasis of Katia, with its palm hods and springs extending many kilometres to the southern inland desert.

> Armies advancing upon Egypt have always been
> under the necessity of seizing the Katia wells as a
> preliminary to the final stage of their invasion

[Henry Gullett wrote]. This northern route was followed from east to west by Alexander [the Great] in his swoop on Egypt, by Napoleon from west to east more than two thousand years later, and by most of the intervening conquerors who marched from the East upon Egypt, or, as fortune varied, from Egypt towards Syria and the Valley of the Euphrates.[2]

If the enemy could make Katia, there was every chance he could make Suez. This seemed to be the plan of the Turks—or, at least, the Germans formulating the Turkish war plan—who, by January 1916, were observed by British intelligence to have mustered twenty-five thousand troops across the Sinai. By June about twenty thousand of those troops had marched to within 25 kilometres of the Suez Canal.

Despite an obvious urgent need to confront the Turks in Egypt, most accounts strongly suggest that the British High Command considered the Sinai operation to be something of a sideshow to the Western Front, where tens of thousands of British and Anzacs were being killed and maimed in horrific battles by a resilient and resurgent German army. By all accounts Murray was privately angry that his forces were under-resourced, despite the fact that he generously volunteered to send more and more men—including the light-horsemen—to Europe, almost as soon as the call came for reinforcements.

Murray began his desert campaign with twenty divisions of regular infantry and mounted infantry. But almost as soon as he assumed command, ten of his divisions were abruptly shifted, with no serious objection from himself, to the Western Front. The light-horsemen volunteered in droves to be transferred to the 'real war' in Europe, leaving Murray's regimental ranks depleted and reliant on new recruits—novices with little training and no war experience. Indeed, Murray was left with four poorly trained British territorial infantry divisions and six divisions of thoroughly inexperienced, although overly eager, British yeomanry, as well as the more tried, mounted Anzacs comprising Australian light horse regiments and New Zealand mounted rifles.

Despite his badly diminished forces and an erratic chain of supply of munitions and food, Murray brazenly decided he would meet the Turkish threat not by resistance but by confrontation. He resolved that rather than wait for the Turks, buoyed after their victory at Gallipoli, to attack his men, he would take the fight straight to them. It was a courageous and commendable—if not, at times, overly ambitious—plan that would ultimately prove successful against enormous odds. But owing to a string of command failures, a general contempt for his detached, aloof leadership in the ranks (not least among the Australians) and communication blunders that stole what should have been two decisive victories at the ancient fort city of Gaza, Murray would never see the plan out.

~

In April 1916 the Australian light horse had its first major clash with Turkish forces in the Sinai. British airmen had spotted a small group of Turkish infantry and engineers searching for water by sinking bores in central Sinai near Jifjafa, in preparation for their march on to Katia. Jifjafa was a tiny settlement that was being transformed into a Turkish outpost in the central Sinai about eighty kilometres from the Suez Canal.

A squadron of about ninety mounted infantry from the 9th Light Horse Regiment, comprising South Australians and Victorians, was dispatched from its base at the canal defences to capture Jifjafa and destroy the Turkish waterworks. The logistics of this small operation would stand as a signal lesson to Murray and his commanders: of the onerous weight of waging war with men and horses in the desert. Only ninety mounted infantrymen were involved. But they were supported by thirty-two officers, engineers from Britain and Australia, men from the medical corps as well as local guides. In the end it took a column of 320 officers and men, 175 horses and 261 camels to defeat a small force of Turkish soldiers and engineers.

'The actual fighting was simple; the difficult problem confronting the Commander-in-Chief was supplies,' Gullett noted.[3]

A 28-year-old sawyer from Prahran in Melbourne, Colonel SF Monoghan became the first member of the Australian light horse to die in the desert campaign after a Turk fleeing Jifjafa shot him. Six Turks were killed there and five were wounded, while others bolted into the scrub on camelback when the light horse attacked. The stragglers were taken prisoner with little resistance.

Despite Colonel Monoghan's death, the operation was considered a huge initial success for Murray, who immediately recognised just how adaptable the light-horsemen and their animals were to the arduous desert conditions. Not unlike the self-reliant Special Air Service of today, the light horse could set out on a search-and-destroy mission in totally unfamiliar territory many kilometres from their base, and confidently traverse unfamiliar and uninviting terrain—mainly by night—without being detected by the enemy. The light-horsemen could then be upon the enemy swiftly and with little notice, before dismounting, striking quickly and efficiently, and withdrawing just as rapidly.

But some of Murray's other mounted troops would not prove nearly as adept. Their blooding in battle against the Turks would, tragically, be far less glorious.

The reputation of the light-horsemen as ruthlessly efficient desert warriors was born at Jifjafa; only six Turks died in the skirmish, yet it had significant, immediate strategic value for Murray because, from then on, the Turks largely avoided trekking across the central Sinai's 'southern route' in large numbers for fear of encountering the ferocious bushmen again. Instead, they would water at the coastal oasis El Arish, close to the border with Palestine, before marching an arduous 80 kilometres to the oases between Katia and Romani, close to Kantara on the Suez Canal.

The Australian operation at Jifjafa effectively drove the Turks towards the seaboard northern route. Murray's forces were expecting them.

~

Murray was hugely disliked. His men, particularly further down the ranks, regarded him as an aloof and detached commander. This was especially the case among the colonial regiments—not least those from Australia and New Zealand—that constituted the backbone of his war-fighting divisions. The fact that he and many of his immediate subordinates later based themselves at the Savoy Hotel in Cairo—instead of closer to the desert action—didn't help.

'Murray's staff worked in luxurious offices at the Savoy and lived in fashionable hotels or in comfortable quarters very often with their wives and families, in the seductive city [Cairo] with the famous playground at Ghetzireh, which was always over-run with officers close at hand; it was impossible that they could apply to the affairs of the campaign that intimate knowledge and fierce energy which are as essential to victory as sagacity and valour in the field,' wrote R J Dunk of the Anzac Mounted Division's 3rd Regiment, comprising companies of men from Tasmania and South Australia. Dunk was writing after Field Marshal Edmund Allenby replaced Murray as commander of the Egyptian Expeditionary Force in 1917: '"I could not count the times I have shaken hands with Allenby," said a Light Horse Brigade Major a few months after the new leader's arrival. Between the canal and Gaza I never set eyes on Murray.'4

He who leads a military force to victory is invariably revered, while those who precede him are too often forgotten or dismissed as failures. So it is with Murray who, notwithstanding his serious flaws of temperament and personality, laid much of the difficult groundwork—especially in Egypt—for Allenby's eventual success. But by war's end Allenby was also seriously on the nose with some of the light horsemen.

~

Murray realised early during his command that the key to beating the Turks was water: finding it underground, bringing it to the surface and getting it to his horses and his men. And so he hatched an ambitious plan: he would build a pipeline across the deserts of Egypt and eventually Palestine to channel water, from a sweet water canal near Suez, to his troops and horses as they chased the Turks northwards. The 12-inch pipeline would carry water from near Suez to the troops on the front line, while a railway line, also built by Murray's engineers and thousands of Egyptian labourers, would run parallel with it to transport men and supplies to the front.

He pushed the railway and the pipeline into the oases and established posts, using British yeomanry, at Katia, nearby Oghratina and Romani. The yeomanry outposts were obvious targets for the Turkish if they were serious about capturing Suez. So, on 23 April 1916, a force of about five thousand—including many of the hated desert Arab Bedouin who had been co-opted to fight with the Turks—dramatically overwhelmed the British yeomanry deployed by Murray to protect Katia and Oghratina. The hopelessly ill-prepared yeomanry fled while a few Scottish infantrymen held out at nearby Dueidar, barely thirteen kilometres from the Suez Canal.

The Australian general Harry Chauvel was ordered to send reinforcements.

~

The legendary Australian commander of the Anzac Mounted Division, New South Wales–born soldier and Boer War veteran Major General Harry Chauvel, would become a hero of the Middle East campaign and, not least, the Beersheba episode. At that time the Anzac Division comprised three brigades of Australian light horse, each of three regiments, and the New Zealand mounted rifles. Two other light horse regiments, the 11th and the 12th, were sometimes available to him.

Harry George Chauvel was born in 1865 on a cattle station owned by his grandfather, once an officer in the Indian Army, on the Clarence River in New South Wales. Brought up on a farm, Chauvel was a natural around horses. He was short and fine-boned—physical attributes that would eventually enable him to start as an amateur jockey at meetings in New South Wales and Queensland.

He was educated at Sydney Grammar School where he was more focused on sport than schoolwork. Nonetheless, Gullett credited him as 'an eager reader': 'One day at Damascus, almost at the end of the great cavalry drive which had given Palestine and Syria to British arms, he confessed that the two historical heroes of his boyhood were Saladin and "Jeb" Stuart, the great cavalryman of the American Civil War. "I never thought in those days," he remarked, "that I should take part in a cavalry operation greater than anything undertaken by them."'[5]

It is ironic that Chauvel should nominate Saladin as one of his heroes, not least while triumphant, at war's end in Damascus—the place of Saladin's death in 1193. For Saladin was the twelfth-century ruler of Egypt, Syria, Iraq, the Hejaz and Yemen who successfully led the Muslim resistance against the European Third Crusade and recaptured Palestine from the crusader kingdom of Jerusalem.

Chauvel volunteered for the Boer War, serving first with the Queensland Mounted Infantry and later as commander of a composite mounted force of Australian, British, Canadian and South African horsemen. He was, by most accounts, a reserved and modest career soldier who, while being a strict observer of military rules and protocol, related well to subordinates from different backgrounds. This was a trait, Gullett observed, that would serve him well after his 'elevation later in Palestine to the command of Desert Mounted Corps, where, as the leader of a force of Australian and New

Zealanders, British yeomanry and Indian cavalry, he directed with complete success, and always without any apparent effort, one of the most complex and difficult corps commands to be assembled in warfare'. Much is also made of Chauvel's propensity to exude calm. Gullett describes him as 'one of the most imperturbable cavalrymen who ever crossed a saddle. No temporary failure depressed him; no victory, however sweeping and decisive, excited him.'[6]

At the outbreak of war in August 1914 Chauvel was already 49 years old. By the time he was commanding what became known as the 'Desert Column' across Palestine, he was in his early fifties.

~

When he discovered what the Turks were doing to the Brits, Chauvel dispatched the 2nd Light Horse Brigade, under the command of the hulking Brigadier General Granville Ryrie. Ryrie and his men arrived just in time to help the Scots—dogged, fierce fighters that they were—resist the Turks. But they were well and truly too late for many of the yeomanry who, contrary to what their rustic name connotes, were often the over-educated but ill-trained sons of wealthy English landowners. As Gullett observed laconically:

> The wealthy young men of England, when they respond whole-heartedly, as they always do, to the nation's call to arms, tend to treat their newly

acquired military responsibilities in a very sporting manner. They do not in the least mind dying for England, but they like to go to war casually and, if possible, in comfort. They ask that the wretched business shall not, except as a last resort, too seriously alter their regular habits of life. So it was with the ill-fated yeomanry … With slight exception among the officers, all ranks were utter strangers to the desert, and a sharper contrast than that between the desert of northern Sinai and the soft and gracious English countryside is scarcely to be discovered in the world.[7]

It would be some days before the full horror of the massacre of the yeomanry at Katia and Oghratina filtered back to the men in camp. Idriess was among those under Chauvel's command during the early days of the desert conflict. Of the massacre of the yeomanry, he wrote:

The brigade has lost six hundred men. After we relieved Dueidar and news of the disaster trickled in, the 6th and 7th Light Horse away back at Salhia on the Canal hurried to Romani … They found that the Yeomanry at Oghratina and Katia had died hard. Numbers of men had been bayoneted in their blankets. But many others after the first surprise had burrowed holes in the sand and fought to the death. Beside each man was a little pile of empty cartridge cases. The 6th and 7th Light Horse were pretty mad when they found some of the wounded Tommies had been slowly choked to death. The Bedouins had twisted wire around their throats.[8]

It was a brutal introduction to the harsh realities of desert warfare for most of the Australians, many of whom had already been hardened by months in the trenches at Gallipoli. It was also the genesis of a deep, abiding hatred of the Bedouin, some of whom had been forced into the ranks of the Turkish army while others willingly acted as spies and scouts. Idriess's diaries smoulder with hatred for the Bedouin. The hatred would boil over into terrible violence at Surafend two and a half years later.

Such visceral hatred was, however, largely lacking in relation to the Turk—'Jacko', as the horsemen called him. According to the myth, if not the reality as it sometimes unfolded on the battlefield, he was considered a skilled, courageous and resourceful enemy, and a fair fighter who was respectful of his opponents and who largely treated both the wounded and prisoners properly. Gullett noted that the light-horsemen 'knew their prospective enemy' and had 'probed and discovered the Turk's weakness and strength':

> They knew his straight shooting, his efficiency with the bomb rather than with the bayonet, his grim tenacity in defence, his fortitude under punishment, his capacity to make sound warfare under the harshest conditions and to endure on rations which would starve and destroy Western

troops. They knew also his lack of personal initiative and his feebleness as an individual fighter in the open. Every Australian and New Zealander respected the Turk as a soldier; but every trooper felt his man-to-man superiority over the enemy; and that consciousness, natural to men of a superior race, endured throughout the campaign. "The light horseman," said an experienced Australian officer during the campaign, "looks upon the Turk as a superior nigger."[9]

It was clear from Gullett's description of the Bedouin, however, that he regarded them as nothing less than a kind of nigger who 'prowled round the edge of the battlegrounds ready to tear uniform and boots from the fallen and even to dig up and strip the dead'. 'Scarcely higher in civilisation than the Australian blacks,' wrote Gullett, 'these wretched tribes presented a miserable and starved appearance. They seldom carried arms. Their women were particularly unattractive, but nevertheless were almost invariably veiled.'[10]

The Australian historian Ian Jones—a writer and producer of the 1987 movie *The Light Horsemen*, who interviewed many of the original horsemen for his research—describes the 'Arab problem' as a 'thorn in the side of the British and the Turks':

The very word Arab was a signal to transform the light horseman from a man of few words to a bully-beef-box orator—ranting against the Bedouin who helped the Turks and killed wounded mates, the town Arab who stole and cheated, the mounted armies of the Sherif of Mecca who were supposed to be allies but never seemed to be there when needed. They were all Arabs. They were all trouble.

It rarely occurred to the lighthorseman that any member of those three groups would have agreed with him about the other two. The Bedouin, in a pure line of descent from the Old Testament patriarchs, regarded town-dwelling Arabs as dirty, lazy and dishonest. The townsmen saw the Bedouin as fearsome desert raiders and robbers. But both groups were broadly loyal to their Turkish rulers.[11]

~

As Murray's lumbering architecture of war—the pipeline and railway—snaked their way towards Egypt's northern border with Palestine, for the next twelve months the Australian light horse—together with the British forces—fought against the Turks, as well as a smaller number of Germans and Austrians, in the desert. Many contacts between the enemies were mere skirmishes as light horse patrols ventured further north into no man's land in pursuit of the enemy. But others were full-scale battles—including those at Romani, Rafa, Maghdaba and Gaza—that would enhance the reputation of the light-horsemen as fearsome fighters and add to the legend of their commanders, not least Chauvel, Ryrie and Royston.

Granville de Laune Ryrie—at 52, one of the oldest men in the light horse as well as one of the heaviest—was about to forge a reputation as one of his country's most fearless soldiers and finest leaders of men. He is remembered as 'sixteen stone of bull-necked, hulking, ungainly bulk':

> He looked anything but a cavalryman, yet he rode lighter and better than most of his troops—Gullett called him the 'most perfect horseman in Palestine'—and he shot better, skills that he learned as a boy in the Australian bush. He could throw and treat a sick horse as well as any veterinary officer, and wield a boomerang with the best of the Aborigines. In his youth, he had fought in the finals of two amateur Australian heavyweight boxing championships. He was no deep student of war but relied on instinct, common sense and courage to carry him, and from first to last made no serious mistake—a rare record in a dashing mobile force that saw so much action.[12]

Through courage and example on the battlefield Ryrie earned enormous respect and affection. He was no disciplinarian; he loved to eat and joke with his men and tell stories to them. Photographs of Ryrie tell something of the story of the man. One sepia image shows him from a distance in profile, his huge bulk perched astride his horse, somewhere on approach to Beersheba. With a field service cap instead of the more traditional slouch hat crowning his massive head, and his tunic stretched uncomfortably across considerable girth and square, stump-like legs extending to the stirrups, he looks like an inert deadweight.

But Ryrie could apparently move like lightning. He survived Gallipoli, and his prowess in the Palestine campaign, in the saddle and as a commander, would be forged in a string of battles leading to Beersheba, Jerusalem and Damascus. He did, however, miss one of the war's most decisive and bloody 'stunts', as the light-horsemen called their actions: the battle for Romani. To Chauvel's disgust, Ryrie was on special leave in London at the time.

In Ryrie's absence, another man was temporarily given command of the 2nd Light Horse Brigade, and another legend was born in the form of Brigadier General Jack Royston, who would play a decisive role at Romani and serve, like Ryrie, as a lasting inspiration to those under his command. Those who thought Ryrie the oldest and heaviest light-horseman of World War I were wrong. Royston would have that dubious honour. But like Ryrie, Royston could ride, and was fearless to the point of recklessness.

The legends of both Chauvel and Royston in the Middle East were forged at Romani, a battle that tested the light horse like none before it. It would, however, highlight yet again, after the unnecessary tragedies of Gallipoli—not least the Battle of the Nek—the ineptitude of British command.

4

MYSTERY JOE

At the turn of the twentieth century, Beersheba resembled a small outback post in Australia. Situated in the middle of the Negev, south-west from the ancient Mediterranean fortified city of Gaza and in the middle of unforgiving desert between the Dead Sea and the Egyptian border, Beersheba was little more than a dusty camel trading station.

Back then it was an Arab town, surrounded by Bedouin camps. It had a mosque with a towering white minaret and a few administrative buildings, a military hospital and a railway station that served the Turkish army's rail system. Then, as today, the town was ringed with camps inhabited by Bedouin, who wandered the craggy creek-beds and wadies tending their goats.

Surrounded by a series of artificial and natural wells, Beersheba was the last watering stop for traders and soldiers trekking to Gaza. Gaza was seen as impenetrable from both the land and the sea and, by late 1916, the Turks had built an elaborate system of trenches and defences across the 50 kilometres or so of desert between the fort city and Beersheba. These defences formed what was known as the 'Beersheba–Gaza line'.

The British knew that if they were to defeat the Turks on their own patch in Palestine, they would first have to break the Beersheba–Gaza line. In anticipation of attack, the Turks had heavily fortified their positions in and around Gaza. The city itself—with its commanding views to the north, south, east and west across the Mediterranean—offered superb natural defences. All around the city a series of small garden allotments were divided by hedges of prickly pear cactus, metres high and just as thick. Trenches were everywhere. Legend had it that Gaza would be almost impossible for an invading army to penetrate. Today Gaza retains its infamy as the stronghold of the radical Palestinian organisation—and elected government—Hamas. The Israeli military controls the borders of the Gaza Strip, a home to militants who make repeated attacks on nearby Israeli towns and villages. Hamas sends rockets into some neighbouring towns on a daily basis. Gaza is heavily reliant on international aid, but the stand-off with Israel has ensured that many local Palestinians live in terrible poverty virtually under the rule of the gun.

Gullett seemed most unimpressed by Beersheba, a new village that had been constructed close to Tel el Saba, the ancient town known to Abraham and, more likely than not, perhaps the actual site of his ancient well. (A major tourist attraction of modern Be'er Sheva remains 'Abraham's Well'. Only after I'd paid a few shekels to look at it did Rika Ashahi Harel, an Israeli history teacher with a passion for light horse battle sites, tell me she thought Abraham's well was actually at Tel el Saba.) Much has changed in Beersheba since Gullett was there. Today it is a sprawling town of about three hundred thousand that is home to many Russian and Ethiopian Jews. But much has not changed—then, as now, the desert tribes also call the city and its surrounding desert home. In 1923 Gullett wrote:

> The village of modern Beersheba in itself offers no facilities for a prolonged defence. It lies in a shallow saucer at the foot of the Judaean hills, which rise abruptly from its outskirts to the north, with high ground also to the east and south-east. Before the war Beersheba was a squalid trading centre, linking up the hinterland with the port of Gaza, and a distributing centre for camels. In the operations against Sinai it was constantly used by the enemy as a base; many new temporary buildings rose, and the town became the scene of much activity. As the Anzacs first saw it from the hills to the south-east at sunrise on the morning of the 31st, it had, except for its new mosque built by

66

the Germans, the appearance of a struggling township on the pastoral country in Australia. To the dusty ring of mounted campaigners it promised no prize in comfortable quarters or in foodstuffs. But it contained that which was still more essential and coveted, for the village was rich in springs of good water. Perhaps never since the far-off days of Abraham had the water in the old wells of the patriarchs been so needed by parched men riding in from the southern desert.[1]

~

Certainly Beersheba was an unusual place for a young Armenian Catholic to end up in the years immediately after the Turks were expelled. But then again Joseph Hokeidonian was, by the scant accounts we have of his life, a most unusual man. Today his family will tell you that he was a 'spy', sent by the Catholic Church in Jerusalem to keep an eye on events in Ottoman Palestine during the war. No doubt his swarthy Arab appearance would have made him reasonably inconspicuous among the Turks and, perhaps also, with the Arab tribes whose anti-Turkish foment was skilfully harnessed by TE Lawrence 'of Arabia'.

Somehow he managed to lose an eye in the conflict. But this was no impediment to his being awarded a lucrative position under the British Mandate, as the deputy town clerk of Beersheba. It was his job to help rebuild the war-damaged town after the eviction of the Turks. While much of the damage was done by the British and other imperial troops—including the Australians—who occupied the town, the Turks themselves had sought to demolish as much of the infrastructure as possible when their invaders arrived. They detonated charges that had been carefully laid at some of the wells and public buildings. At least one well was destroyed, but their plan to blow up the railway station (still standing, although thoroughly decrepit, today) was foiled at the last minute.

In 1927 Hokeidonian moved to Jerusalem, where his Palestinian wife Rose gave birth to a child, Richard. He was, apparently, a less than perfect father and disappeared soon after the child arrived. Richard would never know his father, and the boy would not learn, until he was an old man himself, of his father's death in a traffic accident in Egypt.

Richard Hokeidonian recalls visiting Beersheba in the 1930s. Despite his father's efforts to rebuild the place, his impression of the town seems little more positive than Henry Gullett's: 'It didn't have much there, not much going for it … it was a dusty, isolated place, perhaps a bit like some Australian outback towns like Broken Hill.'[2]

The striking building—characteristically constructed by the Turks from carved blocks of blond stone—where Richard's long-lost father worked, can still be found midway along the main street of the old town today. The mosque and the station are a little further along the street. And not far from the station, surrounded by highrise apartment buildings, is a cemetery surrounded by gum trees. For more than ninety years, some of the Australians who died while trying to wrest this dusty town from the Turks have rested here.

Some things remain unchanged.

5

LEGENDS OF ROMANI

After overrunning the British yeomanry at Katia and Oghratina in April 1916, the Turkish forces immediately withdrew to the east, leaving the British wounded to their fate at the hands of the jackals of the battlefield—the Bedouin. According to Ian Jones:

> The lighthorsemen were most angered by the living style of the Yeomanry officers. Ryrie wrote, 'They were not the right people to put at this sort of job', naming five English lords whose luxury foodstuffs, abundant liquor and sporting equipment had been left behind in the scramble to evacuate Romani, even though the Turks had not even approached the camp.
>
> For the rest of the campaign, the Light Horse attitude to the Yeomanry would swing from

contempt to tolerance and eventual respect. Their introduction to the Scots as hardy fighters began a remarkable three years of mutual admiration.[1]

While the Turks overran the yeomanry at Katia and Oghratina, they met tougher resistance from a unit of a hundred Royal Scots Fusiliers at the nearby British camp of Dueidar, close to the canal. Dueidar could only loosely be termed a fortification, protected as it was by a small number of shallow trenches and, as Gullett said, 'a few strands of barbed wire'. At dawn on 23 April 1916 the Turks, intending to rush the Scots with bayonets and bombs, began to cut the wire at the perimeter. But a feisty terrier belonging to one of the fusiliers apparently saw what was happening and alerted his owner.[2] In the ensuing firefight seventy Turks were killed and another thirty wounded were left behind. Twenty Scots died.

While the Turks quickly learned that 'the Scotties'—like the Australian light-horsemen—should not be lightly messed with in the desert, they were none the less very quick to boast about their successful raids on Katia and Oghratina, saying it was evidence of their superiority in the desert against the imperial forces. The British prisoners were quickly transported up to Jerusalem and paraded through the streets as evidence of the invincibility of the Turkish forces—and a genuine testimony, it must be said, to the weakness of the yeomanry.

'Coming so soon after Gallipoli, and with the Turkish star ascendant at the time in Mesopotamia [today's Iraq], the success upon Sinai was of great political and moral value to the enemy,' Gullett wrote.[3]

Murray's folly at sending the inexperienced and soft yeomanry to hold the forward positions of Romani, Oghratina and Katia was obvious to all but him. Indeed, it seems he was boasting of the yeomanry's success just a week before they were comprehensively massacred. 'Katia,' he cabled to the War Office, 'is already occupied, and should be finally secured against every attempt on the part of the enemy by the end of the month.'[4]

While Ryrie's 2nd Light Horse Brigade was sent forward from its defensive base on the canal to cover the withdrawal of the defeated yeomanry, Chauvel's newly formed Anzac Mounted Division was then put in charge of defending and helping to push forward Murray's railway and pipeline. Chauvel quickly based a brigade at Romani, which the yeomanry had abandoned (along with their sporting equipment and luxury rations) even though the Turks had not actually attacked it. Instead of basing small units of men in the forward oases at Katia and Oghratina, he instead patrolled them aggressively while bolstering the main forward base at Romani.

~

As the brigades crossed the Suez Canal and moved into the Sinai from their defensive positions across the water, they were following in the footsteps of generations of horsemen before them who had tried—with varying levels of success—to capture Egypt and Palestine.

> As the column hurried through the magical moon-light across the desert, all ranks felt the influence, as they so often did, in the long campaign which followed, of the teeming associations of the route which since the birth of time had been trodden by mighty armies and great personages [Gullett mused]. Here the desert air had resounded with the huge marching hosts of the Pharaohs, the Persians, the Macedonians under Alexander, the legions of Rome, and the matchless revolutionaries of France under Napoleon. With the crossing of the Canal in strength was launched the amazing enterprise of the men of one of the world's youngest Christian peoples for the conquest of patriarchal Palestine.[5]

While it's certainly true that the Australian light horse was traversing a well-worn route on the hoofprints, metaphorically, of armies marching under the banner of the eleventh-century crusades and Napoleonic France, Gullett's historical take on the beginnings of this epic ride, from the canal to Aleppo in northern Syria, is—if not quite over the top—then certainly a deep hue of purple. Most of the men, especially the regulars, while cognisant that they were traversing some historical trails across lands central to the Bible's story, were probably more mindful of—and motivated by—duty or even adventure than nostalgia or, certainly, religion. In fairness, however, Gullett does point out: 'The idea seemed so unreal and ludicrous that many officers and men laughed aloud in the night as they pondered it.'[6]

On 14 November 1914 Istanbul's senior cleric declared jihad, or Islamic holy war, on the Allied infidels, calling on the world's 270 million Muslims to rise up against Britain and its interests. It was a call to arms that dramatically failed, not least because the Arabs of the Hejaz did exactly the opposite by declaring war, in June 1916, against Constantinople. There was another problem for the Turks: consistency. The Turks' main ally was Germany, one of the world's oldest bastions of Catholicism.

The Arab forces of TE Lawrence contributed in no small part to the defeat of the Turkish, and whether Lawrence or the Australian light horse rode into Damascus first remains a point of serious contention. Either way, some Western Christians find an irresistible symmetry between the Australian light horse and the crusaders. The crusaders, primarily Catholics from Germany, France and England, marched into the Holy Land in the late eleventh century to rid the local Christians of alleged persecution by the Muslims. Almost a thousand years later Britain's imperial forces, spearheaded by the Australian light horse, defeated an army whose country had declared jihad on Britain. Some, predictably, cannot resist seeing a parallel between the crusades, the World War I desert campaign and this century's great conflagration between terrorists with twisted notions of Islam and powerful Western Christian nations. But the truth is that, although they might have one important common element in Palestine, they are all vastly different conflicts.

Gullett himself found it necessary to reject the notion that the desert campaign was a crusade. 'Picturesque writers and public speakers during the war often described the British campaign in Palestine as a "New Crusade", and represented our armies as impelled by a strong religious feeling. This was pure literary extravagance. Religious feeling was a factor with the Turks and was exploited by their leaders, but it contributed nothing to the whole-souled energy of the light horse ... The campaign was in no sense a crusade.'[7]

Chauvel, it is said, carried a Bible, bound in wood and with a crusader's cross carved into the cover. In 2001 Chauvel's daughter, the author Elyne Mitchell, still had a similar Bible, bound in wood from the Mount of Olives in Jerusalem, that her father had sent her from the war when she was still a baby.[8] Chauvel's grandson, the historian Richard 'Harry' Chauvel, would later tell me that he believed any suggestion that his grandfather considered himself to be some sort of latter-day crusader was utterly incorrect.[9]

~

By mid-1916 the Australian light horse was clashing with the Turks daily in the desert around the Katia and Oghratina oases, taking dozens of prisoners and killing the enemy in heated skirmishes. Other light horse patrols were destroying Turkish wells on the southern route across the Sinai. A simple logic underpinned this defensive-offensive strategy: if the Turks wanted to take the Suez Canal, they would have to attack by the northern coastal route, by watering at El Arish, then taking the long, dry march to the palm hods and underground waters of Katia and Oghratina.

It was summer in the Sinai. The horses and camels could cope with the brackish water from the oases. But there was never enough; each man was rationed just 1 quart of poor-quality water a day as the temperatures pushed into the forties and desert windstorms—the dreaded khamsin—blinded the men and enveloped their camps in a mist of fine sand. In early August, as anticipated, a Turkish force of twelve thousand troops moved into Katia, the beginning of an action that would culminate a few days later in one of the toughest and most viciously fought hand-to-hand battles, for both the Turks and the British, of the entire desert campaign. It was the Battle of Romani.

The Turkish planned to attack Romani from the south-east and overwhelm the stronghold's southern defences, which were held by the British 52nd Infantry Division—comprising, at that time, about seven thousand men. But Murray and his commanders had anticipated the Turkish moves and hoped to encircle the Turks from the south once they were fully committed against the British infantry. When the Turks attacked at one in the morning of 3 August, yelling their customary battle cry 'Allah, Allah!', they had expected to surprise the British infantry. Instead they were met by two regiments from the 1st Australian Light Horse Brigade at an out-post line that stretched for 5 kilometres across the south-ern approach to Romani.

Dozens of Australians died holding the Turks off in the forward posts before gradually withdrawing, with the enemy in tow, to Mount Meredith, which acted as a natural barrier in front of the infantry. An Australian major found four men who had lost their horses while being overrun by the Turks; he took two of them on his horse and the other two held onto his stirrups while he galloped back through the attacking enemy towards Mount Meredith.[10] The fighting was so close and the visibility so poor that another light-horseman who thought he was lifting a mate onto his saddle later discovered the man was a Turk.[11]

Eventually a small group of Australians perched on the crest of Mount Meredith and shot the Turks as they attempted to clamber, many of them in bare feet, up the steep, sandy surface of the giant dune. The attacking Turks had to dodge their dead on the way up, as those who'd been bayoneted and shot rolled down the dune and banked up at the bottom. Eventually the Turks attacked the ridge from its more gradual slopes, and the light-horsemen fell back in formation; one squadron would dismount and fire at the enemy while another would fall back and repeat the process.

The moon set. At times nothing could be seen except little fleeting flames resembling match-strike, thanks to the phosphorous in the sand, which the bullets struck. Just before dawn Royston arrived with his 2nd Light Horse Brigade, which Chauvel had purposely held in reserve while seriously testing the two regiments from the 1st Brigade throughout the night-time battle.

Bolstered now by Royston's men, the Australians of 1st Brigade fell back to another giant dune, Wellington Ridge, and took firing positions on the crest. By daylight the Turks took the ridge and found themselves within seven hundred yards of the British 52nd Infantry Division camp, just below at Etmaler. By now the sun was blazing, and the Turks were running six hours behind schedule; they had anticipated taking Wellington Ridge by 2 a.m. As the sun beat down they were an easy target for the artillery below at Etmaler, which effectively pinned them just below the crest on the other side of the ridge.

~

As a teenager, the South African–born Brigadier General JR Royston fought in the 1879 Zulu War and, at the outbreak of the Boer War in 1899, he was a sergeant major in the Natal Border Rifles. In 1901 he became a commander of the West Australian Mounted Infantry, after which he commanded Australians in both the Boer War and the Zulu Rebellion of 1908. By the time he was sent to command the 12th Australian Light Horse Regiment in 1916, he was approaching his sixtieth birthday. Like Ryrie, Royston was physically imposing, weighing in at close to twenty stone. He was also deeply wary of military protocol.

On the first day of the battle for Romani, Royston had galloped all over the battlefield, wearing out—or so legend has it—up to fourteen horses in the process. Gullett said Royston appeared to those who saw him that day to be 'insensible to fatigue as he was utterly careless of danger':

> From the moment his force entered the fight at Romani he had fearlessly ridden up and down the exposed firing line. Parties of men crouching low in the sand were cheered again and again to see 'Galloping Jack', as they called him, come racing up to them with yards of blood-stained bandage from a flesh wound trailing after him. 'Keep moving gentlemen, keep moving,' was his constant advice to his officers. And to the men, 'Keep your heads down, lads. Stick to it, stick to it! You are making history today.' To a hard-pressed troop on the naked flank he cried: 'We are winning now. They are retreating in hundreds.' 'And,' said one of the light horsemen afterwards, 'I poked my head over the top, and there were the blighters coming on in thousands.'[12]

Chauvel, according to the official history, was unperturbed that the Turks had made the top of Wellington Ridge because, as the desert sun beat down, 'each hundred yards the Turks advanced brought them nearer to defeat. It was inevitable that, unless they very speedily won the hods and the water at Etmaler and Romani, the great assaulting wave must spend itself and perish on the burning sand.'[13]

Indeed the plan, hatched by Major General Hubert Lawrence, commander of the canal defences—and supported by Chauvel—had been to entice the Turks all the way to Wellington Ridge and then to have New Zealand Mounted Rifles, together with some yeomanry, commanded by Chaytor, outflank and envelop them from the left. But Lawrence had remained paranoid that the Turks might launch a simultaneous direct attack on the canal defences. By mid-morning, however, the exhausted Turks were baking in the sun on the south-eastern side of Wellington Ridge without water, shoes (in many cases) or reinforcements. It was time for Chaytor's counter-attack.

Owing to a potentially disastrous communications hiccup between Chauvel, at the front, and Lawrence, back at Kantara, which occurred after an enemy spy managed to cut the British telephone line, Chaytor's force was late. The Turks had meanwhile taken another sandy hill, Mount Royston. Foot by foot Chaytor's men fought the Turks until, late in the afternoon, the enemy surrendered en masse. About this time the Turks made a final effort to advance over Wellington Ridge, but they were raked by machine-gun fire from the bottom.

By afternoon the light-horsemen, whose thin line arced between the base of Wellington Ridge and the defensive lines at Etmaler, were so close to their camp that the cooks were serving them hot meals as they fought. The battle entered its second night with the Turks still pinned on Wellington Ridge and thinly stretched around to the base of Mount Royston.

Early the next morning Chauvel sent in most of his mounted division as infantry. With bayonets fixed and supported by British infantry, they fanned across the sand dunes while yelling obscenities at their enemy. The loose sand was so heavy-going that many of the Turks fought in bare feet. Some Australians died because their heavy boots dragged their feet deep into the sands. Somehow the Australians managed to charge up and over Wellington Ridge and sweep the retreating Turks down towards Mount Meredith.

By 5 a.m. more than a thousand Turks had been taken prisoner. Those Turks who weren't bayoneted, shot or captured were forced to a full retreat, parched and weary, over heavy sands to Katia, 7 kilometres away. Lawrence now ordered Chauvel to hunt down and kill or capture the retreating Turks as soon as possible.

Idriess, a member of the Townsville-based 5th Light Horse Regiment, recounts chasing the Turks into the oases around Katia and nearby Bir el Abd.

> Through it all we can sense a battle very, very narrowly won. As the columns rode along it seemed to me that these men with their strained, grimy faces, their eyes fever-bright, were living on the terrible excitement of hours before. Some were swaying in their saddles, their heads, like their

horses' heads, drooping for want of sleep. And we
were riding out with these overtired men to deal
another blow at a furious enemy at bay!

... We branched off towards El Katia, chewing biscuits as we rode. Then my neddy snorted at
a Turk who lay with his sand-filled eyes glazed to
the sky; then past a smashed case with its Turkish
ammunition shining on the sand.[14]

At the top of a rise overlooking Katia, Idriess and
his mates are ordered to fix their bayonets. 'By Jove,
what a thrill ran through the regiment! The flash of steel,
the innumerable click, click, clickings and five hundred
bayonets gleamed.'[15] It was the first time in the campaign
that bayonets had been drawn, cavalry-style, by the
horsemen. Although the bayonets couldn't be used effectively from horseback while secured to the ends of rifles,
it was anticipated that the sight of the weapons would
frighten the already severely demoralised Turks into a
quick surrender.

Over to Idriess's left, three brigades of Australian
and New Zealand horsemen had also fixed their bayonets and charged across an open salt-pan at Turks hiding
in the trees. But the first big cavalry charge of the light
horse in the desert campaign was anti-climactically
thwarted when the horses became bogged, somewhat
ingloriously, in a heavy swamp. The men dismounted
and picked their way slowly through the bog.

Meanwhile, Idriess and his men had charged into
the middle of their oasis fully expecting to be met by

enemy gunners and infantry. But the oasis was empty, and instead of a confrontation, the adrenaline-charged light-horsemen found themselves thundering straight through the hods and out the other side onto a plain that was bordered by another big growth of palm trees.

'We breathed,' recalled Idriess, 'then came the sickening thud of bullets into horseflesh.'

The men dismounted and slowly made their way, under covering fire, to the next oasis where the Turkish snipers were taking cover. Here Idriess's diary adopted a tone that captures, like very little war writing, the emotions, the adrenaline and the fear—the pure sensory overload—that a soldier experiences as he prepares for close-quarter combat:

> The Turk was fighting in a snarling fury over every yard of ground. There was no trench work here. You were all concentrated just in your section and often for mad, hysterical moments, just in yourself. You saw a Turk's head in a bush, you saw his moustache, you saw his eye glaring along his rifle-sights. You fired too, with your breath in your belly, then rushed forward screaming to bayonet him, to club him, to fall on him and tear his throat out and he met you a replica of the berserk, frightened demon that was in yourself.[16]

Bitter hand-to-hand fighting continued all afternoon. But the Turks—supported by German and Austrian gunners and artillerymen—were putting up tough resistance. Chauvel knew that unless his men took all of Katia, but especially its wells, by sunset, his men and horses would be stranded without water. He ordered the troops to return to Romani.

The men, many of whom had not slept for two or even three nights, dozed in their saddles as the horses wandered back to camp. Two days later the Turks had retreated to Bir al Abd, 15 miles east of Katia. Galloping Jack Royston led both the 1st and 2nd Brigades this time. But the fighting that day was a virtual carbon copy of the earlier battle at Katia; the light-horsemen were dramatically outnumbered by the Turks, who had dug an elaborate trench system and who were again, after Romani and Katia, well rested and watered.

After another day of bitter fighting, Chauvel ordered another withdrawal. After riding all night and again fighting all day in temperatures likened to those of a foundry,[17] the men, suffering from heat exhaustion, were finally withdrawn. In his diaries, Idriess describes the men as they marched through the night:

Then the order came, 'No smoking, No talking,' and the rest of the weary ride was like a ghostly army marching through silence ... shells would scream by and burst in the rear, all through the long silent ride. All the other men could hear the fight. We were dropping asleep in the saddles. A horse would walk up through the column, his rider, head swaying over his chest, quite asleep in the saddle. A comrade would touch the man, he would wake up with a sudden jerk, there would be a low laugh and the man would wait for his section. At last we reached Oghra Sina [Oghratina], fell off our horses, fed them, rolled on the sand, and listened to the plop plop plop of bullets as they embedded themselves in the sand around. But not for long. Imagination had no chance against that over-powering sleep.[18]

Romani had been a hard-won victory for Murray's forces. But it had been soured by the failures at Katia and Bir el Abd. Murray blamed Lawrence, who had thought it appropriate to try to command the war-fighting operations by telephone from Kantara all the way back on the Suez Canal. Chauvel, meanwhile, blamed Murray, who was trying to run the whole show from the safety and comfort of the Savoy Hotel even further away in Cairo. The Australian men, for their part, blamed both Murray and Lawrence.

~

By 12 August the Turks had abandoned Bir el Abd, and had begun the long, thirsty march north-east to El Arish, close to the Palestine border. It was now clear that the Turks had, for the time being, abandoned their designs on the canal and were playing a defensive game by looking to secure Palestine from British advance. Murray was determined to chase them into Palestine itself.

There is no doubt that Romani was a turning point made possible largely by the Australian light horse and the New Zealand mounted troops. The British infantry, held on reserve in camp, took little part in the hard fighting. If anything it seems, on the basis of Gullett's assessment, that the Australian light horse at Romani was all that stood between the British infantry and the marauding Turks.

Idriess remarked in *The Desert Column*: 'The infantry are as disgusted as we are. One infantry commander on his own initiative sent out several hundred of his men into the fight. The Turks got so close to one of the infantry camps that they plastered their redoubt with shells at close range. No doubt the English have a peculiar way of fighting; thirteen thousand men, fresh, eager for the scrap, and just simply not allowed to go in.'[19]

Murray was, publicly at least, effusive in his praise of the Australians and New Zealanders. But it was not the first time he would praise the Australians publicly and privately credit the British with their achievements. Gullett noted that Murray had sent 'many messages of unstinted praise to the Anzacs both during the reconnaissances and over the period of the actual fighting' at Romani. That is why Murray's subsequent official dispatch had caused 'much surprise'.

If the story of the work both before and during the engagement is read only in Murray's own expressions of opinion in the contemporary official papers, it is beyond all question that the Anzac

Mounted Division fought Romani almost alone. But in the Commander-in-Chief's narrative of the engagement, as sent to the War Office and subsequently published, the decisive work of the light horse and the New Zealanders is slurred over, and the British infantry is credited with activities which were not displayed.[20]

Similarly, most of the military awards and decorations from the Romani battle went to British troops—especially to staff officers who, Gullett points out, 'had blundered in the conduct of the fight from beginning to end. Had no awards been made, the Anzacs would not have complained; but the publication of a list so discriminating and unfair caused much discontent.'[21] This became a theme of the Australian action in Egypt and Palestine, not least at Beersheba, and much later in the Jordan Valley and Syria in the actions leading to the capture of Damascus and Aleppo.

Murray's actions were clearly duplicitous. He was simply rewarding the British for actions they had not performed while denying awards to the Australians who had. The Australians would be denied medals for later acts of bravery, but that would happen for an altogether more sinister reason.

6

GHOSTS OF THE DESERT

After victory at Romani, Murray set his sights on the same place for which all would-be invaders of Palestine had also, by necessity, marched: the ancient Mediterranean town of El Arish, which stands about eighty kilometres from Romani, separated by the unforgiving soft, dry sands of the Sinai Peninsula.

Throughout late 1916 the Anzacs proceeded along the coastal route to El Arish well ahead of Murray's pipeline and railway, thanks to the Royal Navy landing supplies along the beaches of the Mediterranean. But the men still needed to find enough water for thousands of advancing troops and animals. Men like Trooper Pauls and Trooper Simpson, who worked as a carpenter in the Victorian town of Corryong before he enlisted, used ingenious methods to find water in the desert.

'In the desert it was 125 degrees [Fahrenheit] and there was no shade. If you wanted water you had to dig for it. We had to dig for enough water for hundreds of men and horses,' Simpson told me many years later. 'They [the commanders] realised I was as much use as a tradesman as a rifleman.'[1]

On 30 August 1916 Trooper Pauls' week began: 'Commenced sinking wells about $1\frac{1}{2}$ miles away from our camp. Water of fairly good sort is procurable at a depth of 12 to 14ft. We are to sink 14 of these so that 1,000 horses can be watered per hour.'[2]

By the end of the week Pauls was reeling from the news that his brother Charlie had been killed on the Western Front: 'The shock and pain which this news gives me is unbearable. Would that it had been me in his place, such was my love for him. But war is war and fate was against him,' he wrote on 8 September 1916. He got on with the job of digging wells, writing on 10 September 1916: 'Has been a terrible day here. We have completed our wells. Have completed 9 in all, also 5 at [nearby] Bahdah. Am still very upset, worrying over Charlie's death. Hope they can bear the news at home bravely. Now we have completed this work I expect we will move on.'[3]

~

By September 1916 Murray had all but surrendered hope of using the British infantry to clear Turks from the Sinai. The infantrymen were badly affected by the heat and sank, with their heavy boots and cumbersome loads, in the soft surface sands and dunes. He was determined that the way forward in Egypt lay with the advance of the Anzac mounted troops. British infantry would be used merely to hold—rather than take—advanced bases.

The glacially slow, monotonous advance across the open desert towards the border of Palestine was determined by the excruciatingly tedious progress of both Murray's railway and his pipeline. From then until Christmas the light horse continued moving slowly forward, often in night marches, towards El Arish, all the way sinking wells to supply thousands of men and horses. But there was little contact with the Turks, who withdrew slowly across the desert towards the border of Palestine as the Australians slowly advanced north-east of the Oghratina and Katia oases. The men, it seems, were bored and dispirited:

> Since the Romani operations there was scarcely an Australian who had ridden his horse at a pace beyond a walk. The men were, if not dispirited, at least exceedingly weary of the heat and flies and short water-supplies and heavy sands of the desert. Their progress towards the east after Romani had been constant, but movement had been so slow as to be almost imperceptible; as they shifted camp, they changed only from one sand-dune to another.

For months there had been practically no sign of the enemy, and the only break in the dreary monotony of patrol work was the capture of an occasional Bedouin and a few camels.[4]

Idriess described a typical night march thus:

At one o'clock in the morning we rode out east again, a long column of horsemen. We had no horse chains, we had stripped our saddles and everything we did not want was left behind. It was the usual night march, no smoking, but little talking, and only soft murmuring of the horse feet. Recently riding parallel with us was a long column of Tommy artillery, their caterpillar wheels creaking in the still night. Then we rode through a native village, and wondered at the lights showing in the houses. Then out into the desert again, past a tribesmans [sic] orchard protected by a wall of cactus, then past a long line of ambulance carts and sledges. Ominous, these, all of us going east.

The Desert Column always advances into the rising sun. The small hours of the morning came, and our feet and hands got very cold. As usual we wished for daylight, the warmth to drive the cold away, the light to drive away the wretched, drowsy sleep.[5]

~

Meanwhile, the War Office in London decided, at Murray's request, to dramatically restructure its forces in the Sinai. Murray, concerned about the fomenting internal disquiet about the imperial presence in Egypt, won London's approval for a decision that would utterly undermine his already tenuous standing among his countrymen of junior ranks and with the troops of the dominions. He withdrew his headquarters from Ismailia, near the Suez Canal, to the Savoy Hotel in Cairo. He was now sitting comfortably 225 kilometres from his railhead, and his frontline, at Romani. It was clear that he had not heeded the lessons of near failure at Romani, which had been brought about by the great distance between commanders and troops, and by poor communications and a muddled chain of command.

Murray promptly had Major General Hubert Lawrence, the commander of the canal defences, dispatched to France and replaced by Lieutenant General Charles Dobell. Dobell had successfully commanded small groups of men against native uprisings in Africa. But he had none of the requisite experience to command a planned invasion by thousands of men and animals. Nonetheless, Murray saw fit to base him at Ismailia and appoint him General Officer Commanding Eastern Force. This included every man at the Suez Canal and in the Sinai.

Dobell immediately placed all of the mounted troops into the 'Desert Column', in the command of the respected British cavalryman Lieutenant General Philip Chetwode. Chauvel remained in command of the Anzac Mounted

Division. Chetwode, who had distinguished himself as a cavalry leader in France, was not an immediate hit with the Australians, although he would earn their respect over time. It is little wonder he didn't immediately endear himself to the light-horsemen, because one of his first actions involved complaining to Chauvel about the Australians' carelessness in saluting him. 'He rode about the camps followed by British mounted orderlies, whose smart dress and precise and stiff horsemanship were in strong contrast to the appearance of the casual and desert-worn Australians. "Not only do your men fail to salute me when I ride through your camps," he protested, "but they laugh at my orderlies,"' Gullett wrote.[6]

Chetwode's complaints about Australian discipline would cease after he saw them in battle, just as Murray's gripes about the Antipodeans' attitudes were checked by their actions on the battlefield at Romani.

~

In September the light horse led attacks on Turkish garrisons at Mazar, about seventy kilometres along the main coast route from Romani to El Arish. In October another raid was mounted on Maghara in the Sinai hills. Chauvel failed to overwhelm the Turks in both raids and withdrew his men before the garrisons fell. But the actions served to keep up the pressure on the Turks, who slowly fell back towards the border of Palestine. From then until around Christmas, it was rare for a light-horseman to see a Turk … a living one, at any rate.

On 23 December 1916 Idriess took one of the little notebooks from his haversack and wrote:

When on desert patrol, we sometimes ride across dead Turks. Most of our own boys have long since been decently buried. Their neat white crosses are dotted over the desert.

Afternoon—Well, I'm blest—our troops have occupied El Arish. The Turks evacuated it—we thought hell would be played there. Meagre details are that the 1st Light Horse Brigade, the NZMR [New Zealand Mounted Regiment] Brigade, the 3rd Light Horse Brigade and the Imperial Camel Brigade, the Leicester, Somerset and Inverness batteries, RHA and the Singapore and Hong Kong Mountain batteries, all under Chauvel concentrated on the Old Caravan Road at night and marched the thirty miles to El Arish. But the Turks had just gone.[7]

Gullett describes, with an almost dream-like quality, how the men of the two dominions—Australia and New Zealand—marched under 'heavens thickly sprinkled with stars' from the loose desert sand dunes of Sinai and onto the hard, flat earth on the outskirts or El Arish.[8]

The chief sheikh gladly handed over El Arish to Chauvel, who ordered the establishment of outposts around the town. His superior, Chetwode, meanwhile landed at El Arish by sea and ordered Chauvel to proceed immediately to pursue the Turks to their nearby strongholds of Rafa and Magdhaba. They were the two remaining impediments for the Anzacs' entry to Palestine.

Chauvel's men—a second night without sleep and a long march ahead of them—anticipated what lay ahead. While Chauvel prepared for battle, an otherwise quiet day became tragically eventful when two members of the 1st Light Horse Brigade blew themselves to pieces while bathing in the sea, when they accidentally detonated an anti-submarine mine that had washed up onto the beach. 'A thumb was the biggest part of them found,' Idriess noted.[9]

No sooner, it seemed, had Chauvel's exhausted Anzac Mounted Division arrived in El Arish than it set off, at Chetwode's insistence, on the 40-kilometre ride for Magdhaba. At dawn the horsemen stopped about seven kilometres from Magdhaba. The Turkish campfires burned in the distance, and smoke hung low in the chilly desert air. The brigades of horsemen and cameleers—also under Chauvel's command—took on the appearance of ghostly apparitions as they verged wide and prepared to enclose the town.

The Anzacs fought all morning and took hundreds of prisoners. But the Turks continued to put up a spirited defence, and by afternoon Chauvel had become concerned that if the men did not take the town by evening, they would have to march 40 kilometres back to El Arish for water. He ordered his leaders to break off the attack. But the commander of 1st Brigade, General Cox—'Fighting Charlie' to his men—ignored Chauvel and, in a wild race with the cameleers, charged towards the Turkish trenches. Hundreds of Turks surrendered.

Galloping Jack Royston, now the 3rd Brigade's commander after Ryrie's return from leave, decided to ride with his 10th Regiment at Magdhaba that day. His legend grew, as it seemed to do, each time he led men and horses into battle. By the end of the day his regiment had taken more than seven hundred Turkish prisoners. At one point he hastily cobbled together a gang of men and horses, and mounted an ad hoc charge on a group of Turkish gunners who were using a dry wadi as a makeshift trench. Legend has it that as the old Boer War veteran confronted the startled Turks he waved his riding crop at them and barked: 'Hands up!' in Zulu. They surrendered.

As the brigades poured into Magdhaba from every side, Chauvel suddenly had an unanticipated victory on his hands. By 4.30 p.m., as a winter's night closed in, Chauvel and his men had taken the town and thirteen hundred Turkish prisoners. The competition for prisoners was so keen among the various regiments that an indignant French military attaché, Captain Count St Quentin, who had been riding with the light horse, was himself taken captive.

But there wasn't enough water in the wells for the parched men and horses, which had been at least twenty-four hours without a drink. At midnight Chauvel turned the column back towards El Arish. For some, it was the third night on the march without sleep. Across the ranks, the dozing horsemen reported strange apparitions as they meandered mounted on their horses, tooth to tail, back to the coast. Gullett noted that it was the 'third, and with many of the regiments, the fourth, night without rest, and there were very few officers or men who did not sleep as they rode'. But he did not detail the delirium that apparently beset the men and their officers.[10]

Idriess, calling it a 'very peculiar story', describes in *The Desert Column* how, after being enveloped in blinding clouds of dust,

> Hundreds of men saw the queerest visions—weird looking soldiers were riding beside them, many were mounted on strange animals. Hordes walked right amongst the horses making not the slightest sound. The column rode through towns with lights gleaming from the shuttered windows of quaint buildings. The country was all waving green fields and trees and flower gardens. Numbers of the men are speaking of what they saw in a most interesting, queer way. There were tall stone temples with marble pillars and swinging oil lamps— our fellow could smell the incense—and white mosques with stately minarets.
>
> It is strange to hear the chaps discussing what they saw ... I don't think they would talk so openly had it not been for a general riding with his staff. Suddenly he and his companion officer galloped off into the darkness. It has just come out that both officers suddenly saw a fox and galloped after it![11]

Chauvel wrote the foreword to Idriess's book. Perhaps this is why Idriess did not identify the esteemed Australian general as the officer who'd chased the fox. But there is no doubt it was Chauvel. In a letter to his wife on 7 February 1917, Chauvel recounted:

Yes, we were all rather tired leading back to El Arish after Magdhaba and were all seeing things whose existence was doubtful! I even galloped after a fox once and am not really sure now that it was there. We were all asleep once ... and went off the track. As Brown had volunteered to lead I had gone to sleep and woke up suddenly to find I could not see the telegraph poles, which had been our guide and found that Brown was asleep too and that the telegraph poles were nowhere to be seen.

However we had not been looking for them long when we heard the dogs barking in El Arish ... our horses must have got bored with following the telegraph and bee-lined across the desert for the wells.[12]

In an earlier letter to his wife about Magdhaba, Chauvel—ever the disciplinarian—said: 'The papers made a song about the lack of water and the men's sufferings at Magdhaba, but it was only the poor horses that suffered. If any man suffered, it was his own fault as all started from El Arish with full water bottles which ought to last anyone for 24 hours in this weather.'[13]

But many Australian horsemen, especially the 117 wounded, did suffer at Maghdaba. The wounded were left for collection by the ambulance men while the column went back to El Arish for water. Even if they survived the bone-crunching ride back to El Arish on the camel cacolets, they were still 48 kilometres from the railhead at Romani and, from there, another 80 kilometres back to proper treatment at the canal.

Despite the surreal ride back from Magdhaba, however, the operation was a great success. In twenty-four hours the Anzacs had ridden 80 kilometres over unfamiliar ground to surprise and fight—mounted and as infantry—a strongly placed enemy. As Gullett said: 'The engagement brought out all the effective qualities of the Light Horsemen.'[14]

~

Two weeks later, Chauvel's men finally crossed the border of Palestine on their way to attack Rafa, the last significant Turkish stronghold between the Egyptian border and the Beersheba–Gaza line. Chetwode rode with Chauvel for the attack and, curiously, the fight was almost a carbon copy of that at Magdhaba. By late afternoon, with the horsemen and cameleers unable to penetrate the Turkish redoubts and the men low on water, Chetwode ordered Chauvel to retreat. But while Chetwode turned his horse for El Arish, the New Zealanders and the cameleers, ignoring the order to withdraw, began rushing the trenches. More than 1500 Turks surrendered and 200 were killed. Chauvel lost seventy-one men, and another 415 were wounded.

As the light-horsemen entered the dry, open plains of Palestine, Murray decided to create a second division of mounted troops. It consisted of the newly formed 4th Light Horse Brigade (itself comprising the 1st, 12th and 4th Light Horse Regiments), the 3rd Brigade and two brigades of British yeomanry. To the disgust of the Australians, Murray called it the Imperial Mounted Division and put in place as its commander a British officer, Major General HW Hodgson. Chauvel's Anzac Mounted Division would be bolstered with another yeomanry brigade.

By the beginning of February the light-horsemen, buoyed by their string of battle successes across the Sinai, were preparing for the advance upon Gaza and then, inevitably, Beersheba. The prospect of defeat had probably not crossed their minds.

7

BADLANDS

As the light horse commanders planned their inevitable attack on Gaza, Idriess contemplated the historical and strategic Mediterranean city that then, just as it does today, held such critical implications for the future of Palestine.

> This city of Genesis is one of the oldest in the world. It is Samson's city, the strong man of Israel who when his foes were upon him tore down the city gates and carried them up the hill of Ali Muntar. At Gaza, when chained to the pillars of the Temple of Dagon, he pulled the roof down on top of three thousand Philistines. Delilah was his girl [he wrote].
>
> Gaza has ever been the fortress city of southern Palestine. Alexander took it, after an historic

siege. It became a mighty fortress against Pharaoh's
armies. It was a huge city under the Romans …
But what interests me is that the youngest nation
in the world will soon be thundering at its gates.[1]

~

More than ninety years later I am contemplating Gaza
in the distance from much the same spot as Idriess. We
drive past a sign. 'BADLANDS', it says.

It looks like home. On one side of the dusty gravel
road a wheat field stretches to a gentle rise that is
fringed with young eucalyptus trees. Head-high wattles
in full bloom line the road to our right while on the left
the gravel falls away steeply to a series of dusty, furrow-
ing creekbeds or, as they are known here, wadies.
Except for the lonely camel tethered beside a Bedouin
camp, typically made up of corrugated iron, plastic and
canvas, we could be driving through the Mallee at the
beginning of summer.

There is not another car and not another soul. As the
road rises to a crest, Gaza stands before us and, on this
brilliant cloudless day, the Mediterranean sparkles azure
behind it. Badlands. As it was in 1917, so it is today.

We are looking for a memorial to the light-
horsemen and the New Zealand mounted riflemen who
fought in the second of two battles for Gaza in 1917.
The memorial, funded by Jewish donors in Australia
and New Zealand, is towards the coast from a sulphur
mine and the Kibbutz Be'eri, which has, in recent times,

become a constant target for rockets fired from Hamas-controlled Gaza City.

In the past fortnight tensions between Hamas and the Israeli military have been higher than usual, and a tit-for-tat cycle of violence has enveloped the region we are driving through. It began when Hamas militants attacked a fuel depot close to the border crossing between Gaza and Israel, killing two civilian workers and closing the terminal through which fuel for all of Gaza's 1.5 million residents must pass.

The Israeli military struck back with an air strike on Gaza, killing two militants. Hamas, predictably, retaliated, ambushing three Israelis at the border post. In turn, the Israelis mounted another airstrike and sent tanks and troops into Gaza, killing twenty Palestinian militants and children. And so the violence was destined to continue ... until later in the year when Israel would mount a full-scaled military invasion of Gaza. And still the rockets continued ...

I had sought the advice of my friend Matt Brown, then the Middle East correspondent for the Australian Broadcasting Corporation, about travelling in this part of the world. He'd been covering the Israeli strikes on Gaza. 'Should we drive down to the memorial near the sulphur mine?' I asked him.

'It should be fine,' he said. 'But then again you might get shot.' It was not unheard of, he said, for Hamas snipers to take pot-shots from the taller buildings in Gaza at people and cars along the other side of the border. 'My advice—go, but be careful,' he said.

Kelvin Crombie—a dedicated Christian, an author, an amateur historian and a Beersheba expert—is driving. In the back seat is Susan McMinn, an Australian artist.

'I've got to admit I'm a bit wary driving through here—there's just nobody about and usually there's families, all sorts of people, around here—especially during Passover holidays,' says Crombie, who has spent almost half his life in Israel—much of it on the trail of the light-horsemen.

He's driven through Badlands many times before. But today he's toey.

~

We reach the Anzac Memorial. It is a vast, wave-like, concrete, vaguely A-shaped structure that is hollowed at the bottom, allowing the eye to look through and beyond the tops of the eucalypts and into Gaza City, perhaps a kilometre away. The monument incorporates a lookout. But today we won't be going up there.

'We'll stay in the car today. Snipers—you just never know,' Crombie says.

We get out of the car, but we do not stand between the monument and Gaza. And we do not climb the lookout. From where we stand I notice for the first time the towering prickly pears between us and Gaza.

'A lot of blokes had real problems with the cactus back then,' says Crombie. 'It gave them a hell of a time.'

Looking through the monument at the ancient fort city, it is easy to see why in 1917—as it is today—Gaza would be such a difficult city to wrest from an enemy. As Henry Gullett noted, the Beersheba–Gaza line, 'which barred the gateway to the Philistine Plain and to Palestine as a whole, lends itself admirably to defence':

> Few cities have changed hands so frequently as Gaza. Its conquest has, since the beginning of civilisation, always been a preliminary step for the invasion of Egypt from the north or for an advance from the Nile towards Palestine. One of the five cities of the Philistine league, it has been assailed and captured by the Hebrews, the Pharaohs, Assyrians, Ptolemies, and by Alexander and Pompey and Napoleon ...
>
> Most of the villages of the Philistine plain are more or less surrounded by a network of tiny fields, enclosed by wide, tall cactus hedges, which are not only capable of bringing infantry to a halt, but are in large measure proof against machine-gun and rifle fire. For some miles around Gaza the sprawling cactus stands eight or ten feet high, and from six to fifteen feet across.[2]

We don't stay long. Frequent incursions by Hamas militants have ensured that the road along which we are driving, and the brief stretch of wheat-covered land between us and Gaza, is no man's land today.

So, too, was it no man's land in early 1917 as the British forces prepared to attack Gaza, in what would become an inglorious military farce. The fiasco at Gaza also marked a formidable start to the countdown for Beersheba. If Beersheba was to mark a high, a turning-point in the British campaign for Palestine, then Gaza was, truly, the low.

~

The first battle of Gaza was a disaster in all but name for the British forces, including the Australian light horse. An unnecessarily convoluted chain of command and abysmal communications between the Anzac mounted infantry, the British regular infantry and the artillery would doom the attack to failure and repeat the well-established mistakes that nearly cost them victory at Rafa and Magdhaba.

Lieutenant General Dobell, the newly appointed and ill-experienced commander of Eastern Force, was in charge. Chetwode would direct the regular infantry that was under the command of yet another general, Major General CA Dallas. Chauvel was commanding the Anzac Mounted Division, whose job was to encircle Gaza and its surrounding villages from the north while the infantry made a direct inland attack on the city's main defence: an ominous, well-fortified peak called Ali Muntar.

The attack was scheduled for early morning. The light horse of the Anzac Mounted Division led the Imperial Mounted Division in the movement north of Gaza. After setting out from camp near Belah at 2.30 a.m., they had reached the coast, inside the northern line of the Turkish defences, by 10 a.m. After some skirmishes with Turkish outposts, they were ordered to wait for the infantry attack on Ali Muntar.

The British infantry of the 53rd Division was ready to attack by 8.30 a.m. But Dallas wasn't. By now the fog, which would have offered the infantry a natural cover, had lifted, and Dallas was inexplicably intent on having a meeting with his commanders. As it began at 10.15 a.m., he issued the order for his infantry, sweltering in the spring heat, to attack.

But the attack was again postponed because Dallas, believing his infantry was not properly in place, suddenly changed his mind. The guns were, in fact, trained on Gaza already. But when the artillery began to blaze, it struck an old cemetery wall behind and to the north-east of the fortifications at the top of Ali Muntar.

Undeterred, however, the British infantry raced towards the Turkish lines and were soon fighting the Turks in the cactus hedges below.

At 1 p.m. Chetwode finally ordered Chauvel to ready his Anzac Mounted Division for the attack on Gaza. But there are suggestions that Chauvel didn't get that order until 2 p.m.[3] and that he took at least another hour after that to organise his brigades for the attack. 'But we massed Australians and New Zealanders for hours were spectators of the fight. It made our hearts bleed. Here we were gazing right down into the city—and not allowed to enter it!' wrote Idriess.[4]

At 4 p.m. Chauvel's men, led by the 5th Light Horse Regiment, attacked. Before long they were in vicious running hand-to-hand battles with Turks in the cactus hedges. The Turks were surprised by the attack from the north so late in the day and offered only piece-meal opposition. They traded shots with the Australians throughout the cactus mazes. '"The Turks," said one of the officers afterwards, "ran in and out like rabbits and we shot them as they ran."' An old sergeant found him-self cornered in a field with an impassable wall of cactus ahead of him. His horse nibbled at the grass while he remained in the saddle to shoot at the Turks in the prickly hedge.[5]

Idriess's description of the fighting in the cactuses captures the desperation of hand-to-hand combat and the almost super-human—and subhuman or primal—force that overtakes men staring at death:

I wondered what calamity might happen when we struck those giant walls of prickly pear. The colo-nel threw up his hand—we reined up our horses with their noses rearing from the pear—we jumped off—all along the hedge from tiny holes were squirting rifle-puffs, in other places the pear was spitting at us as the Turks standing behind simply fired through the juicy leaves. The horse-holders grabbed the horses while each man slashed with his bayonet to cut a hole through those cactus walls. The colonel was firing with his revolver at the juice spots bursting through the leaves ... Then came the fiercest individual excitement—man after man tore through the cactus to be met by the bayonets of the Turks, six to one. It was just berserk slaughter. A man sprang at the closest Turk and thrust and sprang aside and thrust again and again—some men howled as they rushed, others cursed to the shivery feeling of steel on steel—the grunting breaths, the gritting teeth and the staring eyes of the lunging Turk, the sobbing scream as a bayonet ripped home. The Turkish battalion simply melted away: it was all over in minutes. Men lay horribly bloody and dead; others writhed on the stained grass, while all through the cactus lanes our men were chasing demented Turks ... How we thank, now, our intense training.[6]

Further outside the town, the 3rd Light Horse Brigade under Galloping Jack Royston was engaging the first of up to six thousand Turkish reinforcements who had made the long march from Beersheba. The British infantry, meanwhile, was inching against the odds towards the crest of Ali Muntar after a series of reckless bayonet charges.

By early evening Australians and New Zealanders were in the centre of the town, destroying and capturing Turkish and Austrian gun emplacements. The town officials were preparing a banquet to welcome those they anticipated would, by nightfall, be the new occupiers of Gaza when a nervous Chetwode—supported by Dobell— made the order to withdraw.

Chauvel strongly protested. The order reached Ryrie and the New Zealand commander, Major General

Edward Chaytor, just before the British infantry reached the top of Ali Muntar. Chaytor immediately demanded that the order be repeated to him in writing from Chetwode while an indignant Ryrie cursed the British commanders and obstinately refused to budge until every one of his men—active, wounded or killed—was accounted for and recovered.

> Never will I forget the utter amazement of all troops—we simply stood gazing down the streets of Gaza—officers shrieking for signallers to confirm the order lest it be the work of spies. The sun was right down—repeated signal after signal came: 'Retire! Retire! Retire!' ...
>
> We know that General Chauvel protested vigorously when the Big Heads ordered him to retire the mounted men. We would never have forgiven Chauvel had he taken that bewildering order quietly. The En Zed General Chaytor refused to retire his men until he got the order in writing. Our Old Brig. [Ryrie] swore like a trooper; then point-blank refused to move his brigade until every man of us was safely collected.[7]

The return march of the mounted brigades from Gaza that night, as the exhausted Turkish reinforcements were permitted to pour back into the city unopposed, was, wrote Gullett, 'one of the sorriest movements undertaken by Australians and New Zealanders during the war'. Months later, a Syrian doctor who had been captured by the light horse asked Ryrie why the British had pulled out of Gaza when they'd won the town. 'You can damn well search me,' Ryrie said. The doctor replied that when the Turkish commander at Gaza, Tala Bey, learned the British had pulled out, he had 'laughed for a long time'.[8]

Dobell and Murray, meanwhile, both seemed to be in denial about the blunder at Gaza. Murray's dispatch to the British War Office focused on the fact that he had now advanced his troops to a point 'five miles west of Gaza, to cover the construction of the railway' after being 'heavily engaged east of Gaza'.[9] He dramatically overestimated the Turkish losses at between six thousand and seven thousand and made no mention of the fact that the Australians and New Zealanders had actually taken the city. The War Office, perhaps sensing Murray's obfuscation, asked for more details. He responded, concluding: 'It was a most successful operation, the fog and the waterless nature of the country just saving the enemy from complete disaster. It has filled our troops with enthusiasm, and proved conclusively that the enemy has no chance against our troops in the open.'[10]

~

Three weeks later Murray, now with tanks and automatic Hotchkiss machine-guns at his disposal, would make another attempt on Gaza.

Gullett's writings strongly suggest that Murray and Dobell, besides having convinced themselves that the first Gaza attack was a success, were now in serious denial about the dangers of attempting to take Gaza a second time. The Turks had heavily reinforced the city with new men. They had also built another series of elaborate redoubts across the plain from Beersheba.

Despite a heavy bombardment of Gaza over several days, the British infantry could not penetrate Ali Muntar, and many light-horsemen became trapped, dismounted, with no cover as they attacked from the east of the city. The tanks proved useless, doing little more than leading scores of infantry to their deaths before being stuck in wadies and specially designed traps.

Trooper Pauls, whose 12th Light Horse Regiment had been moved forward to participate in the action, recounted the events of 19 April 1917 in his diary:

> The infantry on our left swept on under torturing shell fire, then a 'Tank' put in its appearance and waddled into action driving the frightened Turks before it. It got onto a big Redoubt and poured in its stream of lead on to the Turks, all the while it was under high explosive shell fire. After two hours in action it got on to a trap set for it, a mine, which exploded putting the tank out of action by 9 a.m. We had advanced three miles having driven in all the Turkish and were now facing their main position. Then they opened up all their artillery on to us, at very close range, mowing our boys down in heaps, while we pushed on. The 3rd Brigade was driving the Turks in on to us, they charging

them on horseback with fixed bayonets. The Turks in retiring opened rifle and machine gunfire on to us. This, besides the severe shell fire, was cutting our Regt up severely.[11]

Amid the shrapnel and the snipers Trooper Pauls 'awaited death, but my luck was in'. Two men beside him were seriously wounded, and he retired from the action to help get them to a medical station. He had a 'couple of hours having a touch of shell shock and was almost un-nerved'. He eventually returned to his regiment to find that while it had advanced slightly, the casualties were heavy: 'The country hereabouts offered no protection whatever and the ground was too hard to dig in to with pick and shovels. At 4 p.m. we had retired trying to draw the Turks into our nets, but he didn't show out. This was the most terrible day of slaughter I have ever seen and to have come through without a scratch is a miracle.'[12]

The second assault on Gaza was a conspicuous disaster for Murray's British forces. Murray, despite some of his good efforts—especially establishing the pipeline and railway—would subsequently be relieved of his command of Palestine and Egypt. His men in the field were all but set up to fail that day.

But there were countless efforts—both charted and unrecorded—of bravery and gallantry, not least among the members of the Light Horse Field Ambulance. They were the men who followed the battle to identify the dead and clear the wounded from the field. Gullett noted that 'hour after hour the fearless stretcher bearers worked in the open with no hope that the enemy could, under such conditions of fighting, respect their humane mission'. He singled out the efforts of Albert 'Tibby' Cotter, the international fast bowler who played test cricket for Australia, as 'prominent all day among the stretcher-bearers'.[13]

After the battle, Idriess took to his diary again—this time to excoriate the Bedouin:

> This morning there were two hundred of them all attempting to rush the big stacks of grain. They would come from all sides. While we were driving off one lot, fifty others would be among the stacks behind us, ripping up the grain sacks and carrying off the grain as fast as their legs and arms would let them. And these are the people that the British Commander is so anxious to protect, and penalises us rough brutal Australians [over]. They snip our wounded, and dig up our dead, and steal everything they can lay their hands on. But far worse than this, they are spies. They spy for the Turks, and Turkish and German spies dress up in their clothes ... And yet we are warned to leave the Bedouins strictly alone.[14]

The second battle was managed on both sides from a series of hills and vantage points on the Beersheba–Gaza line that effectively represented the front line. Frequently vantage points were mounds built on old townships and villages (all with the prefix 'Tel', which loosely translated, colloquially, means 'old town'), most notably Tel Jemmi and Tel Hareira.

Ninety years later I would stand atop Tel Jemmi while Israeli fighters and a helicopter gunship roared overhead en route to Gaza City in the near distance. The Desert Column had its headquarters at Tel Jemmi for the second Battle of Gaza. It offered a commanding view barely fifteen kilometres due north to the ancient Mediterranean fort. But as the commanders turned to face south-east, they would find themselves staring into a vast abyss of gnarled, dry creek beds and roughly tussocked desert. Somewhere out there was Beersheba. Back then, it couldn't be seen as it can—owing to its vastness—today.

But despite another defeat at Gaza, it was to be the next stop for the Australians who—from top to bottom—had by now comprehensively lost faith in the British command. The harsh landscape of Palestine claimed Murray's near-sighted command, just as it would forge the already formidable reputation of the British cavalry-man, General Sir Edmund Allenby, who took over as commander in chief of operations in Palestine. Allenby would come to love the Australians during the next act of the war: Beersheba.

8

THE BULL ARRIVES

Nobody believed Murray when he wrote that the total number of British casualties at the Second Battle of Gaza was 6444. This, it seems, was nothing more than a dramatic underestimation in order to hide the truth: that perhaps four times as many British and imperial soldiers had been injured or killed.

Murray, his staff and commanders, were now viewed with open contempt by the men of the light horse and the New Zealanders. The British infantry, having copped most of the casualties at both Gaza battles, was also indignant. Back in London, meanwhile, the British Government was convinced that Gaza had become a 'second Gallipoli', such were its forbidding natural defences, which allowed an inferior and tired Turkish army to inflict such monstrous casualties on the British and dominion troops. Murray's immediate response after the second Gaza engagement was to sack Dobell and promote Chetwode to the command of Eastern Force.

Already knighted on the battlefield after Romani, Chauvel now gained the distinction of being the first Australian soldier with the rank of lieutenant general on being put in command of the thirty-four thousand men, horses and camels of the Desert Column—or the Desert Mounted Corps, as it was then called.[1] It was the biggest mounted army since Alexander the Great traversed the same land.

The Desert Column comprised the Anzac Mounted Division and the Australian Mounted Division, as well as yeomanry and Indian troops. Chaytor succeeded Chauvel as commander of the Anzac Mounted Division, which now comprised the 1st and 2nd Australian Light Horse Brigades and the New Zealand Mounted Rifles Brigade. The Australian Mounted Division (whose name would, at the insistence of the Australian Government, be changed in June from the 'Imperial Mounted Division') comprised the 3rd and the 4th Australian Light Horse Brigades and the 5th Yeomanry Brigade.

As soon as he assumed Eastern Force command, Chetwode set about drawing up a blueprint for breaking the Beersheba–Gaza line. Chetwode's *Notes on the Palestine Campaign* outlined a simple enough plan, whereby the Turks would be deceived into thinking that there would be a third British attack on Gaza. But rather than attack Gaza, the British would actually strike at Beersheba and, using it as a base, wage a series of battles, row by row if necessary, across the lines of Turkish to trenches to Gaza. Water—not least the seventeen wells in and immediately around Beersheba—was the key. As the weather grew hotter, the light-horsemen and their engineers, including Lionel Simpson, roamed the desert south-east of Beersheba to mark the vital water points.

Beersheba's wells were fed by underground springs connected to the Wadi Saba, which snaked down from the hills of Hebron. Their supply was said to be limitless. Not so, however, the series of ancient Bedouin wells and springs throughout the desert to the south, which were capable of supplying water to only a few hundred men and animals. The key to a successful attack on Beersheba, therefore, lay in finding enough watering spots in the desert within a day or—at most—two days' march of the town, and moving the men and horses forward in groups small enough to be sustained by the water supplies.

~

After the Second Battle of Gaza, the Anzac and Australian mounted divisions had set up a forward base at Shellal, an oasis with a brackish water supply roughly halfway between Gaza and Beersheba and just south of the Turkish trench system.

The Australian troops were now on a three-month rotation. For one month they would comb the desert in the no man's land outside Beersheba for water and parties of Turks. For a month they would then rest in and around the coast at Rafa or back at the canal at Kantara. And for the third month they would undergo intensive training.

In late May engineers from the Desert Column made the 42-kilometre trek from Shellal north-west of Beersheba to Asluj, south-east of the Turkish stronghold. The engineers carefully laid explosives under a Turkish bridge that linked the railway line from Beersheba to Asluj. Although the railway line had not been used by the Turks since the second engagement at Gaza, its continued existence left open the possibility that the Turks could use it to outflank the British forces as they attempted to attack Beersheba.

While the engineers blew up the bridge, two brigades from the Anzac Mounted Division and the entire Imperial Mounted Division (soon to be the Australian Mounted Division) marched around the south of Beersheba. The British infantry, meanwhile, moved towards the Gaza end of the Turkish lines to similarly distract the enemy from the work of the engineers.

The engineers' primary aim was the surprise destruction of the railway line. To ensure secrecy the 6th Light Horse Regiment encircled the remote Bedouin village at Khalasa, so that its inhabitants—who spied for the Turks—could not tip off their masters.

Having successfully destroyed the Turkish railway, including 21 kilometres of line and six ornate Ottoman-style bridges, the engineers went on to survey the wells and springs at both Asluj and Khalasa. What they found made the so-called Chetwode Plan a possibility. Both sites were well serviced. At Khalasa there was a series of ancient stone wells, the main one about a hundred feet deep. At Asluj, meanwhile, the light-horsemen found a natural oasis of palm hods nestled beneath a towering hill that offered natural cover for a covert army advancing on Beersheba. Spilling out of the earth at the base of the mound was an abundant natural reservoir.

After the engineers reported their findings, Chetwode immediately determined that two entire divisions of men and horses could be watered at Asluj and Khalasa on their way to Beersheba. It was, suddenly, a workable plan. But it would come too late to save Murray, who was inevitably relieved of his command in favour of General Sir Edmund Allenby.

Allenby automatically inherited and embraced Chetwode's audacious plan and set about making it a reality. He arrived in late June 1917 with an outstanding reputation as a cavalryman and cavalry commander in the Boer War and in the early battles of the Western Front. He later commanded the Third Army in France with, as Gullett notes, 'indifferent' success, which would not have been known to most men under his command in Palestine. Known as 'the Bull' because of his fiery temperament and imposing physical presence, he was a cavalryman's cavalryman. And Palestine was a war that would be determined by cavalry.

Banjo Paterson, who had first encountered Allenby in the Boer War, next came across the cavalry leader in Palestine. By then an established writer, Paterson, also a handy horseman, had enlisted in the Australian Imperial Force for the Great War. He worked in Egypt in a remount unit, whose job it was to break new horses and care for the wounded animals for the light-horsemen. In his later book *Happy Dispatches* Paterson wrote:

> It was a changed Allenby who came to take command in Egypt fourteen years after the South African war. He had been through the shambles of Mons where he had dismounted his cavalry and thrown them into the fighting line in a vain effort to stop the German rush. He had lost his son in the war; and being a full-fleshed man, the heat of Egypt tried him severely, and made him harder than ever. Where he had been granite before he was steel now.
>
> He came to inspect our horse depot—a great lonely figure of a man, riding silently in front of an obviously terrified staff.[2]

Sergeant Charles Doherty of the 12th Light Horse Regiment wrote that, after Murray's departure, 'a decided improvement in the entire organisation was at once apparent and quickly reflected ... the revived interest and confidence shown throughout the army in general. The following months saw a continuous and thorough preparation for the coming attack against a natural and tremendously strong, fortified line of defence, manned by a large army with two previous victories to its credit.'[3]

After his arrival, Allenby quickly set about meeting as many brigadiers, regiment leaders and troopers as possible—a move that endeared him to his subordinates enormously. He did the same with Chetwode's infantry. Yet more than anything, perhaps, what made Allenby most popular was his decision to immediately move his headquarters from the luxury of Cairo's Savoy Hotel to the front-line area at Kelab, between Rafa and Gaza.

The times would suit Allenby. First, he had inherited Murray's achievements but not his failures. Second, he was bequeathed a plan that would decisively and inalterably turn the operation in Palestine against the Turkish army just as Romani had in Egypt. Third, he had in his commanders a group of battle-hardened, highly experienced men who were remote from the worst of Murray's tactical failures. And, last but not least, with the Australian light horse and the New Zealanders he had the type of tough, battle-forged shock troops who could—and would—set the Turkish army on what was, effectively, a permanent course of retreat to Damascus and Aleppo.

~

On a clear, hot spring day ninety years later, the dusty four-wheel drive carrying me pulls into what seems to be another picturesque Israeli tourist park set in what I assume must have been an artificial oasis.

It is a Passover holiday. Hundreds of Israelis have laid blankets on lush lawns under towering palm trees. Israel is home to a people who, perhaps even more so than Australians, love to barbecue. And so, while the women lie on blankets with dozy children to read books or sing, shaded from a blasting sun by the palm fronds above, the men set up portable barbecues, ignite the charcoal and begin cooking chicken and fish. Corks are extracted from wine bottles. The big children, meanwhile, shriek and splash in what at first glance looks like a giant swimming pool. This is Shellal, and the kids are swimming in the natural spring that watered the Australian horses before they set out for one final drink at Asluj or Khalasa before the long thirsty, night ride to the hills outside Beersheba.

About a hundred metres from the spring stands a lookout, which I climb. There is a sign on top that reads: 'The top of this hill, the site of a Turkish machine-gun post, was captured by Australian soldiers on April 17th 1917, during World War I. The post was dug within the remnants of a Byzantine Church with a great mosaic floor.' Chauvel was most taken with the mosaic when his men discovered it, writing to his wife: 'We discovered a very handsome mosaic floor in the Turkish works at Shellal about 400 AD.'[4] Today the tiles, having been carefully removed and shipped to the other side of the world, adorn a wall behind a glass screen at the Australian War Memorial—testimony, perhaps, to the maxim that in war the winner takes the spoils. Regardless, the Shellal Mosaic was, indeed, a sparkling talisman for what lay ahead at Beersheba on 31 October 1917.

9

BEERSHEBA

As the sun rose over Palestine on 31 October 1917, Chauvel was under orders from Allenby to have the Anzac and Australian mounted divisions ready for battle on the east and south-east approaches to Beersheba.

The job of the light horse at Beersheba seemed straightforward enough: after Chetwode's infantry attacked the town from the north soon after dawn, the Australian and Anzac divisions were to block the main escape route to Jerusalem via the Hebron Road, attack the enemy strongholds on the high ground at Tel el Saba and Tel el Sakati and, finally, push through the southern trenches into town.

Despite the simplicity of this plan, these movements required months of planning and weeks of implementation, as thousands of men and horses (aside from Chetwode's infantry) moved east from their camps along the coast and inland towards the target. Elaborate and highly successful efforts were made to reassure the Turks that nothing was afoot; when the light-horsemen abandoned a camp, they left tents standing. Each night the camp fires continued to burn and lamps were even lit inside the tents, while a skeleton crew stayed behind to hoax Bedouin spies and Turkish forward scouts.

As D-Day for the Battle of Beersheba approached, Gaza was shelled relentlessly from the big British guns to the south or from Royal Navy ships on the Mediterranean. It was all part of the ruse to make the Turks believe the British were going to launch a third infantry attack on Gaza and reinforce Constantinople's confidence that the absence of water made an attack on Beersheba virtually impossible.

Camels carried vast quantities of water to Esani, roughly halfway between Shellal and Khalasa, in preparation for the forthcoming massive troop movement. The potential water supplies at Asluj and Khalasa also had to be developed in the ten days before the battle for Beersheba. Perhaps as a safeguard more than in anticipation of an imminent attack, the Turks and the Bedouins had tried to destroy the wells at Asluj and Khalasa by filling them with rubbish and rubble. For more than a week Ryrie and his 2nd Light Horse Brigade worked constantly, clearing the wells at Asluj, sinking new bores and pumping water in preparation for the other brigades. Khalasa's wells were also cleared. The men of the light horse engineering corps were greatly buoyed when Allenby, having ridden all the way from his headquarters at the coast, visited Asluj and Khalasa—something Murray would not have contemplated.

Meanwhile, vast quantities of water were being moved across the desert and stored in anticipation of Chetwode's infantry, who, attacking Beersheba from the unforgiving, trench-lined hills to the town's north, south-west and west, would enact the opening scenes of the battle come 31 October.

Surprise was to be the critical factor at Beersheba, so Chauvel had to assemble six of his brigades, replete with thousands of additional camels and donkeys, as well as native labourers, outside Beersheba virtually under the enemy's nose—all without his knowledge. This meant that after a massive troop movement from the coastal camps, the horsemen would set out from Shellal in the late afternoon of 28 October en route to Khalasa and Asluj, 22 and 26 kilometres respectively, due south of Beersheba.

On the afternoon of 30 October, Chauvel reached Asluj and completed final arrangements for the forty-kilometre night ride to the outskirts of Beersheba. What lay before him must have seemed excessively daunting: by early next morning the horsemen must be ready to fight a long, pitched battle against the Turks after a sleepless night in the saddle spent crossing forty kilometres of unfamiliar desert. As it transpired, by the time some of the horsemen entered the battle, their horses would have been without water for at least twenty-four hours.

Despite all this, Chauvel had reason for confidence in his troopers and their commanders. Together with the New Zealand Brigade, the 1st and 2nd Australian Light Horse brigades were, according to Gullett, by that stage 'without peer among mounted troops engaged anywhere in the war'.[1]

The 3rd Australian Light Horse Brigade was similarly experienced but, for the most part, the 4th Light Horse Brigade had come late to Palestine, having mainly been involved in the operations in Egypt, including defending the canal. Despite coming late to Palestine, the 4th Brigade had operated convincingly at the Second Battle of Gaza and had a disproportionate share of 'originals'—men who had been with the light horse since it first deployed from Australia in 1914. By the time preparations for Beersheba were being finalised the Desert Column's 4th Brigade also included the reconfigured 4th Light Horse Regiment. Raised in Victoria at the outset of the war in 1914, the regiment had fragmented after deployment to Gallipoli. After returning to Egypt, it was again broken up and deployed as regular infantry to the Western Front. It was the only regiment to fight on all fronts of World War I.

The reconfigured regiment was commanded by the brash and daring 'Swagman' Murray William (Bill) Bourchier, a farmer from Strathmerton in Victoria. The 4th Brigade, meanwhile, had a new brigadier in Lieutenant Colonel William Grant, a pastoralist and accomplished bushman from Darling Downs in Queensland. Gullett describes the tall and wiry Grant, somewhat cryptically, as 'more excitable and impulsive than most of the Light Horse leaders' and possessing 'the temperament for the exploit ... which was to give lasting distinction to his name'.[2]

Another significant and potentially detrimental personnel change had also happened. Galloping Jack Royston, the much-loved commander of the 3rd Brigade, was relieved of his post the day before the Battle of Beersheba. According to Gullett, he was given leave to return home for 'urgent personal business'.[3] But there is another, more colourful, story about Royston's departure that seems more consistent with his recklessness in the saddle and his penchant for looking out for his men in battle: 'Some time before, during a gas exercise by the 3rd Brigade, Galloping Jack Royston had deliberately inhaled some poison gas so he could be sure of recognising its presence. He became seriously ill and, after some time in hospital, was ordered back to England.'[4]

Royston was replaced by Brigadier General Lachlan Wilson, a suburban solicitor from Brisbane. Wilson's 'short and round' appearance and his personal reserve belied his mastery as a rider and, like Royston, he had learned about soldiering in South Africa although, unlike his predecessor, as a trooper rather than a commander.

~

In the days preceding the attack on Beersheba, the sense of anticipation and excitement steadily grew in Chauvel's men.

On 29 October Trooper Pauls wrote: 'Soon we will be making the big thrust. A heavy bombardment was on at Gaza last night. Our aeroplanes are unusually busy to-day.' The next day he wrote: 'Last night we moved ... to Khalasa where we camped for the day making all final preparations and receiving instructions ... All units are ready now to make the big flank attack.' On the day of the battle, having watered his horse for the last time before the long night march from Khalasa to the outskirts of Beersheba, Trooper Pauls took to his diary again.

> We are now ... right behind the enemy's line of retreat, thus when the infantry advance from the front we will attack the retiring forces. The Anzacs are at present endeavouring to capture two enemy redoubts [Tel el Sakaty and Tel el Saba]. We are awaiting orders and at any moment we may enter into the full fury of a pitched battle in which the odds are very much against the Turks, who will eventually have to give in or retire to new positions.[5]

Lance Sergeant Patrick Hamilton of the 4th Light Horse Field Ambulance kept a detailed diary during the desert campaign, which he later turned into a brief but compelling record of the field ambulance's exploits. In it, he described the methodical movement of thousands of men and animals towards Beersheba and the details of waiting, with his ambulance mates, for the battle to begin. 'Am now riding a camel with the tent division,' he wrote on 30 October:

Joined the sand cart ambulances last night. Moved out from Esani at dusk. A complete full moon but rotten slow trip. Transport blocked up for miles, halting every few minutes. Thousands of camels in convoys. Reached Khalasa, 12 miles out, about 1 p.m., and turned in ... then stood all day to avoid being seen from the air. Boiled billy and had a good meal of curry and fried onions with Bill Taylor and Norm Challis. Moved out at dusk and travelled all night without a rest. Reached Asnlj [Asluj] 12 miles out. Then pushed on fast. A rough ride, covering another 15 miles.[6]

Sergeant Charles Doherty of the 12th Light Horse Regiment described riding all night on 29 October, stopping just before dawn for 'a short sleep' before embarking on the long ride in preparation for battle on 31 October. 'Throughout the night we continued our long ride over rugged, stony country, changing directions frequently; until shortly after daylight when we stopped near Iswauin [Iswainin]—some seven miles north of Beersheba.'[7]

Idriess, whose 5th Regiment was ordered early on 31 October to seize the high ground at Tel el Sakaty, north-east of Beersheba, described the vista from the Judaean hills as thousands of mounted troops began the attack: 'As the brigade cantered out of the abrupt Judaean hills the battlefield unfolded like a panorama— a four-mile wide plain, then the low hills fronting Beersheba, and running away to our right the white

Beersheba–Hebron road between frowning hills ... Hiding in a depression behind the hills was Beersheba, the white dome and minaret of the great mosque and the railway station, barracks, and numerous buildings growing plainer to us.' Idriess said that, while he knew a tough battle lay ahead as they galloped on to Tel el Sakaty, 'most of us laughed when the first shells screamed towards us ... I think all men get scared at times like these; but there comes a sort of laughing courage from deep within the heart of each, or from some source he never knew existed; and when he feels like that he will gallop into the most blinding death with an utterly unexplainable, don't care, shrieking laugh upon his lips.'[8]

Beersheba was defended by an elaborate trench system that stretched from Tel el Saba, itself standing behind the dry bed of the Wadi Saba, east of the town, through a series of detached trenches to the south and south-west. The trenches in the south and south-west—although close to three metres deep in part—were not secured by wire. More trenches and dugouts twisted through the hills in the west and north-west.

~

At 5.55 a.m. Chetwode ordered his artillery to begin bombarding the trenches south-west of the town. The guns quickly found their targets but, because it was a perfectly still morning, vast columns of dust rose above the trenches and hung low in the sky above. This gave the

Turks cover, but it also allowed British scouts to move forward, unseen, and cut the barbed wire that the shrapnel from the shells had missed.

The giant howitzers echoed around the Judaean hills. When the dust and smoke finally cleared, the Turkish trucks could be seen frantically ferrying troop reinforcements to the front. Another column of enemy troops and guns could be seen abandoning the town on the road to Hebron.

Much of the country to the south and south-west of Beersheba is hilly. Even today, traces of the Turkish trench and dugout systems are still identifiable. It is not difficult to imagine, while driving or walking through this area, how potentially unforgiving and disorientating it must have been for the infantry as they moved forward in a pall of dust and smoke while the Turks sniped at them. Small valleys, and crags within them, twist and wind their way across dry creek beds. Knolls and hills within those valleys, with trenches hacked into their flanks, would have made it tortuously slow-going for the British infantry. The redoubt system further west and the hills to the north of the town were similarly forebidding.

But by 8.30 on the morning of the big battle, the British infantry had captured a strategic high point south-west of the town—Hill 1070. Soon after midday Chetwode launched the main infantry attack west of the town with four brigades. A short time later his 74th Division cleared the Turks from their stronghold in the northern hills above the town. By early afternoon the infantry, having achieved all its objectives, was ordered to hold its positions. The job of the foot soldiers was effectively done for the day, but not without significant casualties and deaths. An estimated twelve hundred British troops—mostly Scottish, English and Welsh—were seriously injured in the hills around Beersheba on the morning of 31 October 1917. Perhaps a third of them died. Many more Turks were injured and killed.

By early afternoon it was time for the mounted troops, including the light-horsemen, to play their part.

~

The charge of the light horse was certainly the most decisive event of the Battle of Beersheba. By its very nature it also provided a dramatic and emphatic crescendo to one of Britain's most daring operations in Palestine.

But it was not entirely unparalleled that day in terms of bravery and determination. Indeed, the capture of Tel el Saba by members of the New Zealand mounted rifles and the Australian light horse was an almost textbook example of soldiers scoring a resounding victory against seemingly impossible odds. Had Tel el Saba not fallen, the next phase of the battle that day—the charge—probably would not have happened. And had the charge not taken place, Beersheba would not have fallen that day. Had Beersheba not fallen that day, many more horses and men would have been required to march back to Asluj or Khalasa for water. This would have inevitably delayed another attack on Beersheba by which time the Turks probably would have reinforced defences across the south and south-eastern approaches to the town or fled to Gaza.

Tel el Saba—the original village of Beersheba—stands perhaps a hundred metres above the northern bank of the main river, Wadi Saba, which winds its way into the town as Australian soldiers would have seen it. Standing just under five kilometres due east of Beersheba and nestled between the banks of Wadi Saba to the south and Wadi Khalil to the north, it offers a perfect point from which to rain gunfire on those who would attack Beersheba from the east, the south or the north-east. It offers a commanding view of the immediate surrounding countryside, much of which is undulating until it reaches the foothills, and the boulders on top give perfect cover to machine-gunners. On the southern side of the *tel* facing the deep northern bank of Wadi Saba, a sheer cliff face runs from almost the top of the mound to river level below. The Turks had cuts two deep parallel trenches into the cliff face. The dugouts were manned by scores of Turkish infantry with a perfect view of any aggressor below. Tel el Saba was totally inaccessible to horses.

Chauvel, meanwhile, had situated his battle head-quarters 6.5 kilometres south-east of the town. As the Australian general looked west from 'Chauvel's Hill' he could see the sand-coloured buildings of Beersheba directly before him. A little over three kilometres to his right the Turkish fortification at Tel el Saba was clearly visible. From where he stood Chauvel could see the Turks steadily reinforcing Tel el Saba, all the while moving a steady stream of men, horses, supplies and artillery out of Beersheba on the north-eastern highway to Hebron.

Earlier that morning he had ordered Granville Ryrie's 2nd Light Horse Brigade to cut the Beersheba–Hebron road and to take another nearby high point, Tel el Sakaty, north-east of the town. Led by the 7th Regiment, Ryrie's men—including Trooper Idriess—came in under the Turkish artillery. Not a single light-horseman was wounded as they careened through a Bedouin camp, scattering donkeys, camels, sheep, goats and chickens in their wake.

Idriess recounted sweeping 'among the mud houses of a Bedouin village to the rush of cowled figures, scattering camels, donkeys and goats' while shrapnel screamed overhead: 'Suddenly a Turkish cavalry regiment with four mountain-guns appeared almost in front … evidently coming out to seize the Hebron Road. They stared amazed, then wheeled and galloped back hell for leather … They got in behind the Tel el Sakaty redoubt, thrashed their gun-teams up a hill and wheeled around in action just as the 7th and we plunged down into an old wadi-bed facing the action.'[9]

English and Scottish artillery pounded Tel el Sakaty until, about midday, the 2nd Light Horse Brigade took the mound and cut the Hebron road. As the cloud of fine red dust settled around Tel el Sakaty, Idriess and his mates could see the fierce battle for Tel el Saba in the distance.

A heavy barrage of British artillery fire from close range was intended to soften up the Turkish defences on

Tel el Saba. But Australian and New Zealand horsemen from the Anzac Mounted Division who had been ordered to take Tel el Saba were relentlessly peppered with machine-gun fire from the top of the great mound. The New Zealand mounted rifles attacked from the north-east under heavy fire while the 1st Brigade's 3rd Light Horse Regiment began moving in slowly from the south-east. Their aim was to make their way down Wadi Saba, albeit under the sights of the Turks on the *tel*, climb the banks of the dry river and rush the cliff face. It was, in any soldier's language, almost a suicidal order given the commanding view the Turks held of their advance.

The 3rd Regiment comprised men from Tasmania and South Australia, under the command of Lieutenant Colonel George Bell, a Boer War veteran and Tasmanian grazier who would later serve with distinction in Federal Parliament. After initially dismounting and inching along the floor of the wadi, the Tasmanians and the South Australians—including Private Edward Harold O'Brien, a signaller from Tunnack near Devonport—managed to train machine-gun fire on the Turkish trenches in the cliff face above. Bell is mentioned by Gullett as having led a 'spirited gallop' under heavy fire to 'within 1,500 yards' of the Turkish position before he and his men dismounted. This distraction allowed the New Zealanders to win more ground from the east.[10]

At 1 p.m. the brigadier 'Fighting Charlie' Cox ordered his 2nd Regiment to charge the *tel* as well. The men galloped until they reached a point where the Turkish rifle fire made any further advance impossible.

Two advanced squadrons of the 3rd Regiment crossed the wadi immediately opposite the Turkish trenches and accurately trained their Hotchkiss automatic machine-guns on the trenches. Lance Corporal Henry Killalea of Exton, Tasmania, was seen darting constantly out in front of his C Squadron with the Hotchkiss, blasting at the Turkish trenches in the cliff. He was eventually wounded while out in front of his squadron.

For the first time, thanks to the likes of Killalea and C Squadron, the Turks on the *tel* became vulnerable. Taking advantage of the chaos, the New Zealanders at first crawled, then dashed up the back of the *tel* with their bayonets. Soon after, the Australians scrambled up the face of the mound to attack the trenches while others chased dozens of Turks, who were now fleeing towards Beersheba, along the dry bed of the wadi.

Seventy years later, 89-year-old O'Brien, who had served with C Squadron, would recall: 'we looked in there and the New Zealanders got into it with the bayonet'. O'Brien also described the future federal MP, Bell, as a recklessly brave and inspirational man—in the vein, perhaps, of both Ryrie and Royston. 'As I say, he would make for the shell bursts every time. He wouldn't dodge them, he would go for it, you see: he would be far enough away for the shrapnel not to hurt him or anything like that ...'[11]

Today, a railway line crosses the deep gorge of the empty Wadi Saba south of the *tel*; a chasm that the Tasmanians and South Australians fought so hard to cross can now be effortlessly traversed. It is possible from up there on the *tel*, however, to envisage what the Turks saw that day. Despite the chaos on every other front of their town, they must have felt all but invincible up there. The view into the wadi bed, along which the light-horsemen advanced, is absolute. The Australians and the New Zealanders below must have seemed—and felt—like sitting ducks. That they managed to scramble up the cliff face below, even while the Turks were so panicked by the machine-gun fire, is scarcely imaginable.

But they paid a heavy price. The 3rd Regiment lost one officer and ten men in the battle for Tel el Saba. They are buried along with the other Beersheba fatalities in the British War Cemetery in the modern Israeli city of Be'er Sheva. But they, like the hundreds of English, Scottish and Welsh infantry who died taking Beersheba, are rarely mentioned when the big battle is spoken of today. Neither are the other eight New Zealanders who died taking Tel el Saba.

Twenty-five Turks were killed on the *tel* itself, and 132 prisoners were taken. You only ever hear—if you happen to hear anything at all about the Battle of Beersheba—about the thirty-one members of the 4th Light Horse Brigade who died in the charge.

~

By about three that afternoon, with the Hebron Road secured at Tel el Sakaty and the strategic high point of Tel el Saba captured, the final act of the Battle of Beersheba was about to be played out.

Chauvel was becoming increasingly anxious that the fading light might yet—despite the eventual decisive capture of Tel el Saba—impede an overall victory in the ongoing battle. From his hill east of the town, the vista of battle stretched before him. Chetwode's infantry to the south, west and north of the town were holding position, having achieved their objectives. Ryrie's 2nd Brigade was holding the Hebron road at Sakaty. Most of the 1st Australian Light Horse Brigade, having crushed the Turks at Tel el Saba, was poised to the east of the town. But the town had not yet been captured, and the failing light would allow the Turks to bring in reinforcements or escape towards Gaza. The Turks were expecting a dismounted attack, probably from the 1st Brigade, which had, after Tel el Saba, made one unsuccessful attempt to rush the town on foot. 'Had Tel el Saba fallen earlier, as had been anticipated, a dismounted attack would doubtless have been decided upon,' wrote Gullett. 'But with the day on the wane, it was neck or nothing.'[12]

The situation required a creative, unanticipated response. Soon after Tel el Saba fell, Chauvel called a meeting atop his hill with the Australian Mounted Division's commander Hodgson, Grant of the 4th Australian Light Horse Brigade, and Brigadier General PD Fitzgerald, commander of Britain's 5th Mounted (Yeomanry)

Brigade. Chauvel made it clear to these officers that he wanted to launch a mounted 'cavalry' charge to break the Turkish trenches on the south-east and take the town. Grant—by most accounts impetuous, fearless and impulsive—wasted no time in telling the Australian general that he and the men of his brigade were the best at hand to carry out such a high-risk, devil-may-care operation.

Gullett described the following conversation between Fitzgerald, Grant and Chauvel as 'brief but tense'—a euphemism, no doubt, for a heated argument, at least between Grant and Fitzgerald, about who should win the honour of mounting the charge.[13]

Fitzgerald's yeomanry carried sabres, as would be expected of traditional cavalrymen. They were waiting closely behind Chauvel's Hill. But the men and horses of Grant's 4th and 12th Regiments were hiding in a wadi bed at Iswaiwin, about 6.5 kilometres south-east of Beersheba—closer to the town itself than the yeomanry. The 4th Brigade's other regiment, the 11th, was operating further south, close to the yeomanry regiments. The 4th and 12th Regiments had been secure in the wadi all day after the long march the previous evening. The men and the horses were comparatively fresh after resting all day while the battle went on around them. But many of the horses had not been watered for at least twenty-four hours. Unlike the yeomanry, the light-horsemen did not carry sabres. They had just their rifles and long bayonets. Whom to choose?

Chauvel, it is said, gave the issue but a moment's thought. Then he addressed Hodgson who, as the commander of the Australian Mounted Division, was Grant's immediate superior.

'Put Grant straight at it,' Chauvel ordered.

In a split second Grant had swung onto his horse and was galloping back towards his men at Iswaiwin. It was after 4 p.m. when the men of the 4th and 12th Regiments received the order to saddle up. Word spread through the lines: 'Tighten up all your gear ... in ten minutes we are going into Beersheba to water.'[14] 'At 4.10 p.m. we saddle up and received orders to secure tightly all gear to saddles,' Trooper Pauls wrote. 'As we were going to gallop right through the Turkish defences, first stop at town of Beersheba. We lined up behind a set of hills and came out at a gallop. We had 5 miles to go into town.'[15]

The Charge of Beersheba had begun.

10

NECK OR NOTHING

The Australians of the 4th Light Horse Brigade would have to gallop flat out over almost 6.5 kilometres of open bare ground, punctuated in parts by the shallow, dry beds of creeks and rivulets. Then, as today, the approach lay across a vast gently sloping plain that ran from the base of the crest—known then as Hill 1280—behind which the horsemen were assembled, to an elaborate but largely hidden crescent-shaped trench system and on to the Turkish railway bridge and the white-domed mosque beyond.

There was no natural cover. If the Turkish snipers and artillerymen aimed accurately, many of the light-horsemen would die on final approach to Beersheba. Few cared or, at least, showed any fear at that prospect.

Each of the squadrons of the two regiments formed three lines up to half a kilometre apart. They were followed at a distance by the light horse field ambulance stretcher-bearers. It was 4.30 p.m. and the sun was sinking behind the town. The dying light and the pall of fine dust—created by a day's heavy artillery activity and the movement of vast numbers of troops, machines and animals around Beersheba—made visibility extremely poor.

The light-horsemen had set their direction correctly. The barrage of whistling artillery overhead and the 'whizz' of shrapnel past their ears would confirm their course soon enough. But as they set out in formation they were all but blinded by the dust haze and the sun setting directly behind the town.

The 4th Regiment, behind its commander 'Swagman Bill' Bourchier, had assembled on the right; it would hit most of the trenches head on. The 12th, under Lieutenant Colonel Donald Cameron, was positioned on the left. Cameron's men would strike fewer trenches and find a clearer path into town.

But as they topped the crest of the hill behind which they'd assembled, neither Grant, Bourchier nor Cameron knew exactly where the trenches were or which regiment would confront them first. Brigadier Grant led the men over the crest but, as the regiments began to gallop, he dropped back and his regimental commanders moved into the lead.

The 4th Brigade's remaining regiment, the 11th, followed in the reserve lines while Fitzgerald's 5th Mounted Brigade followed at the trot. As the regiments gathered pace, two scouts from the leading squadron of the 4th Regiment, Troopers Tom O'Leary and Alfred Healey, bolted a hundred metres ahead. O'Leary was next seen bee-lining for the mosque, while Healey was said to be the first to jump into the Turkish trenches to attack the enemy with his bayonet.

Sergeant Charles Doherty of the 12th explained what happened next:

> As the long line with the 12th on the left swung into position, the rattle from enemy musketry gradually increased in volume ... After progressing about three quarters of a mile our pace became terrific—we were galloping towards a strongly held, crescent shaped redoubt of greater length than our own line. In face of this intense fire, which now included frequent salvos from field artillery, the now maddened horses, straining their hearts to bursting point, had to cross cavernous wadies whose precipitious banks seemed to defy our progress. The crescent redoubt—like a long, sinuous, smoking serpent—was taking a fearful toll of men and horses, but the line remained unwavering and resolute. As we neared the trenches that were belching forth death, horse and rider steeled themselves for the plunge over excavated pitfalls and through that tearing rain of lead.[1]

As the men raced towards the forward trenches, artillery shells burst overhead. The Turkish guns were aiming long. After galloping just over 3 kilometres, the horses and men were raked by machine-gun fire. No sooner had the English artillery taken care of the machine-guns than some of the Turks in the trenches began finding aim with rifles. Two German aircraft—Taubes—swooped overhead. A bombardier in the back seat tossed his missiles earthwards and the machine-gunner sprayed at the horses' hooves. But they appeared to strike nobody. The dust rising from thousands of hooves enveloped all but the men in the front line of the charge, so that most of the Australians could not see beyond their horses. The only guide for direction was the sound of the gunfire and the white dome of the mosque in the distance.

Men and horses close to the front began to fall. A young Victorian, Trooper Thomas Bell—who had arrived in Egypt less than two months earlier and was immediately assigned to the 4th Regiment—copped a machine-gun round in the leg. He fell into the dust where he lay screaming until the field ambulance arrived.

The 4th Regiment scout, O'Leary, had by this time bolted straight into town, overtaking streams of fleeing Turkish troops and officers on his way. As the forward squadrons of the 4th Regiment came within 750 metres of the first trenches, the Turkish gunfire intensified. But almost without exception it failed to find its mark. The Turks, fully expecting the light-horsemen to stop, dismount and charge at the trenches on foot, as was their custom, had failed to lower the rifle sights as the Australians remained in their saddles and continued charging. It was a fatal mistake.

As the horsemen charged, they kept their heads low and close to the necks of their Walers for cover. In most cases their rifles were slung over their backs and, as they galloped furiously over the final few hundred metres towards the forward dugouts, they cursed the waiting Turks and waved their bayonets overhead.

The dying sun glinting off the blades of the swearing, dust-covered bushmen, made a terrifying sight. As the first line of horsemen from the 4th, led by Bourchier and one of his troop leaders Major James Lawson—a portly Yorkshire-born man who emigrated in 1905 and became a hotelier in the Victorian town of Rupunyip—roared towards the trenches, a wave of stick grenades flew into the air about their heads. Rifles blasted at the horsemen from point-blank range.

Then came an order: 'Action. Front. Dismount.' Lieutenant Colonel Neil Smith in his history of the 4th Regiment wrote:

> Some men charge across the trenches, scattering equipment and tents to the rear. Others dismount to throw themselves bodily at individual Turks as they engage in fierce hand-to-hand combat ... The troopers lash at the Turks with their bayonets, some un-sling their rifles and use them as clubs in the confined space, others manage to fix their bayonet and lunge at the Turks, many get away a few quickly aimed shots and those with hand guns fire repeatedly at fleeting glimpses of targets.

There is pandemonium, men shouting, screaming and cursing, bodies writhing in hand to hand combat, horses rearing and even lashing at the foe … in the forward trenches it is over within minutes.[2]

Just as the first line of the 4th Regiment struck the furthermost dugouts, Staff Sergeant Arthur John—'Jack'—Cox noticed a group of Turks hurriedly dismounting a machine-gun from a mule cart to the right of the charging Australians. Firing at close range from the side of the Australians—unlike the other Turkish guns, which were failing to strike oncoming targets from the front—the gun crew, supported by a back-up crew in case the first group was wounded, could have cut the horsemen to pieces.

Cox was an English-born adventurer who had been a seafarer before fighting in the Boer War and the Zulu uprising. He'd also been a game-keeper and a gold miner in South Africa before emigrating to Australia and joining the 4th Light Horse Regiment on the very day Australia entered World War I.

At full speed, Cox turned his horse in a sharp ninety-degree arc and charged straight at the machine-gun crew as they hurriedly shifted the gun and prepared to fire. Cox, now galloping at a right-angle away from the lines of the horsemen advancing on the trenches, made an easier target for the Turks in the dugouts. They took pot-shots as he charged towards the machine-gun, waving his revolver above his head. As he came close he screamed at the machine-gun crews in every native tongue—including a few words of Arabic—known to him. Somehow Cox bluffed the men into surrendering. He took forty prisoners, including the gun crews. He, too, would be recommended by his commanding officer for a Victoria Cross. It would be inexplicably denied him.

As the first wave of horsemen from the 4th Regiment killed the Turks in the front dugouts, they went on to leap the second, main trench, which was said to be 3 metres deep in parts. The desperate Turks thrust their bayonets skywards at the bellies of the horses. Occasionally the Turkish blades struck home. But often it wasn't enough to stop the excited horses. A number, crazed with the excitement of battle and by the smell of the water in the town's wells, continued to charge, with viscera trailing behind them, until they had reached the centre of town. Only then did they drop dead.

The horse handlers from each troop quickly led the animals to cover while the soldiers leapt into the deep trench and began flaying at the enemy with bayonets. The fighting was savage and brutal. The leading squadron of the 4th Regiment jumped the first two lines of trenches before dismounting. A number of 'originals'—men who had come from Australia with the 4th and served in Gallipoli and the Western Front before going on to Egypt and Palestine—were killed after breaching the second trench. Among them was the young Trooper Edward Cleaver, who been engaged in a desperate battle with the authorities to return home to Australia so he could see his dying father one last time.

'Your brother was in the first squadron that charged (led by myself),' wrote Lawson to Cleaver's sister, two months later, 'and after galloping over two trenches, full of Turks, we dismounted at the third and got in with the bayonet. Your poor brother was killed in the act of dismounting by machine gun fire as were also his troop leader (Lieutenant Francis Burton) and three others in his troop ...' Lawson assured her: 'His death was practically instantaneous and he, with the others, were buried the next day a few yards from where they fell ... A curious thing is that, like your brother, all killed but one, were men who had been with the Regt from the start and stuck through everything.'[3]

Lawson led the surviving members of his squadron into a trench almost three metres deep where, careening on foot through machine-gun fire, they captured or killed up to a hundred Turks. Lawson was recommended for the Victoria Cross but, like all the men who deserved the British Empire's highest military award after that day's fighting, it was also inexplicably denied him.

Bourchier was in the thick of the fighting alongside his men, shooting dead six Turks with his revolver.[4] Burton was shot dead as his horse jumped the second trench. Another troop leader, Lieutenant Ben Meredith— a grazier from Terang and a popular and courageous soldier—was apparently shot soon after he dismounted, possibly by a Turk who had earlier surrendered. The 4th Regiment's war diary records several incidents in which

Turks who had purportedly surrendered again took up weapons amid the chaos and confusion of the charge, and shot at the Australians.

The mounted stretcher-bearers somehow managed to work among this hellish chaos, applying field dressings to the lightly wounded (many of whom threw themselves straight back into the fight) and clearing the more seriously injured. One of the stretcher-bearers, Private Albert 'Tibby' Cotter, was shot dead at close range as he worked close to where the four Gallipoli veterans fell. There were lingering suggestions that Cotter was also shot dead by a Turk who had already surrendered.

Trooper Phil Moon, a member of Meredith's troop, told colleagues many years later that he saw Meredith dismount and followed him: 'He hands his reins over to me and turns with his revolver on one of these pits full of Turks. They throw up their hands at once, but as he turns away one of them picks up a rifle and shoots him in the back.' Moon recalled that few of the bewildered Turks put up much of a fight and that he became annoyed when his horse Jerry began 'looking for grass to eat'. He did not, however, say what happened to the Turk who shot Meredith. But according to some witness accounts, Moon repeatedly bayoneted the Turk while yelling, 'You bastard, you bastard.'[5]

Dozens of Turks were killed by bayonet or pistol shot, while many others threw down their weapons and begged for mercy.

Another field ambulance man, Lance Sergeant Patrick Hamilton, related how a light-horsemen he later treated had told him: 'As soon as we cleared the trenches and dismounted the Turks threw down their rifles and offered gold coins to save their lives.' Another slightly wounded Trooper told Hamilton: 'All I could do was ride my horse, wave my bayonet round and yell. But we were lucky. No barbed wire and none of those horse pits too wide to jump.'[6]

~

Meanwhile, the men of the 12th Regiment—including Trooper Pauls—struck the lines of trenches further to the south of the 4th Regiment. Some men of the 12th apparently rode over and past the trenches almost before they realised they were upon them. But Major Eric Hyman—a grazier from Tamworth—dismounted on striking the first trenches to engage the Turks hand-to-hand. With a dozen of his men, Hyman engaged in one of the most vicious and bloody trench battles between the Turks and Australians since Gallipoli. According to Gullett, sixty Turks were killed in this vicious encounter—'many of whom were shot by Hyman with his revolver'. Only then did the rest surrender.[7]

Just as Hyman entered the trenches, the second squadron of the 12th, led by Major Cuthbert Featherstonhaugh—a South African veteran described as a 'fine old soldier'—was charging at full pace about thirty metres back. When his horse was seriously wounded, he calmly dismounted and—preoccupied with the suffering of his mount—took his service revolver and destroyed the animal. Featherstonhaugh then continued charging towards the nearest trench on foot, where he is said to have emptied his weapon into the nearest Turks. He then fell after being shot through both legs.[8]

While Hyman and Featherstonhaugh attacked the trenches, most of the two front squadrons swung hard to the left and, led by Captain Rodney Robey and Captain Jack Davies of Scone, New South Wales, rode hard for the town. As he and his men approached Beersheba, Robey rode around to the west of the town while Davies and his men galloped straight for the main street.

Although it has been swallowed by the new metropolis of today's Be'er Sheva, the skeleton of the old Turkish town—the town encountered by Davies and the men of the 12th when they screamed in from the desert—can still be found. Back then Davies raced down the main street, Ka Homando, past what is known today as Abraham's Well. A little further up, on his left, was the Turkish hospital and, a little further on the right, the main administration buildings and the mosque.

The ornate arches of the Turkish railway bridge still traverse the dry wadi bed east of the town, although the line has been replaced with a new one that crosses Wadi Saba just to the south of Tel el Saba. Davies and some of his men probably passed under the bridge on the way into town (it features in the photographs of many soldiers, including those taken by Trooper Pauls) before finding the mouth of the main street opposite Abraham's Well. There are signs that the Bedouin were camped in the expanse of flat, dusty plain between the main Turkish trenches at what is today's Bet Eshell and the railway bridge back then.

They are still there today. But today the plain is a vast field of roughly ploughed earth, often covered in litter. There's a Bedouin market opposite the arches, while a car graveyard—replete with the bodies of hundreds of crushed and neatly stacked vehicles—stands just on the outskirts of the town today. An Arab kebab shop stands on one corner of Ka Homando, while a car repair business nestles up against Abraham's Well.

Once Davies and his men checked the mosque for snipers, it was a short ride to the simple Turkish railway station, which stands derelict between towering apartment blocks today. Much has changed. But much has not.

~

Of striking the first trenches near Bet Eshell Trooper Pauls wrote in his diary:

> At about 3 miles we came upon the Turks' first line. Two lines of our men went straight on and the third line took up a dismounted assault on the front line defences. Half an hour after the commencement we were right into Beersheba rounding up large bodies of prisoners, guns, etc. 'Shock action' they call these tactics and very successful as the enemy was taken absolutely by surprise, as will be recognised by the fact that six of our troop captured a whole battery of field Artillery … This

is absolutely the greatest charge ever made in the history of the campaign in this front and will live in history forever.[9]

In the ten minutes or so that passed between the first lines of both regiments smashing into the foward trenches and Davies and his men entering the outskirts of the town, the Turkish forces had been thrown into a state of utter chaos. As the horsemen of the 12th Regiment galloped into town, closely followed by members of the 4th Regiment who'd finished at the trenches, explosions echoed through the streets and the surrounding hills as the Germans set off a series of explosions in an attempt to destroy the wells and other infrastructure in and around the town. Only two of the wells were destroyed, however, because the German officer in charge of the detonations was captured before he could detonate the others.

Turks of all ranks took part in a wild mob rush into the hills north and north-west of the town. Heavy guns were moved out of town as fast as the horses could draw them; even the engineers, who had elaborately wired the wells and important buildings with explosives, abandoned their posts and tried to scramble out of town.

After the fevered bloodshed in the outer trenches, hundreds of other Turks began surrendering to lightly armed Australians all over town. The 4th Regiment scout O'Leary, who had jumped all the trenches well ahead of his regiment before bee-lining for the mosque, captured a Turkish artillery unit by himself. An hour and a half after the charge began, an officer from his regiment found O'Leary down a side street sitting on the big gun (he had made the Turks move it so no other allied unit could claim it as theirs!) while each of the six enemy crew took turns holding his horse.[10]

In a letter to his wife after the charge, Trooper Edward Dengate of the 12th Regiment referred to the effectiveness of the element of bluff in the operation:

> I suppose you have heard how we took Beersheba, tearing up the barbed wire with our bare hands, chewing it up as we raced madly into the town, spitting sparks, so the papers said, or something like it.
>
> Well there was no wire there at all and those who took the town (about fifty or sixty) never got off at all. I was one of 'em … I reckoned I deserved a decoration but as no one else thought so, I never got it … I never fired a shot and no one else did either I think [it] was a huge bluff stakes, we put the wind up 'em properly … We lost a lot of good men there, the bullets were so thick they almost jammed in the air, its marvellous how we got through.[11]

The war diary of the 4th Regiment echoes Dengate's understated description of what many others considered to be a most remarkable military action. The diary for 31 October 1917 reads simply: 'The regiment reached Iswaiwin where it rested till 1600. Headed by

A Squadron with C in close support, the regiment charged at the gallop the Turkish trenches E of Beersheba, which were carried and Beersheba was taken ...'[12] Murray Bourchier, one of the charge leaders, was somewhat more effusive and proud, however, when he wrote to his parents a few days later:

> My Dear Mater and Pater,
>
> Just a hurried line to say that I am safe and sound after our brilliant attack and capture of Beersheba.
>
> *I led my Regiment in a Cavalry* Charge on the position and the boys behaved like angels and 'Australians will do me'. I am sure you will be pleased to hear that I have won the DSO.
>
> Your Aff Son
> Murray[13]

Chauvel—as a man reticent by nature and as a soldier never quick to indulge in self-congratulation— also gave the impression that he was deeply proud of his men, especially Grant. In a letter to his wife the next day, he wrote: 'We had a great battle yesterday and an entirely successful one but it was a long business and a hard fight. Mine was the usual wide turning movement with a long night march and ... all day battle, as we really did not take this place till about nine o'clock last night when Grant's Brigade which I put in as a trial effort, carved the last defences and the town at the gallop in the moonlight.'[14]

Throughout early evening, the skirmish continued between the light-horsemen and the Turks who were fleeing the town into the hills. The horsemen took about twelve hundred Turkish prisoners; another eight hundred were taken by the infantry. About five hundred Turks were buried on the battlefield, although countless others were doubtless left where they fell after clashes with the British infantry, whose losses had also been huge that day. More than twelve hundred Britons were injured in the battle for Beersheba, most of them during the big infantry push for the town on the morning of 31 October. About a third of them died. Their fatalities were almost certainly dwarfed by the number of Turkish dead.

The cemetery at Beersheba has since been the resting place of the thirty-one Australians killed in the charge. But 1250 men, from all corners of what was then a vast British Empire, are buried there too. Most carried out tasks that day that have been largely overshadowed by the pure military daring and *élan* of the last great cavalry charge. Their number includes hundreds of British infantry who, arguably, had a much tougher task in the hills and gullies surrounding Beersheba that morning. Then, of course, there are the New Zealanders and other unsung Australians from the 1st Light Horse Brigade who died capturing Tel el Saba—the impossible high point that turned the day for Chauvel and Allenby when it finally fell.

A German staff officer captured in the battle said: 'We did not believe that the charge would be pushed home. That seemed an impossible intention. I have heard a great deal of the fighting quality of the Australian soldiers. They are not soldiers at all; they are madmen.' Meanwhile, an intercepted wireless message, dispatched by a Turkish commander before he fled Beersheba on the night of the charge, said his troops had run for the hills because they were 'terrified of the Australian cavalry'.[15]

Thirty light-horsemen died on the day of the charge. Another, Bell, died the next day. Although diminutive, he could ride and fight with the rest of them. But he was, at 16, just a boy who was known to his fellow riders by the *nom de guerre* 'Trooper Wickham'. Thirty-six other horsemen were wounded.

More than seventy of the Australians' horses were also killed. Some were disembowelled by Turkish bayonets, others cut up by machine-gun and artillery fire. The scene on the battlefield that evening and the next morning was one of carnage. Numerous horses lay where they fell. So, too, did one or two Australians who had not been found by the ambulance men. Dead Turks lay everywhere. 'The trenches were literally full of enemy dead,' wrote Trooper Pauls.[16]

At least one man was found dead still astride his horse as it wandered the battlefield. The commanding officer of Victoria's 8th Regiment, Lieutenant Colonel Leslie Maygar, who had been awarded the Victoria Cross in South Africa, was last seen alive by his men— including Simpson—when a bomb thrown from a low-flying German Taube fell among them. His grey horse, also seriously wounded, bolted into the moonlight with

Maygar in the stirrups. He was found later that night and died in hospital the next day.

Seventy years later Simpson, then aged in his late nineties and his memory failing, told me he could recollect that on the day of the battle the open spaces in and around Beersheba were filled with bright flowers, possibly poppies and daisies. 'After we'd taken prisoners, we watered the horses and then … I couldn't believe it … some of the men started picking the flowers.'[17]

As the dust settled in the moonlight, a smoky haze from the Turkish explosions hung low over the town. Naturally, there was a rush for the wells by men and horses, some of which had not drunk for thirty or more hours. Chauvel had been desperate to capture Beersheba, according to his orders, on 31 October for the very reason that if he did not, thousands of men and horses would have to turn back to the limited supplies of water in the wells at Asluj and Khalasa. That is why he had employed the daring charge, so late in the day. It remains one of the great misconceptions of Beersheba, however, that the water found there was plentiful enough for all the men and animals. Despite the rains that preceded the battle, there was not, as Gullett points out in his official history, nearly enough water. Gullett reported that the day after the charge Chauvel was 'compelled to confess grave anxiety about water. Great numbers of the horses had received a short allowance at Asluj, and since reaching the Beersheba district on the morning of the 31st many were still without a drink. He obtained Allenby's reluctant permission to send the Australian Mounted Division back to Karm on the following day ...'[18]

The work of the field ambulance men continued throughout the night. At two o'clock on the morning after the great battle, Hamilton—unable to sleep—took up his pen: 'We ... lay down on the hard ground fully clothed for a few hours rest. But I could not sleep with excitement and wrote up my diary.'[19] In just a few hours' time Hamilton's elation at coming through the battle and tending to the wounded would be shattered by a horrible event, of the type that characterised desert warfare.

~

From up in the hills Idriess described the final moments of the charge:

> My glasses showed me the Turkish bayonets thrusting up for the bellies of the horses ... we heard the mad shouts as the men jumped down into the trenches, a following regiment thundered over another redoubt, and to a triumphant roar of voices and hooves was galloping down the half-mile slope right into town. Then came a whirl-wind of movement from all over the field, galloping batteries ... a rush as troops poured for the open-ing in the gathering dark—mad, mad excite-ment—terrific explosions from down in the town.
> Beersheba had fallen.[20]

II

AT REST IN ISRAEL

11

OASIS FOR THE DEAD

The day after the British forces captured Beersheba, 21-year-old Trooper Ernest Pauls took up his diary again. There has been no indication that Pauls or any of the other troopers were anticipating the grand finale that was the charge; rather it seems he was expecting something of an orderly capture of Beersheba. The part played by the 4th Brigade would—while important—be fairly routine and anything but history-making.

The day after the charge, however, his diary portrays a young man with mixed emotions. There was the unique elation—and the inevitable pondering over the role of fate—that comes from cheating death or, in his words, of coming 'once again through battle safely'.

Pauls had survived a series of trying battles over the previous twenty months as the British forces drove the Turks and Germans across Egypt's northern border, into Palestine and across the Negev. Having survived the deprivations, the terrible illness and the trench warfare of Gallipoli, there was little by way of war's horror and cruelty to which he had not been exposed. Nonetheless his account of capturing Beersheba is almost breathless in tone. In such a state of mind it might have been easy to overlook the dead, enemy or allied. But towards the middle of Trooper Pauls' 1 November entry, the emotional tone shifts suddenly from excitement to regret: 'Sad to relate some of the best pals a man ever had went under. Poor old Kilpatrick was fatally wounded early in the charge, as was Flood, Cotter, Cook, Bradbury, Charters, Neirgard, Coley, McClymont and a lot more …'[1]

More than ninety years later these men, whose lives ended in their teens, twenties or early thirties, are still together, since 'the Beersheba Cemetery is in the midst of a very fine lot of Gum Trees[.] I would very much like to get back to Beersheba some day & get a Photo of the Graves and Graveyard,' wrote Private Jim Gallagher in early 1918.[2]

~

It is early morning in Be'er Sheva. There's still just a hint of luxurious desert-night chill in the air. But already the powder-fine dusts of the Negev are rising on the barely whispering breeze to form a haze that hangs like a dirty pall on the horizon. It is barely the middle of spring. But clearly it's going to be unseasonally hot again—the type of day that leaches the fluid from your body and fries your skin, dispatches old dogs and sends even those masters of desert survival, the Bedouin, scurrying for the cover of their roofs. Only the Bedouin donkeys and camels come out in the midday sun here.

It is morning peak hour in Be'er Sheva, a city whose early twentieth-century Turkish architecture was long ago swallowed by a thriving, sprawling metropolis with a population of several hundred thousand, give or take an unknown number of the semi-nomadic Bedouin. The Passover holiday has finished for some. The buses are busy, and the roads are heavy with traffic. Jews, many of them Russian émigrés who came to Israel at the end of the Cold War, are heading early to workplaces that offer the air conditioning they might not have at home.

Drivers negotiate roads with one hand permanently on the horn. Taxi drivers occasionally curse pedestrians. Modern Israeli dance tunes blare from car radios, and commuters hurry to the scant shade offered by bus shelters.

The Beersheba War Cemetery is an oasis among this disorder, nestled between ultra-modern, high-rise residential units and a big children's playground. While the cemetery would have stood on the outskirts of the town, just a stone's throw from the old railway station at the time when Joseph Hokeidonian worked and lived there, it is now roughly at the centre of what is now a vast city known as the 'desert capital'. The Beersheba cemetery, which continued to grow exponentially in the days and the weeks after the great battle, is still surrounded by the gum trees that are everywhere in Israel today, just as they were in Palestine a century ago, having been introduced for the dual purpose of preventing soil erosion around the land's countless wadies and to help drain swamp land.

It's a peaceful place. But, like so many war cemeteries the world over that bookend so many lives that had scarcely begun, it is deeply sad and mournful, too. Even those with no connection to Australia, people who've never even heard of the Charge of Beersheba, weep when they amble past the headstones. So often it's the ages of the dead (19, 27, 20, 16) or the simple inscriptions on the stones ('*Gone But Not Forgotten—Mother*'; '*We Mourn His Loss But This We Know/To Do His Duty He Did Go*') that get to visitors.

The lawn is a brilliant green, moist and lush from the sprinklers that have doused it with precious water. No sooner, however, have the sprinklers been turned off than the blazing sun takes the life-giving stuff back; you can almost see the evaporation rise skywards and, after a minute or two standing there on the soft lawn, your face is dripping and the shirt clings uncomfortably to your back, courtesy not—as you might expect—of perspiration, but condensation.

It's the type of lawn, like thick, soft, carpet, that you'd delight in running on barefoot, as a kid. It is the grass of a thousand backyards in suburban Perth, Hobart, Melbourne, Adelaide and Sydney. It is the grass of countless farmhouse gardens from the Mallee to the

Southern Highlands, from Gippsland to Gympie. It is the grass of childhoods past, of post–Christmas lunch cricket matches and kick-to-kicks.

The Beersheba cemetery has, apparently, been famous for its grass for many years. For just a few days before I arrived here, I sit next to a man I've never met before at a dinner party in Jerusalem. We get chatting and conversation leads, inevitably, to Beersheba and Be'er Sheva.

'Ahh, Be'er Sheva,' says Dr Nitzan Rabinowitz. 'I grew up there and I couldn't wait to leave. The only place in town to play when I was a child in Be'er Sheva was the cemetery. It has this beautiful grass. We would lie in front of the gravestones and play … we were warned against doing this, however, and told that if we lay down like that the spirits of the big Australian horsemen soldiers would rise up and chase us with their bayonets.'

Tablets the colour and texture of bone, row after row of them, punctuate the green. Beneath each headstone is a different plant. Usually it's a burst of colour—a vivid purple creeper, a blood-red rose or a yellow daisy. But every so often you'll find a succulent green, flowerless, shrub or a more unruly lilac forget-me-not straggling over the invisible boundary between its own gravestone and the one next door.

It is close to Anzac Day. Although that's not a big day here in Beersheba, a few stray visitors are expected to wander through the cemetery. The big Anzac Day ceremony in Israel takes place at the Commonwealth

War Cemetery at the Mount of Olives in Jerusalem, where Australian diplomats, soldiers and other dignitaries customarily gather.

At Beersheba, two employees of the Commonwealth War Graves Commission are busy trimming, snipping and rolling the grass, weeding the beds in front of the stones and plucking dead flowers. The place is immaculate; were the mums and dads, brothers and sisters, sons and daughters of the dead to come here they would almost certainly appreciate the ambience the designers of these war cemeteries had intended. Stand here for a moment or two and you'll find yourself thinking that, although Palestine's desert campaign ended so many young lives with shrapnel and bayonet, this is a truly beautiful and reassuring resting place—perhaps even a small piece of Australia in a once hostile and still unforgiving landscape.

Trees from home heighten that sense. Eucalypts and grevilleas—younger, it seems, than the grandpa date palms in the middle—form a perimeter around the cemetery. Eventually they'll shade the headstones.

You don't need to look too far to find those men Trooper Pauls described as 'the best pals a man ever had': Kilpatrick, Flood, Cotter, Cook, Bradbury, Charters, Neirgard, Coley and McClymont. Charters lies second from the end in the front row of the cemetery. Directly behind Charters is McClymont; he is flanked, on either side, by Cotter and Bradbury. Kilpatrick and Neirgard (a reference to a Sergeant E Neegard) are just to their right.

There is nothing exceptional about Cotter's head-stone. Under the rising sun insignia of the Australian Imperial Force, it reads simply:

924 TROOPER
A. COTTER
12th AUSTRALIAN LIGHT HORSE
31st OCTOBER 1917 Age 33
IN MEMORY OF
OUR DEARLY LOVED
SON AND BROTHER

A simple shrub with tiny flowers of vivid blue softens the place where the rich, black earth greets the stone. It seems an understated tribute to a man who had achieved so much in civilian life, including fame—or infamy—on the cricket pitches of Australia and England in the opening decade of the twentieth century.

Cotter, born the last of six sons to an English mother and Scottish father, grew up in comfortable circumstances in Sydney's Glebe. His skills as a fast bowler first came to the fore while at Sydney Grammar School in 1899 and 1900; in the annual matches with Melbourne Grammar he took 6 for 53 and 7 for 57 respectively. By 1905 he was touring England as a member of the Australian test team where in all matches he played on tour he took 124 wickets at 19.8 and had a batting average of 17.6. In a 1909 English test tour he took 64 wickets for an average of 25 runs. In twenty-one Tests

Cotter took 89 wickets. He took 5 wickets in an innings seven times, for an average of 28.6 each. In the Sheffield Shield competition he took 123 wickets at an average of 23.5 runs each.

Cricketing tragics know all about Cotter, for such statistics place him among an elite pantheon of Australian test bowlers, including Glenn McGrath and Dennis Lillee. Yet unlike his successors on the pitch, 'Tibby' Cotter is no household name. After the war a plaque was erected at Sydney Cricket Ground in honour of the only Australian test cricketer to die in World War I. It was removed during a later renovation and has never been replaced.

When Cotter joined the Australian Imperial Force (AIF) in April 1915, he was comparatively old at 31. But his former life as a cricketer made him an ideal recruitment poster boy for the Australian authorities, who—due largely to the absence of conscription for overseas service—were struggling to find enough able-bodied men for the imperial force. Despite his cricketing prowess, Cotter's bad eyesight made him unfit for active duty. According to the Australian War Memorial, Cotter was no great horseman either. His celebrity was therefore, perhaps, a compelling factor behind the AIF's eventual acceptance of him into the 3rd Reinforcements of the New South Wales–based 12th Australian Light Horse Regiment. The 3rd Reinforcements were sent, without horses, to Gallipoli to bolster the 1st Light Horse Regiment in the dying months of the Dardanelles campaign.

Luckily, Cotter didn't get there until November (the Anzacs retreated in December). But any time at all in the hills above Anzac Cove was bad. Cotter was nonetheless more fortunate than many other light-horsemen who were dispatched to Gallipoli and died there. On his return to the light horse headquarters at Alexandria in Egypt, he joined the 2nd Light Horse Regiment and, by the time the AIF was engaged in running battles with the retreating Turks in Palestine in early 1917, Cotter was a mounted stretcher-bearer with the 12th Light Horse Regiment. *The Australian Dictionary of Biography* describes Cotter as 'strikingly handsome … cheerful and modest, he was generous in his praise of others'.[3]

No doubt Cotter's even temperament and physical agility served him well as a stretcher-bearer—a dangerous job that demanded immense courage. Medical supplies were often light on. Battlefield injuries—inflicted by bayonet and shrapnel from artillery shells, dumdum bullets (their lead tips filed off so they would virtually explode on impact with human or horse flesh) and bombs thrown from German aircraft—were frequently horrendous. Cotter's fearlessness on the battlefield was widely recognised; the official history states that he performed 'fine work under heavy fire at second Gaza; he behaved in action as a man with no fear'.[4]

After the second attack on Gaza, Cotter was briefly promoted to lance corporal. At his own request, he reverted to trooper. In the New South Wales Parliament in 2000, the then Liberal parliamentarian Brian Pezzutti remarked of Cotter: 'It is most unusual for official war histories to record the exploits of a private soldier under those circumstances. To be mentioned once is important.'

The second mention came after Cotter's death at Beersheba where, it says, he was killed while attending the wounded around the elaborate trench system that the Turks had constructed to fortify the town. This tells but a part of the story.

There are many allusions in the diaries and letters of the horsemen and in books on the Australians at Beersheba to frenzied revenge attacks on Turks who, having ostensibly surrendered, took up weapons and killed their captors. The official diary of the 4th Light Horse Regiment says there were up to four incidents of Turks attacking Australian forces at Beersheba after supposedly surrendering. There is, however, no official mention of possible revenge attacks by Australians.

The exact circumstances of Cotter's death remain unclear. The historian Ian Jones wrote: 'In at least four separate incidents, Light Horsemen were killed by Turks who had already surrendered. When one member of a [Turk] gun crew shot a stretcher bearer, the entire crew was killed.'[5] Cotter is the only stretcher-bearer known to have died that day, although three members of the light horse field ambulance were also killed— perhaps after the Turks deliberately targeted them—the next day.

The cricketer died near the Turkish trenches on the south-eastern approach to Beersheba. There's nothing picturesque about this spot today, and there probably wasn't then. It's a flat, dusty stretch of ground leading to the flank of Beersheba. Back then, as today, Bedouin wandered around with camels and goats. The field has been ploughed over many times since 1917. But a metal detector and a shovel will unearth bucketfuls of the type of shrapnel souvenirs that were stripped from Gallipoli Peninsula three decades ago.

~

Standing here at Beersheba War Cemetery in front of the test cricketer's grave at Plot D50, the relentless mid-morning sun cooking the back of my neck, I can't resist reaching into my satchel and extracting perhaps the most evocative and provocative war photograph I have ever seen. It is not an action shot of the type that characterised the early photojournalism at Gallipoli, the Western Front and other parts of the Palestine conflict. Similarly, it exudes none of the pain and frenetic motion of the Americans at Guadalcanal, nor the terror and the horror of the more iconic Vietnam War photographs. No. This image is remarkable for its absolute passivity, for what it says about the great, enduring division between the winners and losers in war—the living and the dead.

The grainy black-and-white image, far from perfectly composed, is of some of the Australian dead. They are neatly assembled in a row of perhaps twelve, lying side by side, their legs splayed and their faces to the sky, covered by what appears to be in some cases surgical cloth and random items of clothing in others.

Most have their boots on. Five other men are standing around the dead. At least two of them seem actively engaged in identifying the fallen. One holds what appears to be a notebook. Or could it be the Bible? There is a pile of personal items nearby, including clothing, water bottles and weapons. It is not known who took the photo or why. But according to the Australian War Memorial, it was taken on the day of the charge. This makes sense; the charge finished close to sundown, and the shadows here—possibly including that of the photographer—are long and obstructive. It is not a professional job. But that only adds to its striking, unsettling candour.

It is a picture that conveys just how prosaic war and its associated human indignity become for those who've seen too much of it. It says to me: 'The war dead are the war dead and the living must deal with their inconvenience.'

Cotter is fourth from the right. His long legs, the left bowed at the knee, protrude from what appears to be an army blanket. Somebody, having pulled the blanket back from his face, has failed to replace it properly. Cotter's left shoulder remains uncovered. So, too, does the left side of his face; his semi-closed left eye peers up at those inspecting him. His trousers appear to have been removed. A rough attempt at dignity has been made by covering his trouserless trunk. But none was achieved. In death Albert Tibby Cotter is a curiosity.

At first you think it's a mistake. But it's not; a small X has been deliberately, carefully, drawn in pen or pencil directly behind his head. The caption explains: 'The dead bodies of Australian soldiers killed in the charge on Beersheba lie in a row on the ground. The dead men were members of the 12th and perhaps the 4th Australian Light Horse Regiments. The body marked with an X is that of 924 Trooper (Tpr) Albert Tibby Cotter of the 12th Light Horse Regiment (12ALH). Tpr Cotter, who came from Glebe in Sydney, had been a noted cricketer before the war. His elder brother John had been killed in action in France less than two weeks before.'

~

Four more stretcher-bearers died the next day, after an attack by one of the German Taubes—open-cockpit, dual-wing aeroplanes from which a bombardier would throw his deadly missiles.

Just as Idriess had emphasised in *The Desert Column* the importance to the light horse of the four-man section, Hamilton in his account of the field ambulance's exploits explained the importance of the groups of four stretcher-bearers and horses in each ambulance unit. 'Firm friendships developed, especially with your "half section"—your mate and yourself,' he wrote:

> With him you shared your one hole in the ground as shelter from the frequent bombing raids, or your one 'bivvy', a hastily erected flimsy shelter, in the incessant dust above ground; worked constantly on

the horse lines together, cooked and had meals together, rode together, talked endlessly together, and wherever possible carried a stretcher together.

My stretcher bearers were dedicated young men, and all volunteers for this special task. They came from a wide range of civilian life—university students, qualified clerks and artisans from the city, and experienced horsemen from farms and sheep stations. Among these were Norm Challis, almost straight from school, our youngest and a great favourite. Also Lake and Maitland, Bill Taylor and Brownjohn, Corporals Oates and Carney, and others who teamed together.[6]

Hamilton details an almost flawless medical operation, as the field ambulance followed the light-horsemen into battle at Beersheba and treated the many wounded as they fell. After treating the wounded, he finally lay down to sleep in newly captured Beersheba, about 2 a.m. on 1 November.

The next day tragedy struck Hamilton's men. He spares no detail in his descriptions of the injuries sustained by his friends and colleagues when a Taube struck on the outskirts of Beersheba:

Saw the observer leaning out of the cockpit and the bomb leave the plane a few hundred feet up. The bomb burst on impact with the hard ground— a direct hit on our bearer lines. In the black dust and smoke, horses were rearing and neighing in terror while a few galloped madly away. Men were running and shrieking. Grabbed my medical haversack and ran about twenty yards to reach Brownjohn. His left leg blown off above the legging. Bleeding badly. His hand also wounded. We got a tourniquet on his thigh in quick time and dressed the stump.

A great crowd had gathered from the regiment nearby. It was a horrible sight. About six horses lay disembowelled, blood running everywhere. Here I heard someone mention Norm Challis.

'Oh no, not Norm,' I said.

'Yes, Challis, Carney, Schmidt and Lake, all killed instantly. Shockingly mutilated. We've wrapped their shattered bodies in blankets and laid them over there.'

Others were attending Oates, his right arm blown off, and Hay with his left buttock cut clean away. Found Hamlyn being dressed with a bad wound over his heart. In great pain. Gave him a shot of morphia ... Bill Taylor was one of the worst types of casualty—shell shock. Apparently standing between two horses, only ten feet from the bomb, he was not hit. But we placed him on a stretcher, a pathetic, incoherent, weeping wreck, unable to walk.

Oh God it was terrible, terrible. Everyone very shocked and upset. But we have to keep going. Turned in about 9 p.m. Mourning for my bearers, I pondered on the meaning of life and the fortunes of war. Why, so often, should the youngest and more recent arrivals go first? Was it fate, destiny or sheer luck that I had been spared?

Further, why was it that the Ambulance had been attacked from the air three times in 24 hours? It was well known that normally the Turks respected the Red Cross. Was there any truth in the rumour going around that our airmen had inadvertently bombed a Turkish hospital and that the Turks were seeking a reprisal? Who could say?[7]

Hamilton goes on to describe the burial of the dead: 'Here in the Holy Land, steeped in Old Testament biblical history, the lament of King David over Saul and Jonathan came to mind—*They were lovely and pleasant in their lives, And in their deaths they were not divided.*'[8]

Schmidt, Carney and Lake lie side by side in the front row to the far left of the cemetery. Challis is nearby. Hamilton's men are still together.

~

Trooper Edward Randolph Cleaver, the son of Edward and Mary Cleaver from bucolic Ferntree Gully in Victoria, lies in the front row of graves at Beersheba. Cleaver joined the 4th Australian Light Horse Regiment in August 1914, like so many, soon after the outbreak of war. He was 'an original'—one of an ever-decreasing number of men who had joined up at the start of the war, served at Gallipoli, returned to Egypt and been with the light horse for the duration of the campaign through Egypt and Palestine. If it wasn't for the bloody-mindedness of those Idriess contemptuously referred to as 'the heads' (a generic, dismissive reference to commanding officers or, indeed, just about anyone involved in the management of the war), Cleaver might not have been in the charge.

While it was clear that he was a professional soldier, he was never mentioned by name in dispatches, although the incident that took his life is referred to by Gullett. Death deemed him to official memory as little more than a statistic—one of the eleven members of his regiment killed in the charge. Few, it can be assumed, were aware of the emotional turmoil he was experiencing around the time he died.

Letters between himself and his sisters Millie and Addie, and occasionally jointly to his father and sisters, offer an insight into his desperation to return home to see his dying father. In a letter identified only, for security reasons, as having been written 'somewhere in Palestine' on 10 June 1917, the trooper says the Palestine campaign is 'not near so bad as Gallipoli as there the enemy was always firing shells and bullets at you day and night ... We heard over here that the recruiting committee was trying to get 5000 new men to take the place of 5000 men who came [in the first deployment of 1915] and give us six months furlough to Australia, but I do not think there is such luck.'[9]

His next letter, again from 'Somewhere in Palestine' on 27 August 1917, mentioned the terrible heat and the dust before moving immediately on to what was clearly preoccupying the young soldier: leave.

> We are all waiting for the furlough to Australia what [sic] was so much talked about for a while but died out again ... I think we deserve it after three years service without a spell and roughing it as we have to do ... You need not worry about me as I can get along in this battle of life alright ... If I have the luck to get back alright, I do not think I could care for the butchering again for a while anyway ... I see there has been a few ships been sunk with some of our mail on it, it is very disappointing to learn your letters have been sunk after all the trouble there is here to write them as we do not get much time to ourselves we are often away from our bivouac for days at a time and me gets very tired after a long ride and lot of fighting and it takes day to two to get over it again and of course we have to look after our horses between times ...[10]

By 9 October Trooper Cleaver seemed ever more desperate to return home, and he was asking for 'compassionate leave' for reasons that are not altogether clear.

> You say there is a chance of us first contingent chaps or what is left of us getting a holiday back to Australia by Christmas, I also thought there was

A column of British troops on the beach, possibly near Belah, Palestine, before the first and second Battles of Gaza in early 1917. (Ernest Pauls)

Ernest Pauls (back right) and regimental pals, including Harold Seale (front right, pointing revolver), posing for the camera on the eve of the Charge of Beersheba, October 1917. The man next to Pauls died in the charge. (Ernest Pauls)

The view from Chauvel's Hill towards today's modern city of Be'er Sheva, formerly Beersheba. (Susan McMinn, *Towards Beersheba from Chauvel Hill*, sand, encaustic and oil on canvas, 158 × 119 cm, 2008)

Last drinks: Australians, possibly from the 12th Light
Horse Regiment, watering horses at the spring at Asluj
about a day before the attack on Beersheba, October
1917; children at the same place today. (Ernest Pauls;
Paul Daley)

Men of the 7th Australian Light Horse Regiment on the eve of the Battle of Beersheba, near Asluj, October 1917. (AWM/P05093.026)

New Zealand engineers from the Anzac Mounted Division repairing the wells at Khalasa to enable horses to be watered before the push on Beersheba, October 1917. (AWM/J02836)

Brigadier General Granville de Laune Ryrie, Member for North Sydney and Commanding Officer of the 2nd Light Horse Brigade, smoking a pipe while mounted on his favourite horse, Plain Bill. At one point the inspirational leader was the oldest and heaviest man in the light horse. (AWM/P01778.009)

Australian light-horseman Ernest Pauls poses in front of a Bedouin house in Palestine, 1917. 'Me and some natives,' Pauls wrote on the back of the photo. (Ernest Pauls)

An Australian light horse unit, its pennant stuck in the sand for the purposes of the photograph, with a captured Turkish commander outside Beersheba on the morning of the big battle, 31 October 1917. (AWM/J06569)

Turkish prisoners captured on the outskirts of Beersheba on 31 October 1917, just before the town fell. (AWM/J03167)

This photograph, purporting to depict the Charge of Beersheba, has polarised light horse aficionados. Many believe it was taken when the charge was recreated for a cinematographer in 1918. (AWM/A02684)

Horses, probably killed during the charge of the 4th Light Horse Brigade at Beersheba, lay dead on the approach to town after the battle, October–November 1917. (AWM/P02400.026)

Around the time he was killed in the Charge of Beersheba, the Gallipoli veteran Private Edward Randolph Cleaver of the 4th Light Horse Regiment was desperately seeking leave so he could return to his dying father in Sale, Victoria. (AWM/P05693.002)

a chance when we first knew of it but things are totally different now ... I had to attach Addie's letter to it to show them the reasons why I wanted [compassionate furlough], but I suppose it will take a good while as it has got to go through a lot of different departments, you know what a lot of red tape there is in anything the government have anything to do with ... there is a terrible lot of trouble to get it but it will be worthwhile if I can only see you all again if only for a month.[11]

The next day, Cleaver wrote a short letter to his sister Millie. He talks about the patrol work—'the stunts'—involving his regiment, the colder, darker days as winter found its way to the Negev and the constant deprivations of army life. He then talks about the possibility of leave again: 'It would be grand to be home for Christmas if only for a few weeks to see Papa once again before he is taken from us as he has been a good father to all of us and sometimes I cannot hardly realise him being so sick as he always looked so healthy.'[12]

On 26 October, just five days before the charge, Trooper Cleaver wrote his last letter home. All hope of seeing his dying father one last time was gone.

Somewhere in Palestine 26.10.17
Dear Papa and Addie,

Just a few lines to let you know how I got along with my application for furlough ... I had bad luck and my application was returned to me marked insufficient evidence, as I told you I attached Addie's letter and there was something about me not receiving a parcel and saying that you heard that the fat officers are not backward in keeping them for their own use.

I was brought over the coals for it and severely reprimanded as they said he writer was liable to prosecution but my C. [Commanding] Officer did not seem to mind as he is a worldly and level-headed man and he reckoned that is what spoilt my chance of the furlough but never mind I suppose all will come right in the end, a fellow might just as well run his head at a brick wall as try and fight them as they have the best end of the stick by far every time, the only chance one has is to take things kindly.

I remain your loving son and brother
Randolph[13]

~

14.1.18
Dear Miss Cleaver,

As we have just finished the first phase of operations and are back resting men and horses, I take this chance of telling you how your late brother met his death. At Beersheba on 31 Oct a determined resistance was being put up by the enemy about two miles from the town so our Brigade was ordered to take the trenches mounted.

Your brother was in the first squadron that charged (led by myself) and after galloping over two trenches, full of Turks, we dismounted at the third and got in with the bayonet. Your poor brother was killed in the act of dismounting by machine-gun fire as were also his troop leader (Lieutenant Burton) and three others in the troop. His death was practically instantaneous and he, with the others, were buried next day within a few yards of where they fell ... A curious thing is that, like your brother, all killed but one, were men who had been with the Regt from the start and stuck to it through everything. Allow me to convey to you the deepest sympathy of all the officers, ACOs and men of the Regt in your sad bereavement. Your brother was one who at all times and circumstances was willing and ready to do anything he might be given to do, whether in the field or out of it and by his conduct won the esteem and respect of all who came in contact with him. He is a great loss to the Regt and is missed by all but especially by those who left Aust with him in Oct 14, I myself being one.

Believe me, yours very sincerely

Lawson MAJOR Acting CO[14]

~

There's scarcely a shadow in the cemetery now as the sun moves directly overhead. One of two men tending the graves wanders over. He smiles and extends his hand.

'Ahmed,' he says. 'I'm Ahmed. Welcome. Come—you like some tea or coffee?'

Ahmed leads me to a small stone building at the far end of the cemetery. It is screened by a row of bushy grevillea and rangy eucalypts, flowering with crimson brushes. Pointing to a flower I say, to myself as much as to Ahmed: 'This is wattle.'

'What is?' he says.

'Wattle.'

'What you do with wattle?' he asks.

'You can stick it in a bottle.' I laugh. He doesn't. Maybe he thinks I have sunstroke.

He looks at me quizzically and says: 'Us Bedouin, we go into the desert and find all sorts of herbs and plants. We mix them up and put them in a bottle to make you better. They are Bedouin medicine. Should we put wattle in the bottle to make you better?'

'No, no—you put the wattle in a bottle and then you put the bottle on the bench and stand back and look at it. You look at wattle because it is beautiful.'

'So, it makes you better if you look at it?'

'Yes, I suppose, because wattle is beautiful. It makes you feel good.'

He nods, smiles.

Ahmed's mate shakes my hand and points me at the water cooler while he makes syrupy Bedouin tea, sugary and pungent with mint.

Ahmed brings out the visitors' book and lays it before me on the linoleum table. There's not many entries and it doesn't take long to flick through. One entry reads:

WO2 G.I. Craggs
Australian Contingent Sinai
A relative lies here

The relative, Trooper Earnest Craggs of the 12th Australian Light Horse Regiment, lies in the front row just along from Cleaver, his headstone virtually in the shadow of one of twelve recently planted, smaller date palms. Craggs was 19 when he died, possessing the soft face of a boy and wide doe eyes, and wearing a uniform that seemed to hang limply from his scrawny teenage frame. In a letter to Craggs' mother soon after his death, the commanding officer, Lieutenant Edward Ralston, said that the day before the charge her son 'was laughing and joking as usual and was full of spirit all through the long ride':

> He rode into action just behind me and the last I saw of him, he was standing in his stirrups and cheering … he and I were wounded at the same time, he was hit in the head and chest. I helped him under the cover of his horse which was killed. I held the poor boy's hands while he passed away. He only lived about ten minutes after he was wounded and did not have any pain, Thank God.[15]

When we finish the tea, Ahmed asks: 'Have you seen the boy?'

At first it's easy to miss his headstone because he died a day after the charge. Most of the Beersheba fatalities happened on the day of the charge itself and, as you wander through the rows of tombstones, you find yourself looking for 31 October 1917.

H.T. BELL SERVED AS
3650 TROOPER
H.T. WICKHAM
4TH AUSTRALIAN LIGHT HORSE
1st NOVEMBER 1917, AGE 16

Little is known about Henry Thomas Bell's life or death. The farm boy from Walpeup, near Ballarat in rural Victoria, joined the 13th Light Horse on 17 April 1917. Although it is said that he stood just 5 feet 4 inches and weighed 8 stone, the AIF recruitment officials, impressed by his riding skills, believed the boy when he listed his age at 21. His AIF enlistment form tells the story of a tragic hoax. He enlisted as 'Harold Thomas Wickham' but after his death, an official has written in red ink 'Bell Harold Thomas'. Next to 'Bell', in the same hand, is written 'alias'. Bell listed his next of kin as an 'uncle', Mr Thomas Bell of Walpeup, Victoria. Again the red ink tells a story within a story. 'Uncle' is crossed out, the word 'father' inserted.

Other AIF service records show that Bell embarked for Egypt on 22 June 1917, just as the British forces, under the new command of Allenby, pushed forward with a strategy to break the Beersheba–Gaza line. If the boy, Bell, wanted action he was not going to be disappointed. After arriving in Egypt in early August he was dispatched, along with others from his regiment, as a reinforcement for the 4th Regiment. Assigned to a Hotchkiss machine-gun section, he was required to care for a packhorse carrying the heavy weapon and relevant supplies, such as ammunition.

He was but one of sixteen Australians who died the day after the Charge of Beersheba. The official death toll of Australians on the day of the charge stands at thirty-one. But that figure includes only members of the 4th Australian Light Horse Brigade, comprising the 12th and 4th Regiments. The Beersheba War Cemetery is the resting place of fifty-five Australians from a variety of regiments who died that day.

While the charge at Beersheba was undoubtedly a tactical success, the often-quoted death toll of thirty-one is misleading in another sense, too; it gives no indication of the vicious fighting involving troops from other countries—mainly England, Scotland and Wales—who died in other battles around Beersheba on 31 October 1917. And so, when you walk around the Beersheba cemetery, you'll find a row of men from the Suffolk Regiment and behind them twenty or thirty from the Welsh Fusiliers, the Kensington Battalion and the Civil Service Rifles.

And then there's another untold story altogether: the Turkish dead. Just a few hundred metres from the war cemetery you'll find an obelisk-shaped monument to the Turks who died at Beersheba that day. It says that 298 soldiers of the Ottomans were killed on or around the day of the charge. This figure seems a highly implausible underestimation of the true Turkish death toll, especially in light of the hundreds and hundreds of imperial troops who died at Beersheba on that day or of injuries the next.

Unlike the imperial forces, the Turks did not mark their dead with individual graves and tombstones. They took the more pragmatic approach of leaving them for the enemy to deal with or burying them on the battle-field in mass graves. Dozens, perhaps hundreds, are deep under the ploughed earth between Bet Eshell—the site of the main Turkish trenches—and the old railway bridge flanking the town, where the Bedouin wander today.

The unassuming Turkish memorial is one of few obvious reminders that the Turks actually established Beersheba, on its current site, early in the twentieth century. It stands next to the now-derelict railway station that was mined by Turkish and German engineers, and set to be detonated on the day of the charge.

At the gardeners' insistence I go back into their cottage for cold water, and while there I leaf through the visitors' book.

'Many died so that Israel can live,' wrote an adviser to the mayor of Be'er Sheva in 1992.

Then I see a familiar name—Cox.

'Lovingly kept memorial for those who willingly gave their lives that others may live in peace and security,' reads the message. It's signed by Nancy and John Cox. Cox? Cox—the armourer who captured the Turkish machine-gun single-handedly, only to have the British heads deny him his Victoria Cross. Arthur 'Jack' Cox.

12

FATHERS AND SONS

A pristine sky perfectly accentuates the figures in white as they meander purposefully about the lawns. The soothing mid-morning sun, the cloudless aquamarine above and the vivid green underfoot combine to lend the bobbing broad-brimmed hats and flannels—pressed, starched and spotless—an almost luminous, phosphorescent glow. Elderly bodies gingerly crouch and bend forward so slowly and intently, with the fluidity of cresting waves, that, watching them closely, it's as if every other frame of this moving picture is missing.

There's a slight chill, and the faint breeze remains thick with last season's eucalypt. But as you drive to this bowls club on a Tuesday morning of such good-to-be-alive glory, you keep spotting decidedly non-native, towering date palms, straining forward, splitting the surfaces of ludicrously top-dressed lawns that burst their borders like over-yeasted, green-iced cupcakes. These trees are lost. Surely their homes are in the desert? Not this comfortable Sydney suburban patch, a blissful oasis though it is, for retirees and pram-pushers.

But then again, I remind myself, I'm looking for clues. I'm on the lookout and I'm here at this bowls club, with its blond brick, smoked glass and clipped lawns, with its electronic symphony of pokies and its eight-dollar schnitzels, to hear a forgotten story of the desert.

In a basement at the back of the bowls club, enclosed by hospital-blue walls and psychedelic purple and gold carpet, there's a Probus Club meeting in progress. Probus, a hybrid of 'Professional' and 'Business', aims to restore purpose to the lives of former accountants and small businessmen, bank tellers and clerks, teachers and police officers, some of whom—having yearned so long for a second superannuated life beyond paid labour—find themselves, instead, trapped in a lonely void of trivial pursuits and thoughts of mortality.

It's a pitiful cliché that the search for meaning is a young man's quest. Blokes, no matter their age, don't like to admit they're lost. But such clubs, in Australia and elsewhere, bring together men—some of surprising middle age—who need to rekindle the camaraderie, the focus and the meaning that age, retirement, or both, conspire to deny them.

The meeting has just dealt with the final pressing matters of business: a bus trip to the bush with the wives and a night out in town to see 'Circus de Soul', by which the man at the microphone means Cirque du Soleil.

They break for tea and individually cellophane-wrapped Scotch fingers. Cups are delivered to the older and less mobile blokes of whom there are several; the atmosphere is alive with heartfelt fraternity. Post-middle-aged frailty is treated with the sort of no-fuss, blind-eye dignity here that it is not necessarily afforded on the bus, in the street, in the supermarket queue—or at home.

Curiosity and anticipation heighten as the guest speaker materialises next to the lectern. Arriving, as he does, dressed in a well-cut dark suit, white shirt and black tie, and with a briefcase extending from one arm, John Cox carries a certain formality into this room of hush-puppied, polo-shirted, shiny-pated brethren. At the beginning of his ninth decade, Cox is trim, dark-haired and well kept—testimony, it would seem, to a life of order, routine and self-discipline. Despite his proud appearance, he is modest, warm and friendly. His dark eyes shimmer with a light bred of knowledge that life can and should be truly extraordinary, a journey that is the sum of what you make it.

We all carry something of our fathers in our hearts, if not our minds. We might not resemble him, physically or emotionally. We might not even like him or know him. But every man is a part of his father just as something of every father lives on in his son. John Cox is a living embodiment of this maxim even though, to an outsider, he seems not much like his long-departed dad at all. As an old man, John Cox still ponders this paradox.

John left school at 15 to join the bank, whereas at 15 his English-born father, Arthur John—'Jack'—Cox went to sea as a cabin boy from his home at Gossport near Portsmouth in Hampshire, England. As the ship carrying Jack rounded Cape Horn to fish the treacherous waters of the Pacific, a savage storm blew up and the vessel listed perilously. A wave, higher than the mast, struck while Jack and another cabin boy, Tom, furled the sails. Jack, clinging to the yardarm, made a pact with God that, should he be allowed to live, he'd never go to sea again. Tom and two men were swept away. Jack was spared. God, however, might well be disappointed; while Jack never worked the oceans again, his subsequent adventures belied the promise of sedate caution that was so implicit in his pact with the Almighty.

John Cox stayed in the bank for forty-three years until retirement in his late fifties, when, together with his wife, he finished high school, earned a Bachelor of Arts degree and travelled the world. John smiles, shakes his head and laughs at the mystery of how father and son could seem so profoundly unalike.

'Dad was an adventurer, but I spent forty-three years in a bank,' he says matter of factly. He laughs, screws his eyes shut and shakes his head.

After surviving the storm Jack, at 17, together with his twin brother Herbert, enlisted in the Imperial Yeomanry just in time for the outbreak of the Boer War in 1899. Herbert died in South Africa, shot through the head. Jack survived—again. But Herbert's death haunted him. Both boys had promised their mother they'd keep each other safe; now Jack felt too guilty to return to his parents in England. His wanderings began. He'd never return home. Instead, Jack Cox's adventure continued through the gold mines of South Africa and into the South African Constabulary where, in 1906, he helped put down the second Zulu rebellion. After that he became a park ranger in the Transvaal until, twelve years after he left home for the Boer War, Jack decided to try his luck in New Zealand and Australia.

Australia, early in the second decade of Federation, would seem an unlikely place to find a connection with those lost generations of warrior horsemen of the Sinai and Negev. But that is where it began for Jack. And it is that connection that brings his son John to the lectern in the basement of this bowling club almost a hundred years later.

Less than a week after Australia declared war on Germany on 4 August 1914, on the very day recruiting opened, Jack volunteered and received orders to attend Broadmeadows Camp on the outskirts of Melbourne, the base of the 4th Light Horse Regiment. Just over three years later that regiment conducted a war-fighting operation so audacious that it is recognised by military historians the world over as the 'last great cavalry charge'.

John Cox has made it the work of his twilight years to ensure that as many Australians as possible know about it. In so doing, he hopes, history might eventually come to grant Beersheba a rightful place among the pantheon of names—Gallipoli and the Western Front, Kokoda and Long Tan—that have helped define Australia to itself and the world. Cox, his audience well and truly aboard for the journey in his father's desert footsteps, explains just how desperate the situation was.

'Now these light-horsemen, these mounted infantrymen, were being asked to attempt to do something that had never been done before in the annals of military history—a 6-kilometre charge over open ground, bare of any cover, of any growth, against a well-trained, well-prepared, well-entrenched enemy, who was being supported by artillery, by machine-guns and by German planes,' he tells them.

'How could such an action be made by men untrained for such an action, riding horses which had been almost fifty hours since their last watering? How could it possibly succeed without terrible, terrible casualties?'

The story that John goes on to recount—his father's life in the military and with, perhaps, his most remarkable moment at Beersheba—is not based on the diaries and letters of Jack who, like so many of the light-horsemen, wrote home regularly to detail events on their trail through the deserts while fighting the Turks. For after Jack died in 1959, six years after suffering a stroke, his distraught wife Agnes got rid of all his letters and writings about the war. It is, however, a remarkable oral history, much of which was recounted to a son by a father on his deathbed.

John explains it best. 'He took a stroke which left him paralysed. And for some reason my mother thought that she and I could nurse him. He was a 16-stone dead weight and he was murder to lift. And anyway, at night he wouldn't sleep. And I'd hear him talking to himself, or I'd come in to change his sheets because he'd wet himself, and I'd get up out of bed and sit in the room and just listen to him,' he says. 'And he used to talk about these amazing things to no-one, just talk away into the night. He didn't even know I was there. And over a period of eight years, a lot of it sort of stuck in my memory ... I've got twin boys, and I (later) started telling them about Dad's adventures, and they said, "It's no good telling us—you've got to put it all in a book."'

~

John's story about his father resonated with me. Just a few weeks before John and I first spoke, I had sat by my father's bedside over four long days while he died.

Much that had been previously unspoken between us was said.

~

In 1993 John Cox went to Beersheba. He visited the Commonwealth War Cemetery, wrote in the visitors' book with Nancy and saw the tombstones bearing the names of all those comrades his father had mentioned so many times as he raved into the night. Then, in 2001, John published *The Miraculous Lives of a Man Called Jack*. As a testimony of a son's love and admiration for his father, it's hard to beat. John sells the book when he speaks to groups like this one, in the basement of the bowls club.

Jack died nearly fifty years ago. Anyone who experiences the death of a parent carries it with them until it becomes part of their fabric. In that, John Cox is no different. Jack, perhaps unknowingly, perhaps not, bequeathed his son a recollection of the charge and, within it, the story of an amazing thing he did that day when he distracted and took prisoner a Turkish machine-gun crew who were about to change the course of the famous charge. But then it was a day for amazing actions, about which the perpetrators spoke rarely after returning from the war in 1918 or 1919 to settle back into civilian life—some seamlessly, others less so.

'Now, you gentlemen want to tell your children about that charge at Beersheba, you want to tell your grandchildren and you want to tell your friends,' he says.

'The Charge of Beersheba was perhaps the greatest charge in military history. Now can you imagine if they'd been American troops who'd won such a victory? How many books, how many poems, how many songs would have been written? But because it's Australian, it's not in the history books, it's not taught to our children in school and perhaps 90 per cent of Australians have never even heard of it.'

There's a murmur of agreement among John's audience. Heads nod, and there's a few embarrassed whispers as some men check whether the blokes next to them have ever heard of the charge before.

John Cox is not, of course, the only descendant of an Australian light-horseman to inherit a record of the Australian military operations in the Sinai and the Negev, leading up to the Charge of Beersheba and on to the capture of Jerusalem less than two months later. Many Australian families have letters, postcards and diaries written by relatives who fought in Egypt and Palestine from 1915 to 1918. The Australian War Memorial in Canberra has some of these writings. Others are closely held by the descendants, some of whom have visited the light horse battle sites in Egypt, Israel, the Palestinian territories and Syria to follow in the trail of their forefathers. They include members of the Australian Light Horse Association, a group of aficionados that includes direct descendants of the charge—such as Rob Unicomb—and others who have simply been captivated by the actions of Australian troops in the World War I desert campaign.

~

Rob Unicomb and Grant Pyke are mates today, brought together by a chance meeting in Israel as each retraced the ninety-year-old steps of his respective relatives.

Unicomb, a builder with an easygoing temperament, has embarked on what he considers to be an odyssey of self-discovery through reading and rereading the war diaries of his grandfather. His granddad is Ernest Pauls—'Ernie'.

'I was about six when he died so, you know, I was old enough so I can remember the old bloke today but I wasn't really old enough to talk about anything but the basics back then,' Rob says. 'Reading his diaries has been a way for me to get to know him in a way that I couldn't then—you want to work out where you're coming from in life.'

Rob, like his granddad, has always been a keen horseman. Similarly, he left school early to make his way in his chosen trade of carpentry. He's been enormously successful in recent years as a builder on the New South Wales Central Coast. But like many men, when he struck middle age, Rob began to ponder the meaning of his success and wealth.

Ernie had always kept a box in the shed at his rented home in Raymond Terrace, north of Newcastle. It contained all of his World War I memorabilia, including bits of his uniforms (leggings, hat and bandoliers included), many of his letters and hundreds of photographs and maps. As his five children and grandchildren grew, they would pilfer the box for original photographs and other keepsakes for school assignments about World War I. When Ernie died in 1967 his wife threw out the box. Only his diary and a handful of his photographs and hand-drawn maps were saved.

The diary, transcribed from his handwriting into type and bound, is bookended by two photographs. The picture at the front shows the young Pauls in 1915, sitting in Sydney's Crown Studios in his khaki tunic, with a bandolier draped across his chest from the left shoulder. Under the broad-brimmed digger's slouch hat featuring the emu plume, Pauls stares off to the right. His full lips seem poised to smile. There is much of his grandson in that picture.

The picture at the back depicts an older man—a wiry old rooster—in a broad-brimmed hat and whites, intently peering down the green through his glasses as he prepares to release the ball. If you look carefully at his left hand as it rests casually on his knee, you'll just make out the roll-your-own cigarette between the index and second fingers.

'Handsome bugger, wasn't he?' says 46-year-old Rob. 'I'm not kidding when I say that all of this has completely changed my life. He never talked about the war to anybody, except maybe his mates at the RSL. Today perhaps blokes in his situation would be offered counselling or something … but I think that is why the RSL was so important to Ernie and his mates. It was a place they could go to share experiences with other blokes who understood—who'd been through it.'

Rob, like John Cox, wants young Australians to read about the travails of the light-horsemen in Egypt and Palestine because he believes there is much to be learnt from their resilience and improvisation through-out enormous hardships.

'I know when things have been tough … I've read the diaries and thought "What I'm going through is nothing." You read about youth suicide and find it really confusing … Surely today's young people can take something from the story of these other young people who were fighting to survive every day and watching their mates die in the most terrible conditions.'

One of the pictures retrieved from Ernest Pauls' box in the shed before it was tossed out features four young soldiers. They are posing before an open tent. Two of the men are slouched across the earth behind a Hotchkiss machine-gun while two others crouch behind them. The men at the front have their revolvers drawn and pointed, in mock fashion, at one another. One of the men at the back is Pauls. The man leaning across the ground directly in front of him is Harold Seale, a wool-classer from Sydney's Mosman.

Seale's great nephew is Grant Pyke. Pyke, an accomplished horseman like his great-uncle, was one of about eighty riders who participated in a re-enactment of the charge on 31 October 2007—exactly ninety years to the day after the charge itself. The re-enactment was performed at dusk, and the riders—mostly from Australia and England—cantered, rather than charged, from Bet Eshel to the outskirts of Beersheba.

It is there that he and Unicomb realised the connection of their forefathers.

'He's not the normal sort of person I'd mix with, but anyway …' Grant explained to others at the time.

'Yes, it's turned out to be divine intervention. He's lucky to meet me,' Rob responded.

~

Divine intervention? Rob Unicomb was kidding when he said that. But others, including some members of the Light Horse Association, believe that the light horse charge at Beersheba was just that: an event orchestrated by God to turn the war against the Turks, oust the Ottoman Empire from Palestine and return the land—as prophesied in the Bible—to the Israelites. For some of the new light-horsemen, the quest is about personal and genealogical discovery. For others it is historical. For others it is religious. For others still it is both religious and historical.

Unicomb and Pyke have a family connection with the Charge of Beersheba. But blood ties are no prerequisite; many men and women have found, for whatever reason, that the story resonates with them like no other in military history. There are stories and rumours—hard to pin down but delightfully compelling—that some Australian and Israeli light horse aficionados believe they are actually reincarnations of the original soldiers.

I came across a man like this at Bet Eshel. A crowd of Australian and Israeli officials including the mayor of Be'er Sheva, Jacob Terner (an elderly former ace fighter pilot who is said to be, occasionally, prone to donning a feathered light-horseman's slouch hat to welcome Australian visitors) had come to celebrate the opening of a so-called Anzac Trail, linking the battle sites and watering spots of the original horsemen.

The crowd was gathering under the swelter of a tarpaulin in the 'ruins' of Bet Eshel village. The 'ruins' had been hastily reconstructed to coincide with the opening of the Park of the Australian Soldier, a privately funded memorial to the Australian Light Horse bankrolled by the Australian Jewish industrialist and philanthropist, Richard Pratt.

Bet Eshel was among the first of three Jewish settlements in the Negev in 1943 and was subsequently abandoned after bitter fighting against Arabs—including those from nearby Beersheba—during the War of Independence in 1948.

'Psst—there's the horseman,' an Israeli official says to me *sotto voce*, gesturing to a man leaning up against the wall at the back of the gathering.

He is relatively young—perhaps 45—and wears a khaki shirt and trousers, which are tucked into long boots. His midriff is girdled with webbing. There's a water bottle, a long dagger and what appears to be a bandolier across his chest. He is conspicuously unarmed in a country where so many are. A broad-brimmed hat is perched on his head. But this is light horse *chic*. He is not wearing the original gear that has been begged and borrowed by members of the Light Horse Association who are also present; eccentric—no, odd—as some of the *real* light horse impersonators are, this guy is a tryhard or a genuine weirdo.

I look at him, and we lock eyes. As he watches me he turns and walks gingerly around a collection of sitting officials, directly behind the then Australian shadow Minister for Veterans' Affairs, Bronwyn Bishop. The

Minister for Veterans' Affairs, Alan Griffin, is speaking. In order to move towards this *faux* horseman I'll have to walk in front of the officials and draw attention to myself. I decide to wait until Griffin has finished.

As the applause begins, I move. But he's wise to me, moves quickly and turns out of the ruins. I'm no more than twenty seconds behind him. But he's gone. Vanished. I think I saw a man who wasn't there.

~

Serendipity is the faculty for making 'chance finds'; it's a notion drawn from Horace Walpole's 1754 fairytale, *The Three Princes of Serendip*, whose heroes 'were always making discoveries, by accidents and sagacity, of things they were not in quest of'. When I first mentioned this book to veteran journalist and Australian Jewish community leader Sam Lipski, he predicted I would encounter 'many serendipities', saying cryptically, 'The more you learn, the more you'll see what I mean.'

Lipski, as it turns out, has become a critical force in activating interest in the Charge of Beersheba. Throughout his life—not least because he is both a Jew and an Australian—he has experienced great emotional resonance with the events of 31 October 1917. Today, as chief executive of the Pratt Foundation, he represents the philanthropic interests of one of Australia's wealthiest men, Richard Pratt, who died in 2009. In that role Lipski helped plan an Australian Light Horse Memorial at the multimillion dollar, purpose-built Park of the Australian Soldier in Be'er Sheva. The construction and on-the-ground planning for the memorial, opened in early 2008, was overseen by the Pratt Foundation's Israel director, Peter Adler.

Despite his vast wealth and philanthropy, Pratt— a Polish Jew who arrived in rural Australia almost seventy years ago—had been plagued in recent years by allegations of corporate impropriety, and criminal charges were laid against him just two months after his park was opened. Many people who knew and respected Richard Pratt had hoped the park would, regardless of how the criminal case against him ended, stand as a citadel to what so many Australian Jews believe to be an enduring emotional and historical link between their country and Israel. That link is Beersheba. Some also saw it as a monument to his unquestionably great philanthropy. They had also hoped that it would mitigate, in some way, against the damage caused to a formidable reputation by what they saw as a conspiracy to bring down a great Australian.

As a gentile, as a former defence writer and an occasional trouble-spot correspondent, but not least as a fairly ordinary Australian man, I had my own formative fascinations with the Australian Light Horse and the Charge of Beersheba. But I was surprised to discover, both in Australia and the Middle East, just how profoundly the Beersheba story has captivated and, in some cases, changed the lives of those who are drawn to it, even men (and a few women) with no direct experience of the military. Some dress in the full uniform of the light-horsemen as they retrace their battles through the deserts, and on the Western Front and Gallipoli where many of the soldiers also fought and died. What might, at first, be easily dismissed as role-playing pageantry is significantly more complex for some of these people who, along with many evangelical Christians from Australia, Europe and America, also believe the light horse literally did God's work by paving the way for the restoration of Israel.

Israeli military academics, while almost universally united on the extraordinary tactical daring of 'the charge'—encompassing, as it did, the most highly prized war-fighting tactic of surprise—are more divided on its historical contribution to the establishment of Israel in 1948.

To stand, at sunset, at Bet Eshel—the very point where the 4th Light Horse Brigade breached the first line of Turkish trenches on 31 October 1917—is to stand on layer upon layer of Israeli and Palestinian history. There are still trenches at Bet Eshel today. But most Israelis will tell you that they were built by their army and the citizens' militia that won the battle for independence against significant odds in 1948. Stand there with most Israelis and they will say it was an against-the-odds victory over the Arabs in the 1948 War of Independence that delivered Palestine to the Jews. The truth is that the trenches used by the Jewish independence fighters in 1948 were probably refash-ioned Turkish dugouts.

It is impossible not to be struck by the way each event connects with the other and how the architecture of two world-altering battles have found synchronicity in the dusty earth outside Beersheba. Just as Sam Lipski had said.

13

SERENDIPITY

Joseph Hokeidonian and Granville Ryrie probably never met in Palestine, although, who knows? They might have done, given the Armenian man's mystique. Both were part of a circle that would close with the 1996 election that ushered the Howard Government into power in Australia.

Joseph's son, Richard Hokeidonian, after serving with the British Army in Palestine during World War II, emigrated to Australia with his Palestinian mother and brother in 1948. On arrival he changed his name from the Armenian Hokeidonian to the anglicised 'Hockey'. Richard, his mother and brother established a continental deli in Sydney's Bondi. It was the type of store that suddenly proliferated in Australia in the 1950s thanks to the influx of immigrants from Europe and the Middle East; dried fish, smoked meats, olives, thick crusty loaves and aromatic cheeses made an exotic contrast with the white-bread culture of post-war Anglophile Australia.

A young Australian woman, Beverley, occasionally shopped at the deli. She and Richard connected, despite the repeated warnings of her mother to stop speaking to that 'new Australian' at the local shop. They married, settled in Sydney and had four boys. They named the youngest Joseph after his mysterious paternal grandfather. He is Joe Hockey, a former senior member of the Coalition government of March 1996 until November 2007. Today he is spoken of as a future Liberal Party leader.

Hockey easily won what was then the safe Liberal seat of North Sydney in the anti-Labor landslide of 1996. On 10 September 1996 he began his maiden speech in Federal Parliament by saying he was in Canberra because he wanted 'to make a contribution to the future of Australia': 'It all happened around eighty years ago. On 31 October in 1917. One hour before sunset. Above the sounds of heavy artillery and machine-gun fire, you could hear the steady rhythm of horses' hooves—800 tired and thirsty horses, ridden by 800 tired and thirsty men. This was the 4th Light Horse Regiment, hurtling through the smoke and dust towards the Turkish stronghold of Beersheba.'

Hockey went on to describe the charge as 'an act of pure faith in the future—and perhaps our finest illustration of that quality that we call the Australian spirit'.

I feel proud to be able to stand here and tell you that its spirit can still be touched by every Australian. I feel proud to think that future generations can have that same defiant spirit surging through their veins. And I am proud to be able to tell you that my grandfather recognised that spirit too. You see, he was in Beersheba not as an Australian, not even as a soldier, but as the deputy district commissioner rebuilding the town after the Turks had been driven out.[1]

~

Joe Hockey is not alone in thinking that Beersheba deserves a unique place in Australia's cultural psyche and warrants greater public acknowledgement than it currently gets.

The charge happened more than two years after a date—25 April 1915, the day of the catastrophic Anzac landing at Gallipoli—that has become seared, like no other, into Australia's collective consciousness. Casualties at Beersheba were few and, unlike Gallipoli—which received blanket newspaper coverage domestically, thanks largely to the sympathetic prose of CEW Bean—Beersheba received scant coverage back home. For the most part the Australian newspapers reported the fall of Beersheba with little mention of the actual charge. Most credit was given to British troops—not those from its dominions, Australia and New Zealand, without whom the town would not have fallen. Sydney's *Daily Telegraph* of 3 November 1917 carried the front-page headline 'BEERSHEBA. OCCUPIED BY BRITISH', under which read: 'An official dispatch from Egypt reports:—after a night march we attacked Beersheba yesterday morning. While the infantry attacked the western and south western defences, our mounted forces made a wide turning movement through the desert and approached from the east. Beersheba was occupied in the evening despite a determined resistance.' At the end of the main report another headline reads 'AUSTRALIANS IN IT'.

A single sentence credits the role of the Australian mounted troops in the fall of the town: 'Earlier advices [*sic*] from New York stated that Beersheba was captured by the Australian and British troops operating in Palestine.' It took until 5 November 1917 for a Reuters report, headlined 'Mounted Anzacs Take Part', to describe the fall of Beersheba. 'A report issued from headquarters shows the state of the veil which has obscured happenings on the Palestine front for some time past. Beersheba is ours—that ancient city which marked the southern boundary of Palestine, and where the patriots, Abraham and Isaac, lived their peaceful and godfearing lives is now occupied,' it began, before stressing the importance of secrecy and deception to the battle plan.

Perhaps it is not surprising that the local conscription debate, events in Europe—including the invasion of Italy, the bitter fight for Passchendaele and the air raids on England—and the Melbourne Cup all but overshadowed

Australia's part in the fall of Beersheba and the subsequent occupation of Gaza.

Two weeks later General Allenby's report of the British operations in Palestine mentioned the Australians' participation, although not prominently: 'The Londoners and dismounted Yeomanry made a dashing attack on October 31 and gained the whole of the enemy's first line of defence at Beersheba, the fighting lasting all day long. The Turks at evening held trenches a mile to the eastward. The Fourth Australian Light Horse (Victoria) charged these, which were eight feet deep and four feet wide, and galloped over them ending all resistance.'[2] While mention of the Australian participation was scant enough, no credit was given to the part played either by the New Zealanders at Tel el Saba or by the 12th Australian Light Horse Regiment in the charge itself.

~

Nobody is advocating any change to Anzac Day, which falls on the anniversary of the landings. The loss of life at Gallipoli was so shocking and so well documented that it was, quite literally, white Australia's first blooding. But among the growing number of groups with a stake in the Beersheba story, there is a quest to ensure that the last great charge in military history becomes more than a mere footnote to the Gallipoli-centric Anzac legend.

An extraordinary photograph of prisoners at Beersheba brought home by Robert Unicomb's grandfather, Trooper Ernest Pauls, shows that some Turkish officers captured in the battle proudly wore the Turkish army's Medal of Gallipoli, indicating their service on the infamous peninsula, while fighting the Australians at Beersheba. Knowing that they were facing many of the same Turkish soldiers against whom they had fought at Gallipoli must have lent some of the Australian troops a sense of resuming an incomplete fight.

It is that desperate undercurrent to the Beersheba story that has captured Joe Hockey's imagination. For him, 'Beersheba was a symbolic moment in the transition of Australia from, in my mind, a colony to a nation in its own right … Because in the Dardanelles we were still under the command of the British and it was only when Monash took control on the Western Front that we really started to develop our own military leadership. But the reckless … the calculated indifference of the Australians at Beersheba was based on the lower level leadership of a very impressive Australian [Chauvel].

'I think we celebrate Gallipoli because it was the first extraordinary display of Australian courage. And time passes and our resentment towards British command grows and our diggers become victims … and that's why, when the whistle blew, they went over the top knowing they were going to die and at that time they were doing it for God, King and country.

'Whereas it seems that at Beersheba we had control of our own destiny in one sense … I think many Australians probably feel in their hearts that if it was any other nation they wouldn't have had the courage to charge the guns. That's the difference and that's one of the reason why we should celebrate it as a great symbol of Australian mateship and that capacity for Australians to dig deeper and harder and to do more than any other soldier in the world ... Their leaders were incredible, inspirational men, too.'[3]

Which brings us to Ryrie. Although the unconventional Ryrie was already an extremely popular leader by the time of the Gaza engagements, his reputation for doggedness and unflinching loyalty to those in his command was forged at that ancient fortress city. It's a reputation he might have forged earlier, at the terrible Battle of Romani in August 1916—had he been there. But the hulking Ryrie was replaced as commander by the heavier and even older Royston. Ryrie, much to the chagrin of Chauvel and others, had taken leave to attend an Empire Parliamentary Conference in London. Besides being an experienced soldier, Ryrie was also a federal parliamentarian. Elected to the House of Representatives in 1911, the ultra-conservative Ryrie was regarded as a fine, if earthy, orator. His natural capacity as a raconteur was as popular with his constituents and his parliamentary colleagues as it would ultimately prove to be with the men in his command.

On the outbreak of war in 1914, Ryrie (who had served in the Boer War) re-enlisted and was immediately given command of the 2nd Light Horse Regiment. His constituents pitched in and bought him a Waler, Plain Bill, a beautiful and impressive animal that was the envy of many regimental commanders. After the war, in December 1918, Ryrie was appointed commander of the

Anzac Mounted Division before returning to Australia to resume his parliamentary duties in late 1919. For a short time he was an assistant Defence minister. He remained in Federal Parliament until 1927, when he was appointed High Commissioner to London. His appointment was widely seen as a reward for vacating his safe seat of North Sydney in 1922 to facilitate the move from Bendigo of the then prime minister, Billy Hughes.

North Sydney is the seat that Joe Hockey held since 1996.

'Ryrie was this larger than life character … I didn't know much about him, I admit, when I won the seat and then someone came and gave me this book [a biography of Ryrie] and I thought, "This is amazing"—a connection with Palestine again … you know, the circle meets,' Hockey says.

Richard Hockey, born in Jerusalem in 1927, has no memory of his father, who left the family home immediately after he was born. For the best part of sixty years he wondered what became of Joseph Hokeidonian after he walked out on the family. Then in 1986, while visiting an Armenian church in London with his family, a stranger approached Richard.

'What's your name?' the man asked.

'Hockey,' Richard replied.

'I knew your father … your father died in Egypt. He was shot in the war, the last war, and then later he was run over by a car in Egypt crossing the street.'

Joe Hockey recalls his father's distress. 'He was deeply upset—this was the last time Dad heard anything about his father.'

~

Two decades later Joe Hockey stands on Chauvel's Hill on the outskirts of Beersheba and looks towards the town that his mysterious grandfather helped rebuild after World War I. A small group of Israeli soldiers, all young women, with weapons and satellite navigation equipment, are up there too.

'And there was some irony in the fact that all those years before, other military people—Australians—had been standing on top of the hill and now, here [are] these young Israeli women on top of the hill with weapons and navigational equipment,' he says. 'And it just goes to show that the more things change, the more they stay the same.'

14

COBBERS

One of the things that doesn't change is man's capacity to find friends, and even to find himself, in adverse circumstances. War is the most adverse of all circumstances. The omnipotent threat of death, the physical hardships, the killing of others—soldiers and bystanders—all about, serve to constantly test and challenge the human condition. And it brings out the best and the worst in people. The Australians who fought with the light horse regiments in the Middle East were, undoubtedly, capable of enormous heroism and almost unfathomable physical courage of the type displayed at Romani, at Gaza and Beersheba and later in the Jordan Valley and Syria. But some otherwise decent men were also capable of cruel, inhuman acts that would be unthinkable in peacetime.

'You know, you do things you wouldn't normally do ... Those sorts of things, you'd do them and you wouldn't think anything,' Private Harold O'Brien of Tasmania, who served in the 3rd Light Horse Regiment, confided in the later years of his life. 'In your own private life you never want to speak of it again ... But these things happen.'[1]

As a metaphor for life, therefore, war is irresistible.

~

The taxi driver is persistent and insistent. He wants to know why we're heading for the United Services Club. The guy is a talker. During a short trip from the airport he's tried everything to engage me.

The conversation went something like this:

'Where'd you fly in from?'

'Melbourne.' (Canberra.)

'Waddaya do for a crust?'

'Public relations.' (In my next life, should karma frown upon me.)

'Follow the footy?'

'Nope.' (Collingwood.)

'Got kids?'

'Yeah, seven.' (Three.)

'So what's the story with the services club—you interested in the military, or what?'

Silence.

'You know, mate, it's *my* club,' he says. It's not a question—more a demand that I ask him why. I know he won't volunteer it. But, clearly, he wants it known that he's a Vietnam vet.

'Really? How so?'

What followed was an abridged version of the driver's Vietnam story; he was there in 1972, in the transport corps, for the last six months of Australia's involvement in the war. Then I decide to share. I tell him I'm not actually in public relations, that I'm writing about Beersheba and I'm due to meet an esteemed former soldier, Digger James, a one-time president of the RSL who is patron of the Australian Light Horse Association. It turns out the taxi driver was in a cavalry division in Vietnam that is linked by history to one of the original light horse regiments.

'Those guys—what they did at Beersheba was amazing … to me they represent the very best of Australian values,' he says.

I tell him that I reckon the men who fought at Beersheba didn't think themselves special, even though most knew that the charge was an extraordinary event. Even those who weren't well educated, I tell him, wrote beautifully evocative diaries and letters home not only describing the scenes of battle and the details of military life in the desert but also chronicling their emotional responses to it all.

'Most soldiers don't write like that any more,' I say. 'Email and texting has changed the way they communicate—there won't be a record of the blokes in Iraq and Afghanistan in the same way that there was in World War I and World War II—even Vietnam.'

'But they're still the same sorts of guys—they'd still write the same sorts of things about their emotions, I reckon,' the Vietnam vet says.

'No—I doubt it,' I say. I immediately think about how the military closed ranks around poor Private Jake Kovco, the soldier from the 3rd Battalion Royal Australian Regiment who shot himself through the head (accidentally, we're implausibly asked to believe) while mucking around with his mates in Iraq in 2006. The two other soldiers in a room the size of a shipping container claim to have seen nothing and, as far as anyone can tell, they wrote nothing privately that would give up the truth. Neither, it seems, did the tormented dead man (a risk-taker whose emotionally crippled behaviour before he died was nothing if not a cry for help) articulate his turmoil before he accidentally or otherwise ended his own life.

No. If Kovco had died in Palestine in 1917, somebody would have eventually written or said something about what happened. Even if it took sixty years, someone like Trooper Ted O'Brien would say something— just as he did about the massacre of the Bedouin by Australians and New Zealanders in 1918.

The driver drops me at the services club, an elegant old building of grand stairways, dramatic pitched roofs, porticos and sprawling Queensland-style verandas, on Brisbane's jacaranda-lined Wickham Terrace.

'Mate,' the Vietnam vet says as we pull up outside, 'that Digger James is an amazing bloke—got his balls blown off in Korea, you know? Ask him about it.'

I will, I promise. I will.

~

His name is William. But nobody calls Digger James by his real name.

'Major General,' I say.

'Digger—Digger James,' he insists.

Long before he entered the army, the boy William James donned a hat fashioned from newspaper and his father, an orchardist in Shepparton, dubbed him the 'little digger'. His mum and his brothers started calling him that, too. In the end it was all he answered to. It was never William. Not even Bill. It was Digger. He's been Digger ever since. It's the perfect name for an Australian soldier, especially one such as James—a holder of the Military Cross who served first as an infantryman in Korea, where he was seriously wounded in combat, and later as a medical officer in Vietnam.

We are sitting on the veranda of the club, having a beer and surveying Wickham Terrace. He is softly spoken and thoughtful. He struggles to be heard over the traffic noise. As he begins talking, he hands me a 67-year-old black and white photograph. It shows the school he attended in Shepparton. The little boys in the front row sit cross-legged with scabby knees and gap-toothed grins while the older ones in the next row kneel with their arms folded across their chests. The pig-tailed and plaited country girls stand behind the boys with their teacher.

'I thought you might ask me about him, so I brought the photograph along. It's the most terrible picture you've ever seen in your life. But it shows us. That's Richard there—that little fellow there. And that's me there. He was four years younger than I was. That was taken in '41. That's Little Richard. The story of Richard basically goes back to my father who was an orchardist in Shepparton,' Digger explains.

'During the war Dad was asked if he would help settle some Jewish refugees, whether he would help by being a mentor, you know … So about six months later they brought out a husband and a wife and a little boy. And that was Richard and his Mum and Dad. They'd just arrived from Poland. They only spoke Polish, no English. The end result was that Dad said he'd be a mentor to them and they bought the property next door. Just a hundred yards away—the houses were very close.

'So Richard became, in effect, my little brother. I was the fifth kid in my family and he became the sixth. He ate at our table frequently, slept in our bed with my brothers—you know the way it was, on the veranda. I took him to school and it didn't take him long to learn English and he became the only English-speaker in the family and he would, you know, help look after the family business arrangements—that was the start of it all. I think when he was about six he was going to the bank with his father.

'And of course he grew into an Australian-speaking, foreign-born young man with no accent at all. So that's our story and we've been cobbers, very close cobbers, ever since. My life was army and his life you know ... he is my oldest living friend.'[2]

Digger is talking about Richard Pratt, the billionaire entrepreneur famous for his philanthropy in Australia and Israel. As a child he quickly became fluent in English while his father Leon established a paper recycling business that would become the biggest privately owned company of its type in the world. At Melbourne University in the 1950s, Pratt was an accomplished footballer, playing for the Carlton Reserves and the Under 19s. He also made a name for himself as an actor for productions staged by the Union Repertory Theatre— so much so that in 1957 he toured London and New York for a production of Ray Lawler's *Summer of the Seventeenth Doll*.

After his father's death in 1969, Pratt—honouring the older man's wishes—gave away professional acting and took over as chairman of the family business. At his death he was Australia's fourth richest man having amassed a fortune of some $5 billion, significant amounts of which he gave to charity and dispersed through the Pratt Foundation. Together he and his wife Jeanne were keen patrons of the arts. They also opened their home, Raheen, to charities and to politicians for fundraising.

Richard Pratt had, by all accounts, been a man whose life had been well lived in a spirit of community-mindedness and generosity—a corporate philanthropist who would be remembered for public works and for reinvesting his wealth in the community. In later years, however, the billionaire's existence took a most unwelcome turn. First came the newspaper revelation that he had fathered a child with a so-called Sydney socialite in the late 1990s. He maintained a silence around this episode that was dignified enough to protect his marriage.

Then in 2007 he made a negotiated settlement over charges brought by the Australian Competition and Consumer Commission for price fixing with a competitor. His company was fined $36 million. But something else—the damage to his good name and character—seemed to hurt him a good deal more than the fine.

'My reputation is something I have been building for 50 years and so I am worried that the general public will now see me as a rich person who has made his money doing something that is wrong in the eyes of the law,' he lamented at the time.[3]

In early 2008 he voluntarily handed back his Order of Australia—after discovering that he would have to mount a case before the Council for the Order of Australia to keep it—in light of the price-fixing episode. Suddenly, there was also a question mark over his role as president of his beloved Carlton Football Club. He would later relinquish this title, too.

Despite all that, Pratt's family and friends—not least Digger James—had rallied their support and were working tirelessly behind the scenes to support the big man who, unknown to the public, was suffering serious illness at the same time as the corporate regulator was pursuing his company.

A major step in that rehabilitation process undoubtedly became his patronage of the Park of the Australian Soldier at Be'er Sheva, although the memorial was conceived well before controversy enveloped his business dealings.

~

There is a curry buffet and a good red by the glass. We sit at a discreet table for two in the dining room of the United Services Club. On the wall behind Digger James is a copy of a remarkable canvas painted in 1924 by the World War I official artist Septimus Power, the original of which hangs in the Australian War Memorial.

The canvas vividly depicts the episode for which the only Victoria Cross of the Sinai and Palestine campaigns was awarded to an Australian. In the foreground a single-engine biplane bearing British insignia, smoke streaming from its under-carriage, lurches and splutters into the air. It carries two men. In the rocky desert just below, a column of Turkish cavalry gives chase, all the while shooting skywards at the fleeing aircraft. In the background another British aircraft burns on the ground.

On 20 March 1917 the plane flown by Captain Douglas Rutherford was forced to land after being hit by Turkish rifle fire. Another Australian pilot, Lieutenant Frank McNamara, saw Rutherford crash. He landed his aircraft nearby, helped the injured

Rutherford aboard and was himself shot through the thigh in the process. But McNamara—a 22-year-old schoolteacher from Victoria—could not, owing to his wounded leg, properly control his plane and crashed on take-off. He and Rutherford scrambled out, set fire to the plane and returned to Rutherford's damaged aircraft, which McNamara somehow managed to take off, just as the Turkish cavalry approached.[4]

'It is unbelievable what they have done to Richard,' Digger says *sotto voce* as he leans towards the centre of the table. 'The way they have pursued him is malicious.'

A subsequent case against his friend Pratt for alleged perjury relating to the initial price-fixing case against Visy would be seriously undermined by some questionable investigatory and interview techniques. The criminal case against Pratt would be dropped on the grounds that it was no longer in the public interest, as the accused lay on his deathbed.

~

While Richard Pratt finished school in Shepparton and went on to pursue acting and football at university, Digger James joined the army and went to Duntroon. He served in the Korean War where, as an infantry captain in November 1952, he was seriously injured by an exploding mine while leading his unit in an otherwise successful attack on an enemy position.

'I lost my leg below the knee and I got some shrapnel in my hands. I was lucky, though—I kept the family jewels and everything just below the waist,' he explains with a soldier's candour that relieves me of the need to pose the taxi driver's awkward question.

He spent a year in hospital. Richard visited frequently. Digger eventually went on to study and practise medicine after leaving the army. He rejoined to serve as a medical officer in Vietnam and finally retired from the army in 1985. For a short time in the mid-1950s he was attached to the 12th/16th Regiment of the Royal Australian Armoured Corps—the Hunter River Lancers. The unit's heritage was the 12th Australian Light Horse Regiment, which played such a seminal part in the Battle of Beersheba in 1917.

Some of the original members of the 12th would occasionally turn up to regimental dinners, Digger recalled. 'They didn't talk much about what they'd done, but of course we'd read all about it and we were immensely proud of them. They were reticent in talking about it—but to them this was all part of the job ... they served their country and didn't talk about it and that is the way many people were about their service.' Digger retains a close connection with the Lancers and is today the patron of the Australian Light Horse Asociation.

In 2006, over lunch with Pratt—who was about to fly to Be'er Sheva to collect an honorary degree from Ben Gurion University—he mentioned the Charge of Beersheba. It was the genesis of the Pratt Foundation's Park of the Australian Soldier.

When we spoke a few weeks before the park opened, Digger James pondered why Beersheba scarcely registers in Australia's consciousness. He said CEW Bean's promotion of the Anzac legend and the formidable reputation of Lieutenant General John Monash—who decisively won battles at Hamel, Amiens, Mont St Quentin and Péronne—may have overshadowed Australian achievements in the desert campaign. Bean was with the men he wrote about from the time they arrived at Gallipoli. By contrast, Henry Gullett was with the Australian Light Horse only from late 1917. He missed the seminal battles at Beersheba and Gaza and did not receive official appointment until August 1918—barely two months before the Turkish defeat. Much of his research was therefore conducted retrospectively, whereas Bean followed his subjects from the beginning to the end of the war.

'I think perhaps that the publicity that he created with his writings and reports back to Australia were a very significant factor in that he put legs on the whole story, and the horror of it and the bravery and the courage and the futility of it. And the foul-ups, you know, they landed at the wrong spot [at Gallipoli] and all those things went wrong … I think there was a huge promotion by him and he was a very honoured man in our country,' he says.

'I think the second point I'd like to make is that, the campaigns in Gallipoli and the Western Front were horrible, with terrible casualties and that really hit home with people … whereas the [Egypt and Palestine] campaign, where we did so well, particularly with the light horse, we didn't have such vast casualties.'

Of Monash, Digger James says: 'He commanded a brigade, of course, in Gallipoli, and he then went to the Western Front and he was picked out as an extremely bright fellow and so he brought some real science to the campaign and he was unquestionably the best brain they had in the Allied armies, in my opinion. And the victories that he was able to achieve also added colour to the campaign, whereas in the [Egypt and Palestine] campaign they were odd battles here and there ... and the publicity was given to the British in the main, whereas at the Western Front the Australians were seen to be outstanding from day one.'

Over dessert and coffee, James runs through some of the Australians who've been awarded the Victoria Cross. He focuses on McNamara, pictured in his spluttering aircraft on the wall to his back. It was an amazing episode, he says; besides the selfless disregard McNamara showed for his own safety, it involved daring and, perhaps above all, a commitment to saving one's mates.

It must be a familiar theme to James, who led his men into a battle against the communists to recapture a strategically important knoll that had earlier been lost by the Canadians. A couple of the enemy died. After being critically wounded James managed to organise the evacuation of other men in his platoon who were injured and ensure that the rest of his men returned safely. He lost half a leg (and a promising rugby career) in the process.

Then he hands me an envelope. 'I'd like you to read this,' he says.

The envelope contains an article entitled 'Beersheba and philanthropy', by the constitutional monarchist David Flint, also a former chairman of the Australian Press Council and the Australian Broadcasting Authority. It is a strident defence of Pratt, in which Flint argues that the initial action against the billionaire by the Australian consumer watchdog was unjustified and the penalty imposed on his company Visy disproportionate. Flint concluded, 'It seems those affected by the tall poppy syndrome are never satisfied. Recently there was even a call for Richard Pratt to be stripped of his honorary academic awards. This is mean and unworthy.'[5]

~

I find myself moved by James's unflinching loyalty to his oldest friend. Digger exudes the calm, measured and considered air of professional soldiers from the Australian military whom I have met the world over. Just like them, you would want to ride into battle beside him. It is a friendship that was obviously valued and reciprocated by the billionaire, and one that will be marked, in the most symbolic and public of fashions, when the park in Be'er Sheva is opened.

There can be no questioning the Pratt Foundation's altruistic motive for establishing their park in Be'er Sheva. It is a shady oasis, replete with lush foliage and water features, in what seems to be an otherwise bland and working-class part of the city. Most importantly, however, the park had a unique utilitarian function, having been designed specifically to meet the needs of disabled children.

For Pratt, the Park of the Australian Soldier at Be'er Sheva was clearly conceived as yet another in a long line of charitable acts—part of his long-established pattern of corporate responsibility and philanthropy. The park had been planned well before his company allegedly crossed the law. Regardless, it was clear that some of Pratt's friends and colleagues viewed the park's opening as a significant step in his public rehabilitation, a means by which he could perhaps rebuild a reputation for benevolence and public good after the ignominy of the court case.

Beersheba, it seems, means something different to so many people.

15

HOARDING THE LEGEND

In Israel the artefacts of the light-horsemen—their leggings and hats, their weapons and bandoliers, their saddles and their feed bags—are guarded as jealously as knowledge about their movements. There are small collections of their belongings in kibbutzim, private libraries and lounge rooms from Jerusalem to Jaffa. But suggestions that the items be pooled so that a purpose-built museum might be established are often dismissed by some of the owners. This attitude largely typifies the rivalry in Israel among amateur, semi-professional and government organisations for knowledge about the Anzacs.

Despite the launch of an Anzac Trail around Be'er Sheva that aims to connect the sites of light horse significance, many of these places are not easy to locate or reach without expert guidance. Few Israelis and even fewer Australians have the expertise to find them or explain exactly what happened there.

The Society for the Heritage of World War I in Israel is, as its name suggests, dedicated to furthering knowledge about a front of the Great War that was regarded by the British authorities as something of a sideshow at the time. Its members include academics, teachers and former senior military figures. Some of the society's members are generous with their time and knowledge. Others, however, seem deeply protective; even within the society, internecine rivalries threaten a collective approach that might better serve the promotion—and the legacy— of the light-horsemen.

'Tell me what you know about Chauvel,' demanded one Israeli historian when I told him I was writing a book about Beersheba. 'Was he a good commander of his men? Was he a good man? Do members of his family have any more personal papers they have not yet made public? And tell me—was the charge a tactical and strategic success?'

'I'm not a military historian,' I replied. 'I'm not writing a military history—that's been done. I'm asking whether this military action is important to Australians and Israelis.'

The guy looked at me, perplexed. I sense that no answer would be adequate for him.

On another occasion a member of the society harangued my friend, the Australian visual artist Susan McMinn—who was in Israel studying the light horse for a series of works she was undertaking on the warhorse—

when she began talking about the work of Idriess. 'He told me that Idriess had made it up, that his work was fiction. Well, I told him that I'd read the Idriess diaries in the Australian War Memorial and they're not fictitious,' she says. She also had a disagreement with another historian who insisted the 4th Light Horse Brigade, which executed the famous charge, had its origins in Queensland.

McMinn grew up on a dairy farm near Rochester in Victoria. She still lives in the country, and horses have always been part of her way of life; as a girl she would saddle up and ride the 7 kilometres to town, or hook up the gig, 'wrap myself in a granny blanket and listen to the tranny' while riding to her friend's place.

'I've really been interested in the connections that the Australian soldiers, like Idriess, make in their diaries between themselves and the many soldiers that have gone before them over the same lands ... I'm interested in the tension between myth, legend and reality surrounding the light horse,' she says.

'It really was a cruel and harsh war because the light horse soldiers weren't just fighting other men; they were fighting conditions in the desert. So it wasn't a romantic thing as it is now portrayed ... it wasn't like that at all. I have researched the light horse letters and diaries in the War Memorial, which fully portray what hell it actually was for them ... The horses were really thirsty and the men couldn't get decent feed, and got very upset when their horses became distressed. The horses got colic and they had all sorts of problems with disease because of the blowflies.'[1]

When I first meet McMinn at the Hebrew University, she is working in a room piled with the bones of ancient horses retrieved from an archaeological dig at Vadum Jacob near the border with Jordan. Vadum Jacob was a crusader castle, a stronghold built less than a year earlier when Chauvel's boyhood hero Saladin successfully attacked and destroyed it in August 1179.[2] Eight hundred crusaders were killed along with countless horses. Their remains were buried in deep pits, one of which was opened after an earthquake in 2002. McMinn has been studying the horses' remains and creating drawings and paintings partly based on them.

Some of those involved in the Vadum Jacob project had no idea that Australian warhorses had traversed the same country as the crusaders and their animals. There was, however, intense interest from the others involved in the project, who asked McMinn to give them a presentation on the Waler. A lack of general awareness about the light-horsemen in Palestine is probably only compounded by the hoarding of relics, documents and knowledge about them.

'People kept their bits and pieces of what they'd found—light horse relics bought from ebay and a few bullets and buttons, and yet they say that they want to promote what the Australians did there. But the thing is that most of them are not willing to come together to do that … and so I had this guy telling me that Ion Idriess wrote fiction while there was this other guy who was telling me that the 4th Light Horse came from Queensland. So really, I found that some of their information wasn't all that accurate either. No wonder few know about it, even in Beersheba.'

McMinn's charcoal and watercolour work, and her animated short film, exude an evocative, dream-like quality that is now drawing national and international acclaim. Her work depicts the horses first being shipped to the other side of the world, then traversing the desert sands at night, their masters slouching in the saddles, crossing stony wadies and carrying the men to safety from battle.

~

When the Australian Light Horse Association recreated the Charge of Beersheba in 2007, the public face of the event was Barry Rodgers, a former history teacher and horse-breeder from Queensland.

Rodgers is a thoughtful and cautiously spoken man who was instrumental in the ninetieth anniversary re-enactment ride. He has long been fascinated by the military. Both his father and his uncle served in World War II, and he briefly served in the Monash University Regiment while a student—'in the 1970s—at the very height of the Vietnam War', he volunteers, as if to emphasise the unfashionable nature of his commitment back then. He also likes to fly a World War II vintage aeroplane and breeds heritage horses, some of which are directly descended from Midnight, a horse killed in the Charge of Beersheba. Rodgers is interested in war and its political and its sociological impact; it was he who determined that the charge re-enactment should be a 'peace ride' and that bayonets should remain sheathed and rifles slung.

We speak first at the Australian War Memorial in Canberra, then some months later in the bar of a big hotel in Be'er Sheva on the night Richard Pratt's Park of the Australian Soldier was opened. The room is vast and dark, and centres on an oval bar where two young Israeli barmaids—one of whom is about to commence her military service—are serving drinks to Australians dressed as light-horsemen who flock around them. Some are genuine soldiers serving in Australian units derived from the original light horse regiments. Others like Rodgers are members of the association. Rodgers has been sitting alone, however, and he's on the soft stuff, not the beers and bourbons that the women are serving the others. Along with borrowed Israeli police horses that had been transported to Be'er Sheva directly from operational duties along the Gaza border, all of these light-horsemen have just participated in Pratt's pageant.

Rodgers is a tall, distinguished-looking bloke with a shock of white hair and a rather commanding presence. Dressed in light-horsemen's apparel, some of it original, he personifies a significant Christian element within the association that believes the Charge of Beersheba was part of God's plan. They believe that the charge, along with the Balfour Declaration being taken to the War Cabinet on the very same day, were the direct instruments of God to return Israel to the Jewish people, as prophesied in the Bible. But his Christian interpretation of the light horse campaign in Palestine, and especially Beersheba, sits uneasily with many others in the largely secular Light Horse Association. They resent, in the words of one other respected association member, the increasingly pervasive 'God-bothering take' on Beersheba.

Barry explains why he finds the light horse desert campaign so captivating. 'I think there is a romance about the light horse that escapes most people. The campaign of the Middle East was just a brilliant campaign and it was—except for the later battles on the Western Front—totally different from what happened in France and Gallipoli, of course. And the Charge of Beersheba and various other charges made by the light horse during this campaign—well, there's no parallel to them in Australian military history in my view,' he says.

I asked Barry whether he saw a biblical connection between the Charge of Beersheba, the Balfour Declaration and the re-establishment of Israel in 1948.

'I personally do. Others would see it in purely secular terms. But it seems to me that there's been a lot of destiny involved and we have been part of that destiny. I think there is a religious, spiritual connection, a moral dimension, to the whole thing. I think it's quite profound, quite frankly, but others would probably disagree and see it as a chance connection of geopolitical events. But I don't take that view.'

The Australian Light Horse Association, he says, can accommodate all perspectives on the meaning of it all.

'I think at the end of the day they [the members] all acknowledge that these things have taken place and we have had a very integral part in that. Whether it was God-ordained—well, that's another dimension that might overlay it … many have found in their life's journey a faith dimension within this whole thing with Israel and the Balfour Declaration. They can see history unfolding … even the simple fact of the Balfour Declaration being declared by the War Cabinet on the same day, almost the same hour, as the charge, is a pretty amazing thing—it could have been pure coincidence.'

'Do you think it was coincidence?' I ask.

'No, I don't … I think there was more to it.'

~

The Light Horse Association includes plenty of men and women who are not interested in Christian interpretations of Beersheba. Like most military historians they prefer, instead, to see it for what it ostensibly was: an action of remarkable daring that succeeded against the odds to inalterably change the course of the Middle East campaign. Members of the Light Horse Association are motivated by that which drives most amateur historians: a fascination for the earlier lives of others and perhaps a desire to walk in their footsteps. The difference between many historians, however, and members of the association is the desire of the latter to dress as their subjects did in the hope of understanding them better.

Phil Chalker, a no-nonsense policeman from Queanbeyan, New South Wales, is an ex-army sergeant and president of the Light Horse Association. He is a descendant of light-horsemen and served in the Armoured Corps as a member of the 1st/15th Royal New South Wales Lancers, the successor of the 1st Light Horse Regiment.

The first time we talk at Queanbeyan Police Station, he is anxiously trying to coordinate the transport of the Israeli police horses from the Gaza border to Be'er Sheva in time for the opening of Pratt's park. There are inevitable problems, not least with Australia's Department of Foreign Affairs, which is warning Australians not to venture anywhere near the dangerous border with Gaza. Phil sees it as his duty to promote the achievements of the light-horsemen in Egypt and Palestine so that their actions at Romani, Beersheba and beyond become a part of Australia's historical language and cultural identity on par with Gallipoli and the Western Front.

'Yes, Gallipoli is remembered for all the reasons that we want to remember it for—all those clichés, you know, it's where our country was born, where we got our mateship from—all those things. But what the light horse did, not just in Beersheba but in Jerusalem, in Damascus, deserves, to my mind, similar recognition,' he says. 'To put it in context, it was a great success for our military—very few casualties compared to Gallipoli and the Western Front … and yet it's something that's not recognised as a major campaign and an important, formative part of our history.'[3]

The association, he says, has a role in keeping the mounted infantry tradition alive. Unlike other countries, including France, Britain, America and Canada, Australia has not maintained a regular army mounted unit. 'No real traditions were passed on through our military ... but now we've seen in the past ten to twenty years the re-emergence of such things as the slouch hat reissued to our military personnel, and the colour patches returning to the uniforms,' he says. He sees the actions of the light-horsemen at Beersheba through the eyes of a military man. He is generous with his knowledge of the light horse. He speaks at schools, and he keeps in touch with many descendants of light-horsemen.

Somehow we move onto the topic of Lawrence of Arabia and his connection with the light-horsemen and particularly Chauvel. Another neglected chapter in the history of the light horse—or, at least, as it is interpreted by the British—is that Lawrence led his guerrilla army into Damascus after the light horse. It was important for Britain to maintain the appearance that Emir Feisal's Arab force (for which Lawrence acted as liaison officer with the British) liberated Damascus single-handedly and arrived there first. But the 10th Regiment of the 3rd Light Horse Brigade was actually the first unit to reach Damascus on 1 October 1918, less than a month before the capture of Aleppo in Syria and the armistice with Turkey.

Phil recommends that I talk to an elderly lady who lives not far from my Canberra home. He says that I should ask her about Lawrence of Arabia.

~

When Valerie Howse answers the door she is wearing a hot pink skirt and jacket. At 90 she still lives independently, drives a car, tends her garden and has an active social life. Even before we sit down she presents me with a large, cloth-bound book. It is the *Official History of the Australian Army Medical Services 1914–1918*, volume 1: *Gallipoli, Palestine and New Guinea*. Valerie's father, Major General Rupert Downes, chief medical officer for Chauvel's Desert Mounted Corps, wrote the chapters on the Sinai and Palestine campaign.

'I am a light horse baby,' she declares. 'My mother decided she was lonely while my father Rupert was at the war with the light horse. So she went to see him in the Middle East. I was dreamt up at Shepheard's Hotel in Cairo, you see.'[1] She smiles, then purses her lips and raises an eyebrow—mischievously, charmingly.

Major General Downes began his war service as commander of the 2nd Light Horse Field Ambulance and quickly won a formidable reputation as a battlefield surgeon. He was a master innovator, designing and introducing the horse-drawn sled to move casualties across the desert sands of the Sinai and Negev. He faced perhaps his greatest challenge in the Jordan Valley during the 'great ride' on to victory at Damascus and Aleppo: keeping his men as free as possible of malaria and treating them for it.

After meeting her light-horseman husband at Shepheard's Hotel, the pregnant Mary Downes sailed back to Australia aboard RMS *Mongolia*. She sailed at a time when a German cruiser, the *Wolf*, had been stalking Allied ships throughout the Atlantic, Pacific and Indian oceans and destroying them with torpedoes and mines. Just outside Bombay, *Mongolia* struck a mine and sunk. Mary Downes made it to Bombay fifty hours later aboard a lifeboat. And so Valerie Howse is among us today. She went on to marry John Howse, a federal MP for fourteen years and the son of Neville Howse, another soldier-surgeon who won Australia's first Victoria Cross in South Africa in 1900. Rupert Downes and Howse worked together in the Middle East long before their children would meet. Serendipity.

I do as Phil Chalker suggested and ask Mrs Howse about Lawrence of Arabia.

'They never spoke about the war, you know, the men, when they came back. But they had a dim view of Lawrence … that was passed on to me, but not by Dad, because they never spoke to their children about such things,' she says.

'So, what *was* their view about Lawrence, then?' I ask.

In reply she hands me a piece of paper with a type-written message on it. It reads: 'Rupert Downes remarked that "the wonderful Lawrence is a fine murderer on opportunity".'[5] This somewhat cryptic reference to Lawrence is, it seems, as much a criticism of the Arab forces he worked with as of Lawrence himself. Those Arabs were notorious for their appalling treatment of Turkish prisoners, especially the wounded and ill. After Damascus fell, Colonel Downes was charged with caring for almost two thousand sick Turkish prisoners who had been held in appalling conditions and were dying at the rate of about seventy a day in untended hospitals. Downes, by chance, came across Lawrence at the Victoria Hotel where Lawrence said the sick prisoners should be looked after by the Arabs. Downes had orders from Chauvel to care for them himself, however, and the death rate declined dramatically under his authority.[6] This chance meeting between her father and Lawrence at the Victoria is what what Valerie Howse was referring to.

She says, to emphasise the point, 'His view of him [Lawrence] was Rupert Downes thought the wonderful Lawrence is a fine murderer on opportunity. That's what he thought of him. Father and Lawrence met only once in the Victoria Hotel [Cairo]. That was enough, apparently ... also, you know, Lawrence was a bit of a queer. And, you know, I think men of my father's generation would have abhorred that.'

Certainly Chauvel seems to have viewed Lawrence as suspicious, if not even duplicitous. This is apparent in the note Chauvel took of a meeting between Allenby, Lawrence and Feisal at the Victoria Hotel on 3 October 1918. Chauvel's note alludes to deep tensions between Allenby and Lawrence over Feisal's future control of

Lebanon.[7] Chauvel's suspicion of Lawrence is further evident in his critique of Lawrence's *Seven Pillars of Wisdom* when the book was acquired by the Australian War Memorial. 'I cannot see it going to the archives of the Australian War Memorial without drawing attention to some of the inaccuracies contained in it, particularly where they involve injustice to other people,' Chauvel wrote to the War Memorial's director, John Treloar, on 1 January 1936.[8]

On the liberation of Damascus, Chauvel wrote: 'I am personally of the opinion that the first of the Arab Forces to enter Damascus were those who followed Lawrence in and, by that time, an Australian Brigade and at least one regiment of Indian Cavalry had passed right through the city.'[9]

~

When we meet again in Be'er Sheva on the night before Pratt's park opens, I tell Phil Chalker I took his advice and visited Valerie Howse, who told me her father thought Lawrence was a murderer.

'Well, Chauvel and his men didn't like Lawrence,' Phil says. 'The light horse got to Damascus first, but it was always made to look like Lawrence and the Arabs did … just as the British wanted it, for political reasons for the Arabs.'[10]

The Charge of Beersheba happened more than nine decades ago. But as some like Phil Chalker slowly make headway in their efforts to increase public acknowledgement of the light-horsemen's achievements, a battle of interpretation rages around them.

Most Israeli Jews are warriors, thanks to their state's requirement of compulsory military service. The strategic daring surrounding the Charge of Beersheba is still talked about—and even taught—in military staff colleges in Israel and elsewhere. But Israeli military scholars tend to see it as an extraordinary military action that was, arguably, critical to the outcome of the World War I desert campaign. More often than not they do not see it as a formative moment in the establishment of the modern state of Israel. They will acknowledge the tactical importance of the Charge of Beersheba and the courage that underpinned it. Few will, however, afford it a critical role in Israel's formation, preferring instead to talk about the Israeli War of Independence: the outnumbered Jewish soldiers who, against the odds, fought off the enemy all around, with few weapons and limited international support, in 1948.

Traipsing around the World War I battle sites with such men as Eran Dolev and Yigal Sheffy, former soldiers turned historians, you become aware that Israel is a country founded on layers of battles dating to the Hebrew tribes and the Romans, on through the crusades and the Ottomans, to Napoleon, the British and the Australians—and, of course, every battle and war that has since involved the Israeli Defence Force, the Palestinians and the country's Arab neighbours. Dolev and Sheffy have both written books about World War I in the Middle East. Both have strong views about the strategic and military merits of the charge. But neither would say it was a seminal moment in Israel's creation.

Such Australian Jews as Pratt and Sam Lipski, meanwhile, see the link between Australia and Israel as extending beyond the fact that Australians fought in Palestine during World War I and again during World War II. They believe that Australia's part in evicting Turkey from Palestine, and especially the turning point of the war at Beersheba, was critical to the genesis of modern Israel.

~

Lipski is the son of a Polish Jewish immigrant. His father moved to Australia after living in Palestine for almost a decade after World War I. But despite his father's experience, the Australian light horse's role in the Palestine battles was not discussed. Indeed, the first Lipski learned about the Australians' involvement in Palestine and Beersheba was when he saw the 1940 movie about the charge, *Forty Thousand Horsemen*, starring the iconic actor Chips Rafferty.

'You've got to remember this is the 1950s and I grew up in an immigrant Jewish family in Melbourne that was very badly affected by the Holocaust. And you are also talking about just five or six years after the State of Israel had been established ... and so, a lot of my early awareness of the world was built around the establishment of the State of Israel,' he says. 'And then when I'm about 14 I see this film and it tells me that the

Australian troops were in Beersheba, in Palestine ... Well, nobody had told me at any point that the light-horsemen had been in Palestine, let alone that they had done in Beersheba what Chips Rafferty had done in the movie.'[11]

Lipski first went to Be'er Sheva as a very young man in 1956. He was surprised then—as he was on his return about a decade ago in his capacity as chief executive of the Pratt Foundation—to find there was no monument to the Australian Light Horse. While this experience contributed to the genesis of Pratt's memorial park in Be'er Sheva, Lipski's awareness of the full importance of Australia's military role in Israel's security found full historic symmetry during the Coalition of the Willing's invasion of Iraq in early 2003.

The Australian Special Air Service had been unofficially on the ground in Iraq for several days before the American-led invasion, disabling Iraq's missiles. The covert SAS action was aimed at avoiding a repeat of the Gulf War in 1991 when Iraq struck Israel with Scud missiles. The Australian communication facility at Pine Gap, meanwhile, played its own special role in Israel's defence during the Gulf War, during which Lipski—then the editor and publisher of the *Australian Jewish News*—was in Jerusalem.

To coincide with the 2003 invasion of Iraq, Lipski wrote a column supporting the allied military action. 'I basically said that I was no great fan of John Howard, whom I had criticised a number of times, but that I was a supporter of the Coalition of the Willing and a supporter of the war against Iraq,' he told me. 'I said that as an Australian I'd be out there cheering the Australian SAS and as a Jew I'll be out there waving the Israeli flag as well.

'I also said that this was not the first time in history that Australia has been involved ... There have been four decisive turning points where military action by Australia has been decisive in terms of Israel's security. The first was the Australian light horse in Palestine, including at Beersheba, the second was during World War II, then there was the Gulf War and the Iraq invasion.'

While such Australian Jews as Lipski point to these clear links between the Australian military and Israel's establishment and ongoing security, few venture a step further to argue that the Charge of Beersheba was God's instrument to restore Israel. That argument is left to the Christian Zionists and Evangelical Christians.

16

INSIDE JAFFA GATE

The Australian accent is unmistakable. But there is a foreign inflection and another similarly harsh tone also at work there. Israeli.

'Mate, come and see me—I'm just inside the Jaffa Gate.'

It's Kelvin Crombie, a West Australian university drop-out now in his early fifties who moved to Israel in his early twenties. He immediately fell in love with the place, so much so that he even tried to join the Israeli Defence Force so that he could become a citizen.

I've been communicating with him for weeks by email before we meet in Jerusalem's Old City. It is early in the afternoon on a clear, blistering spring day. Jerusalem is in the middle of an early heat wave. I'm staying close by and intend to walk. But as I leave the hotel, Rasheed latches on to me. He insists on driving me. He starts up straightaway.

'Hey, Mr Paul, how many Palestinians does it take to change a light bulb?'

'Tell me.'

'It takes none, because they all prefer to sit in the dark forever and blame the Jews,' he says, repeating a well-worn Palestinian joke.

He is roaring with laughter as we head down the Nablus road towards the Old City. I am suppressing a laugh; it's not the jokes but the man telling them that amuses me. 'The thing, Rasheed, is that you're just not that funny. You really don't make me laugh at all.' I look out the window.

'Well, you are just being offended for the Palestinians … I am making fair jokes, anyway, Mr Paul. I make jokes about Palestinians and Jews, you, see, because they are both the problem here. Look at what is happening in Gaza this week—the Hamas shoots a Jew, the Jews shoot more Palestinians, the Palestinians shoot more Jews and then the Jews send the tanks in [to Gaza]. It never ends. It's the politicians and the men who give the orders on both sides who are to blame. It's just bad for the ordinary Palestinians and Jews. You have to laugh when you live here, Mr Paul, or you go fucking crazy.

'Now, where do you go in the Old City, and *who* do you wish to see?'

'I'm going to Christ Church, and I'm meeting a man called Kelvin.'

'Ah, the British church,' he says, shaking his head disapprovingly. 'I know it.'

~

Kelvin probably knows better than any living Australian or Israeli the exact places where the light-horsemen camped, watered their horses, fought and died. In the lead-up to our meeting he has been inordinately generous with advice on everything from potential battle-site guides and the best books about Beersheba, to affordable hotels in Jerusalem.

He's asked me for nothing in return, but I'm uncomfortable. Perhaps it's my inner Irish Catholic— lapsed and very flawed though it is—that has made me deeply wary of Kelvin from the outset. I challenge myself. What is it about him? There is but one answer, about which I'm later deeply ashamed. All of Kelvin Crombie's emails to me end with the epithet '*Blessings*'. He's clearly a Bible-basher.

A Jewish acquaintance had already warned me about the odd bods, weirdos and religious crackpots who wanted to appropriate or control the story of the Australian Light Horse in Palestine. They speak of the Christian bloke in Jerusalem who seems to genuinely believe he is a reincarnated horseman, and of the evangelical Christians who say that, come the Day of Judgment, the Australian horsemen buried in the Commonwealth War Cemetery on Jerusalem's Mount of Olives will be the first to rise, such was their part in returning Israel to the Jews. Then there are the legions of amateur historians who are jealously staking claim to local knowledge about the light horse as well as related Australian military artefacts. Sometimes their genuine knowledge is scant. Where does Kelvin Crombie fit into all of this?

~

On 11 December 1917 the commander of British forces in the Sinai and Palestine, General Sir Edmund Allenby, rode a grey horse along Jerusalem's Jaffa Road towards the Old City. He was followed by his staff officers and corps commanders, including Chauvel.

Two days earlier, in the face of a British onslaught, the Turkish army evacuated Jerusalem and headed north towards Jordan, so ending four hundred years of Ottoman occupation of the most religiously significant city in the world. Allenby had come to officially take possession of the place.

Just outside the Jaffa Gate he and his men dismounted and walked into the Holy City. He walked past a guard of honour comprising about a hundred troops from England, Scotland, Wales and Ireland and another fifty from Australia and New Zealand. The troops followed as he and his officers and commanders walked purposefully around to the right and into the Tower of David where the ceremony would take place.

As Allenby and his entourage stood on the landing outside the tower, the Australian light-horsemen stood with their backs to the stone wall of the building opposite. That building is Christ Church. Built in 1849 on the then grounds of the British consulate in Turkish Jerusalem, Christ Church embodies the deep belief of British evangelicals such as William Wilberforce and Charles Simeon that Jesus would return only when Israel was returned to the Jews. A missionary group called the London Society for Promoting Christianity among the Jews built the church in the belief that Christianity had strayed from its simple Hebrew origins. The church's philosophy is underpinned by the fact that the Christian prophet Jesus and all of his Apostles were Jewish.

'In fact the New Testament itself was a Jewish document, written by Jewish followers of Jesus ... Indeed the question in the early Church was not could a Jew believe in Jesus as the promised Messiah, but could a gentile believe in Jesus without first becoming a Jew,' the church's promotional literature explains. 'The founders of Christ Church wanted Jewish people to be able to enter the church and see the Christian faith, not as something alien, foreign and gentile but as it was in the beginning—Jewish.'

Today Christ Church stands pretty much unchanged since the day Allenby entered the Tower of David to hear the proclamation of martial law read in Arabic, Hebrew, English, French, Italian, Greek and Russian. Afterwards he walked over to the abandoned Turkish barracks to meet Jerusalem's leaders. Today that barracks is a local police station. Young Israeli police wander in and out of the station. A cluster of swarthy young women in Israeli army uniforms, with weapons slung and wearing stylish sunglasses, toss their hair and laugh. The attraction of Israeli women in uniform is no mere cliché; most are striking and poised enough to begin with, and the khaki and weapons only adds to this edgy allure. There's a beggar or two squatting by the street. Hassidic Jews rush past on their way to shops to buy a few more things before the Sabbath.

The first thing you'll see when you enter the Christ Church cultural centre is an oversized photograph of Allenby's entrance to the Old City. The light-horsemen in the photographs were standing just metres away with their backs to the external wall. The photograph itself hangs on the other side of the wall that it depicts. Nearby, a glass display case contains a pair of light-horsemen's leggings, a water bottle and a horse's feed-bag. As if to complete the symbolism, there is also a copy of the famous letter from the British Secretary of State for Foreign Affairs, Lord Balfour, to a leader of Britain's Jewish community, Lord Rothschild.

The letter conveys to Rothschild a decision by the War Cabinet on the same day as the charge at Beersheba—31 October 1917—to support the establishment of a Jewish state in Palestine. The decision, known as the Balfour Declaration, is regarded as a seminal moment in the restoration of Israel, although thirty-one years of hope, disappointment, war and, of course, the Holocaust, would elapse before Israel was established in 1948. The letter reads:

I have much pleasure in conveying to you, on behalf of His Majesty's Government, the following declaration of sympathy with Jewish Zionist aspirations which has been submitted to and approved by, the Cabinet.

His Majesty's Government views with favour the establishment of a national home for the Jewish people, and will use their best endeavours to facilitate the achievement of this object, it being clearly understood that nothing shall be done which may prejudice the civil and religious rights of existing non-Jewish communities in Palestine or the rights and political status enjoyed by Jews in other countries.

I should be grateful if you would bring this declaration to the knowledge of the Zionist Federation.[1]

While I'm inspecting the light horse relics in the case, I'm startled by the familiar voice behind me.

'Mate, you found me. So, what can I do for you?'

~

Crombie's handshake is like a vice. He has silver hair, a laconic crooked smile and a nuggety build that points to the younger, athletic cricket tragic he once was. His skin is a deep bronze—courtesy of years traipsing around the Israeli desert—and he wears work shorts and a short-sleeved plaid shirt. He looks like a construction worker. His eyes fix yours immediately, and he sizes you up quickly.

He is, I immediately determine, the perfect Australia–Israel hybrid; the laid-back friendliness is underscored by a disarming, matter-of-fact directness. He has lived in Israel for a long time, and it shows. Kelvin is a curious character—a Christian with a knockabout, no-nonsense Australian air that makes me think of two home-grown adventurers, the 'Bush Tucker Man' Les Hiddens and the late Steve Irwin.

But it doesn't take me long to detect a wariness about Crombie that stems, I suspect, from people trying to sap his considerable expertise on the Australian light horse in Palestine. For the past few years everyone has wanted a piece of Crombie's knowledge, from amateur Israeli historians and visiting Australian official delegations, to the Christian tourists and those who dress up as the horsemen. But they haven't always given him due credit. Some want to take what he knows of the history without the religion. Others want more religion, less history.

Such has been the demand for Kelvin's expertise that at times he has been driven close to exhaustion. He is within his rights to be suspicious of the next person— me—who wants his help.

Despite myself, I like him immediately. I would become even fonder of him as we met repeatedly in Jerusalem and Be'er Sheva, before driving into the desert to trace the final movements of the light-horsemen as they prepared to attack Beersheba. However, I'm still expecting to be Bible-bashed.

I don't, however, get the Holy Book. What I do get is a story that is every bit as technically detailed as Henry Gullett's about the war with the Turks and the events leading up to the great charge. But I get more than that which Gullett's writing has imparted to me. Along the way, Kelvin constantly peppers me with questions. They are not designed to highlight my comparative paucity of knowledge about Allenby, Chauvel, Ryrie, Roston and their men, and the Battle of Beersheba. Rather, they are intended to provoke me into thinking about why events unfolded as they did from the perspective of the commanders and the men who participated. He urges me to make critical judgments along the way. He precedes it all with the genuinely modest qualification: 'Mate, I'm not an expert—just a very passionate enthusiast.'[2] But he is more—much more—than that.

Crombie's first-hand knowledge, gleaned over two decades of visits to light horse battle sites and watering spots around Israel, coupled with his own archival research, gives him a unique insight into this story. He has a vast array of maps that are based on his journeys and not (unlike the maps in the many histories that have been written about Beersheba) on those in Gullett's official history. For the most part he is careful to separate the history from his religious views. I soon establish that many in Israel, and some in Australia, are jealous and resentful of Kelvin's knowledge, gleaned as it is from half a lifetime of field trips into the Israeli deserts and painstaking searches through the archives in Australia, Israel and Britain.

He does not equivocate about his own view: in his mind the charge was part of God's plan, as outlined in the Bible, to return Palestine to the Israelites. But unlike other historians, he makes no claim to the story. He sees it, quite simply, as part of his duty—to God and to the legacy of the light-horsemen—to show as many people as possible the remarkable places where the men fought and died, watered their horses, camped, relaxed and trained. His paradigm is a pure synthesis of the Bible, his belief in God and military history. He is, however, lacking in the dogma I would ordinarily associate with someone like him. And so he is willing to discuss pure military history, unfiltered by the Bible, and based singularly on archival research and official history. It's when you ask him what it all means that he explains it through the prism of his Christianity.

Kelvin is a generous and gentle man, with a wry sense of humour and an ostensibly modest view about his knowledge. His one concession to vanity, however, comes when he awkwardly volunteers he is writing what amounts to an autobiography, with a working title 'Journey to Beersheba'. But then his has been a remarkable odyssey, worthy of at least one volume—if not a movie. The book will chronicle his physical, spiritual and historical journey on the trail of the light horse. It will also serve as a testimony to Israel, the country where he has spent more than half his life and where his children have largely been raised. It is clear that Kelvin is an Israeli at heart, although the country he loves—and contributes so much to—will not grant him or his family permanent citizenship.

In recent years Crombie's Christian take on the charge has, meanwhile, become a touchstone for visiting Christian and secular tour groups from America, Britain and Australia, which flock to Israel to tour the light horse battle sites with him and embrace his compelling stories about the diggers' role in returning the Holy Land to the Jews. Since about 2002 he and Barry Rodgers have been running a tour program. Both men clearly see the potential for an expansion of the light horse tours to take advantage of what could be both a commercial and an evangelical opportunity.

In 1998 Crombie published *Anzacs, Empires and Israel's Restoration 1798–1948*. It is a history of settlement in Israel and Palestine, beginning with the Hebrew tribes, and chronicling Greek, Roman, Islamic, Ottoman, British Mandate intervention and, finally, Jewish resettlement.[3] His record of the part played by the Australian light horse in the British campaign is detailed and groundbreaking, and he tells a compelling parallel story of the politics and diplomacy that led to the Balfour Declaration.

For Crombie the timing of events was no mere coincidence. He believes the hand of God was at work, coordinating events so that—according to the Bible—Israel would be returned to the Jews: 'And it all climaxed at Beersheva, a town connected to Abraham, the father of Israel, to whom, the Bible states, God has promised the land of Israel as an eternal possession.'[4]

'I grew up in the West Australian bush on a wheat, sheep and pig farm about sixteen miles inland from Perth. One of our neighbours, old Reg Clapp, he was a Light Horseman—in the 10th Light Horse. But my real interest [in the Middle East] was triggered by two uncles who were over here in the Second World War. One was … stationed at Gaza,' he says. 'I was just a war fanatic as a kid. Anzac Day for me was the best day of the year. And as I got older I just got more and more interested. I had an encyclopaedia set of the Second World War as a young kid and from the age of 12 I had an Israeli family come to live on a farm in the same area. I picked up a lot of interest in Israel from them.

'I had no religious background. My interest in Israel wasn't formed from a Christian perspective, which is why most people … become interested … in my adolescent years I wasn't that interested and then at university I studied history. History—why things happened when they happened—made a lot of sense to me. It was captivating. But I hated university and I made a decision not to continue with study; I thought university was full of snobs.'

It was 1979. Crombie dropped out, went back to work on the family farm, saved his money and travelled on a one-way ticket to Israel. He began work on a kibbutz, which he immediately loved.

'I wanted to stay. I wanted to become one with the Israelis, so much so that I really wanted to go into the [Israeli] army. I thought that … was the entrance ticket into Israeli society. I was on the kibbutz and I was told,

Members of the 4th and 12th Australian Light Horse Regiments killed in the Charge of Beersheba. The body of famous test cricketer Trooper Albert (Tibby) Cotter, a stretcher bearer, is marked with an X. (AWM/ P02279.003)

A picture of Beersheba Railway Station taken by Trooper Pauls a day after the charge. The derelict station still stands today, close to a memorial for the Turkish dead. (Ernest Pauls)

The legendary Lieutenant Colonel Leslie Maygar, commander of the 8th Light Horse Regiment, who was awarded the Victoria Cross in South Africa in 1901. Maygar died after being bombed from a low-flying German aircraft late on the day of the battle. (AWM/H12606)

Australian troops stationed in the Middle East during World War II visit the graves of countrymen killed in the Battle of Beersheba. (Bruce Haigh)

Dead horses lie in the foreground of a light horse transport unit, the result of a raid near Beersheba by German Taube aircraft. Many Australian men and horses were killed in German aircraft raids after Beersheba fell. (AWM/J03178)

A wounded officer, supporting himself with a crutch and wielding a revolver, surveys the battlefield after the Charge of Beersheba while a wounded soldier is tended. (Ernest Pauls)

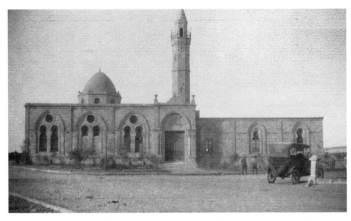

The minaret of the mosque at Beersheba shone in the dying light of 31 October 1917, serving as a beacon for the Australian horsemen charging towards the Turkish trenches while blinded by the setting sun and dust. (AWM/J02505)

Australian light-horsemen make their way along the dry water course into town, after the 4th Brigade took the Turkish trenches about a kilometre behind Beersheba's iconic railway bridge. The bridge is still standing. (AWM/P02268.012)

The main street of Beersheba, taken soon after the charge. The Australian horsemen were said to be unimpressed with the Turkish town. (AWM/P01668.005)

Lieutenant General Sir Harry Chauvel, fine boned and even-tempered, led the biggest column of men and animals across the Holy Land since Alexander the Great. He is pictured here in 1923. (AWM/J00503)

British warships bombed Gaza relentlessly in the lead-up to the attack on Beersheba. An unexploded shell can be seen in the foreground of this picture, which also depicts Trooper Ernest Pauls amid Gaza's ruins. (Ernest Pauls)

Anzac Mounted Division commander Major General Sir Edward Chaytor and Turkish commander Ali Bey Wahaby after the extraordinary 'incident' at Ziza in September 1918, when the Australians joined forces with the Turks for a night to fend off marauding Arab tribesmen. (AWM/B00088)

By the end of the war, the light-horsemen had little but contempt for the nomadic Bedouin (pictured) or the town-dwelling Arabs. (Ernest Pauls)

In a premeditated revenge attack against a Bedouin murderer, the Anzacs raided the village of Surafend on the night of 10 December 1918, bayoneting many of the male inhabitants and later burning the place down. (AWM/H02580)

Mysterious Joseph Hokeidonian became deputy town clerk of Beersheba after the town fell to the British. His grandson Joe Hockey is the federal Liberal member of parliament for North Sydney, the seat once held by Sir Granville Ryrie. (Richard Hockey)

"Well, if you want to go into the army you have to become Israeli." How do you become Israeli? Well, you have to become Jewish. How do you become Jewish? You convert,' he says.

'I thought, "No problems". Until I realised what was involved. It was learning all this religious stuff and going to the rabbis—it just wasn't what I wanted to be in it for. And I said, "No, no, no, it's not for me." And I just didn't know which way to go at that stage. But I had a goal—I wanted to become Israeli,' he says.

Crombie's family was a mixture of Anglican and Presbyterian. While there was some religion at his school—Perth's Scotch College—his background was effectively secular. As a teenager he had, in his own words, absolutely no understanding of personal faith. But then suddenly he was a young man alone in Israel. Inevitably there was a girl.

'A girl came along who was a volunteer with a Christian group. First date—I thought, "You're going to tell me about Jesus." I thought: "What's Jesus got to do with me? What's Jesus got to do with Israel?" I thought: "If there's a God he's the God of the Israelis, the Jewish people and you Christians are hypocrites."'

In 1981 Easter and Passover coincided. Jerusalem was vibrant with religious celebration as the main festivals of the Christian and Jewish calendars aligned.

'Jerusalem then was just humming. I went to all the religious places around town. It didn't do anything for me. And then on Easter Sunday morning we went to a place called the Garden Tomb for a dawn service,' says

Crombie. 'There was an Anglican minister talking about faith. And he was actually the minister from here [Christ Church], although I didn't know that. And he started talking about the ... path to heaven, and he began to talk about ... the Jewish connection ... and I'd never heard it before in my life. And he said the return of the Jewish people to the land of Israel will come before ... the return of Jesus to Jerusalem. I'd never heard that one before. I thought, "What's going on here? This Jesus that this girl's been telling me about—there's a bit more to it than meets the eye."

'That began a process for me whereby I began to seriously think about Jesus and in time become a committed follower. And so I took the regular steps of repentance, and I accepted that Jesus was the Messiah who was sacrificed for my sins and then I was filled with the Holy Spirit. It's just the process that you go through.'

Kelvin became 'a new person'. He stopped drinking and swearing before moving to Jerusalem and working in a hospital for disabled children. About that time, 1982, he made his first visit to Be'er Sheva. That visit became the next step in a process that would tie his new-found Christianity to the deeds of the Australian light horse in Palestine.

~

He leads me from the heritage centre into the church. Christ Church is a physical synthesis of Christianity and

Judaism. The interior of the building itself is reminiscent of a synagogue, beginning with a wooden rerodos at the front, which is strikingly similar to the arc in a synagogue. The Lord's Prayer, the Apostles' Creed and the Ten Commandments are all written on the rerodos— in Hebrew. Striking stained-glass windows are also adorned with Jewish symbols and Hebrew writing.

'This', says Crombie, 'is where it all makes sense.'

Next we are driving through peak-hour traffic up the Jaffa road in Crombie's dust-covered urban truck, en route to collect his youngest daughter from nursery. He waxes lyrical about the joys and difficulties of living in Jerusalem. Despite his significant continued contribution to promoting an understanding of Israel's recent history, Crombie has yet to be awarded permanent citizenship. The recent intifada—with their targeted, random attacks on Israeli citizens—have made security a potent concern, especially for parents.

'But I love it here. I think it's the best country in the world ... and I'm here because I genuinely believe I have a calling to do what I do in relation to the light horse and the Anzacs.'

17

DESERT DOGS

The soccer game continued on the carpet outside my hotel room door for most of Passover. Only on one occasion when my door became a set of goals and a door on the other side of the hallway another, did I stick my head out and complain, grumpily, that I could not be expected to work while this racket continued. The kids looked at me askance. As soon as I shut the door, the game recommenced.

Despite the temptation to quit Be'er Sheva and head back to Jerusalem where I had friends, I stayed for most of Passover. Sadly, Rasheed was correct about the hotel. It had five stars above its entrance, but it was not a five-star hotel. While my inclination was to view the hotel's ordinary food, its grimy carpets, its ubiquitous smoked eel smell and its refusal to sell beer (a yeast product and, therefore, according to Jewish custom, not permitted during Passover) as some sort of hardship, I forced myself instead to focus on the positives. One of the barmaids persuaded me that the kosher red wine was worth a try. And after a few days it seemed not half bad. I spent my days wandering through what remained of the old Turkish town. But often I found myself back in the cemetery with the mates of Ernest Pauls and the names of a lost generation of Australian—and British and New Zealand—men.

After that I'd stop at Allenby Square, where a bust of the great man stood on a stone plinth. It had been repeatedly vandalised in recent years, a young Bedouin man told me.

'Many of the Arabs [Bedouin] around here think Allenby was a pig,' he tells me contemptuously. 'The Palestinians, they hate Allenby ... because of his actions the land was stolen and given to the Jews.'

Elsewhere in the old town elderly Arab men would sit in doorways, while Jewish artisans—tailors and metal-workers—plied their trades in dark rooms half-open to the street. I'd buy pistachios or an Arab pastry and thick sweet coffee, and sit for a while under an awning. I later discovered a fantastic kebab and pide shop, run by local Arabs.

Several nights I went down to the old town for a soft-drink (the local kosher cops apparently ensured that they didn't sell beer during Passover), to watch the passing parade of locals who showed no interest in me at all, and wait for the promised cool breeze to roar in. It never did.

Twice, in the comparative cool of the pre-dawn morning, I walked out to the railway bridge that sign-posted the way into Beersheba for the men of the 12th and the 4th Light Horse Regiments, and watched the local Bedouin set up their nearby market. Standing beneath the bridge and facing west, it was possible to get a fleeting sense of what the Turks might have seen when the Australians came screaming through. From the bridge you can look through the thicket of eucalypt trees at Bet Eshel, grown since the charge, and towards a gently sloping plain that rises to the foothills that gave the regiments cover. Over to the right is Tel el Saba.

One day I take a car and blunder around looking for some of the more famous watering stops. Susan McMinn, the artist, is navigating. We don't realise it when we stumble across Asluj, and we keep driving until the road before the car is nothing but a sand-covered track pointed towards the top of a sand dune, corrugated by the desert winds. We get out.

'This is the sand that they talked about—the fine, powdery sand,' she says.

She's right. So many of the light-horsemen talked of sands that were as fine as talcum powder and clung to your clothes and to your body, and were hell to ride across. If you grab a handful it sticks to your skin. 'The men rode and lived and slept in a fog of dust which seldom settled,' Gullett observed.[1]

We go to the top of the dune. On one side there's nothing but endless dunes. Between us and the oasis that we didn't recognise as Asluj, a big Bedouin village is coming to life. In the perfect, sweltering, serene stillness as dusk starts to eclipse day, narrow ribbons of smoke twist their way skywards from cooking fires.

First you hear them howl and then, from a safe distance, you watch as the brown and black animals gingerly circle the settlement attracted by cooking smells and a remote promise of scraps. The desert dogs.

~

We turn the car for Be'er Sheva just as the sky behind glows with streaks of burning crimson and orange. Before long we're on the highway, then, a few minutes later, on the dual-lane road heading due east into Be'er Sheva. The road takes a steep rise, punctuated by electricity and communications towers, then slowly descends into a long, undulating plain.

Just as the road levels you notice the thicket of trees in the distance to the right. It is Bet Eshel, the location of the Turkish trenches.

As the road dips further, Be'er Sheva's office blocks, housing tenements and shopping malls suddenly ink out this oasis of eucalypts. When the road levels off with the town and Bet Eshel approaches, the dying sun spears its blinding beams straight at you. For a while you can see little.

'This is what they saw—this is it,' I say. 'This is what they must have gone through.'

How the hell, you can only wonder as you drive into the old town towards the mosque, did they ever do it?

~

The Baseiso Mosque is the only formal place for Muslim worship in Be'er Sheva. The problem is that, along with the rest of the town, it was abandoned by the Arabs during the War of Independence in 1948. A plethora of small mosques has been built in the Bedouin settlements surrounding Be'er Sheva in recent years, but there remains no active place of worship for the five thousand or so Muslims inside the city itself. Muslims who want to worship at prayer times must apparently do so in the street, in other public places or not at all.

Built in 1902 after the Ottoman governor imposed a special tax on the Bedouin tribes, the mosque has been the centre of bitter symbolic legal dispute in Be'er Sheva in recent years. Local Arabs want it reopened. The municipality, however, did not, maintaining that to doing so would trigger religious tensions in what is now an overwhelmingly Jewish city. The municipality has argued that the mosque was never intended for use by local Arabs, but was built for the Turkish soldiers who were stationed there.

In any event, the mosque has stood virtually derelict for at least the past fifty years. Each time I visit to take external photographs, the mosque is closed and surrounded by a vast security fence. There are signs of restoration, yet I never see any workmen. Then one evening it is suddenly a hive of activity as the cyclone wire security gate opens for a cement truck, and tradesmen busy themselves all around.

I'm content to take more photographs of the setting sun striking the minaret from outside. But McMinn stands at the gate and beckons the workmen. They open the gate and let her in. I follow. Before I know it one of the men has given her a shawl to drape over her head and shoulders, and we are receiving a guided tour from the friendly middle-aged Bedouin foreman, Kassem Shama.

He uses broken English to establish that we are Australians. 'I don't know all about what happened,' he says. 'But they say the Australians came and took Beersheba away from the Turkish. And then they take Jerusalem and Jordan and Syria. The British used the Australians to take them away.'

We follow him inside the mosque, directly under the great white dome and the minaret that served as a beacon for the charging horsemen. All around us, workmen are rendering the walls, plastering cornices and chipping away at brittle stone and mortar. At the top of the dome sunlight pours in from the large windows that were the suspected posts for Turkish snipers on the day of the great battle. The windows were checked and cleared by the 4th Regiment's reckless scouts, who bolted into town well ahead of the advancing lines to help secure the path for their fellow riders.

The foreman removes a mobile telephone from his pocket. He beckons us to watch the screen, and he begins to play some video footage. The film shows the ninetieth anniversary re-enactment of the charge. The Australian horsemen are cantering in across the dusty plain towards Bet Eshel, their colourful pennants flying high and emu plumes flouncing up and down on their broad-brimmed diggers' hats. As the riders get closer, the video fleetingly pans across some of the men's faces. I immediately recognise Barry Rodgers, Phil Chalker and Robert Unicomb.

'I was there—I saw the Australians come in. It was wonderful, very good to see,' he says. 'This is exactly like the real battle; they are running in from the wadi at the same place and doing the charge.'

We ask him what he knows about the original charge. It transpires that his maternal grandfather, Abraham Caham, was one of the Bedouin who was co-opted to fight for the Turks. His grandfather died in 1975, but not before telling him some stories about the war and showing him the hat of an English soldier.

'My grandfather was here as a soldier, and when the Australians came, he ran away with the Turks to the north of the country. My grandfather he tells me there is two armies: one is British and one is of Australians,' he says. 'He told me that the Indians in the British Army say to the Australian men to leave the Arabic [Bedouin] men alone when they race into Beersheba, and to kill the Turkish men like this [he gestures with one hand holding an imaginary bayonet and the other arm around someone's head].

'My grandfather told me that that the Ottomans took all of the young men from the streets and the villages; they took them in a strong way, and made them fight for the Turkish Army. They didn't want to fight for the Turks, but they made them ... they ran away whenever they could, my grandfather said.

'My grandfather kept the hat of an English soldier that he took that day ... I don't know how, but we still have it somewhere.'

18

THE HAND OF GOD

To follow in the footsteps of the Australian light horse around Be'er Sheva it helps to have a guide with an encyclopaedic knowledge of the official Australian history of the Palestine conflict. It also helps if your guide has a decent grasp of Israeli, Palestinian and Turkish history, a steady supply of cold water, a four-wheel drive with excellent air-conditioning, the best maps in the business and, perhaps more than anything, an ability to bring the past alive by explaining what the light-horsemen did and where. A deep affinity with the Scriptures is, I would discover, an optional extra.

It's another blistering spring day in Be'er Sheva. When Kelvin collects us at dawn, it is already sweltering and the dry, burning, dusty wind is strengthening. It's the khamsin—'the dread khamsin', Gullett called it—which blows in from Libya and Egypt for about fifty days a year. It usually happens closer to summer. When Chauvel was trying to solve the logistic nightmare of supplying water to thousands of horses and men after Beersheba fell, his advancing column had the deep misfortune of encountering the wind. 'The thirst of those wearing days was further accentuated by a violent and prolonged khamsin. For three days and nights the wind, heavily charged with fine dust, blew in hot from the south-eastern desert drying up the rain-pools and distressing man and horse,' Gullett wrote.[1]

Kelvin points the car south-east, and we take off towards the Desert Mounted Corps headquarters or, as it was known, 'Chauvel's Hill'. As we go, Kelvin begins to explain his passion for Israel—and the light horse. He and the Christian girl he met on the kibbutz didn't last. But his relationship with God did. Before too long he met his wife, a nurse from Holland, while he was working in a hospital for disabled children. All the while, he became increasingly immersed in Israeli culture and society. He tried, unsuccessfully, to join the Israeli army again. He first went to Be'er Sheva in 1982, but the 'Australian connection' didn't dawn on him. In 1986 he began working as a local guide at Christ Church. And that is when he experienced an epiphany about Australia's connection to Israel.

'I didn't know anything about the history of the church. It's the first Protestant church in the Middle East [and the] first modern building in Jerusalem. It is located adjacent to the first British consul in Jerusalem, which was the first British consul *per se* in the whole city. It was the first piece of foreign real estate in the whole of Jerusalem. All of a sudden you begin to realise: "Hey, there's a bit of a story here." Christ Church established the first modern school, welfare institutions [and] the first hospital in Jerusalem, and was instrumental in the first agricultural settlement in the country. It's quite a story. So what's happening is that any Israeli in an academic institution who wants to study modernisation of this country has to come here, where it all began.'

A British publisher asked him to write a book about Britain's part in the establishment of Israel, and that was when he stumbled across the Anzac connection. 'So then all of a sudden that dimension of my Australian identity was restored. I'm actually going through a whole cycle again of being Australian when for close to ten years, it wasn't on my radar screen … then I was straight into this light horse thing. It was an absolute awakening for me, and before long I was taking guests, friends mostly, down to Be'er Sheva once a week to tell them what had gone on there.'

~

Kelvin might have been in Israel for more than half a lifetime, but he still drives like an Australian. Every now and then, as he remonstrates with his hands to emphasise a point, the car veers onto the left side of the road … and stays there. Until another car appears at a distance, heading towards us on the same side of the road.

This happens on one occasion when he takes his hands off the wheel to explain: 'You can safely say that the right flank of the 12th [Regiment] would have been pretty close to where we are now.'

Just as he corrects the car, I joke: 'How long did you say you've been here?'

'Maaaate, a lifetime—I've gone native.'

'Yeah, bloody oath—you even drive like a Jew.' (By which I meant, with *chutzpah*, with abandon, with attitude … fast, recklessly. I knew, because I had already driven across the Beersheba–Gaza line with two elderly former career soldiers.)

'Careful what you say about the Jews, mate. Be very careful—because my best friend was a Jew,' Kelvin says.

'Who was he? And what do you mean *was* … what, did he die in a car accident or someth—?'

Kelvin looked sideways at me. As if I was completely stupid. Which, of course, I was.

'Oh, okay, sorry. You mean Jesus. Jesus is your best friend. Okay, I get it,' I say sheepishly.

'You got it, mate. He died for all of us,' Kelvin explained.

'Oh, yeah, right—okay. I'm sorry.'

We turn off the highway and drive part way up a steep, gravelly rise. Kelvin gets his maps from the back of the car, and we walk a short distance to the top of Chauvel's Hill. He opens one wallpaper-sized map before us, and there, plotted on the thick paper in coloured Texta, are the movements of the 4th and the 12th Regiments towards Beersheba. They are symbol-ised by two great thrusting arrows. Just out to our right—figuratively on the map and literally from where we stand—is Tel el Saba. Other arrows represent the New Zealanders and the light-horsemen from Tasmania and South Australia who pushed the Turks off the entrenched mound.

'Okay,' says Kelvin, 'there's a misconception among light horse fanciers and enthusiasts that the 4th Brigade came in to save the day because the Brits and everyone else failed. Not true. No credible source would say the British failed. They won their objectives by taking the Turkish trenches south and south-west early in the day—and soon you'll see how tough that was. And then they held position, consistent with their orders.

'Allenby gets the credit, but it was the infantry commander, Chetwode, who came up with the idea to land the knockout blow from out here. Tel el Saba … took a bit longer than expected and then, as you know, it's after three o'clock and the light is beginning to fade. And so there's a discussion right where we are standing on Chauvel's Hill, where you had all the top brass—Chauvel, Hodgson [Australian Mounted Division com-mander], Grant and Fitzgerald [commander of the British Yeomanry]. All their soldiers were basically backed up around the back of the wadies here.'

At the end of the day Chauvel seemed to have had three options. He could let the light horse make a tradi-tional mounted infantry attack by getting close to the trenches at Bet Eshel, dismounting and attacking on foot, or he could send in Fitzgerald's cavalry, the yeomanry, which were assembled close to Chauvel's headquarters and were armed with sabres. Another alternative was that he could go for the surprise option: a traditional cavalry charge using the light horse.

'So you can imagine that's why Fitzgerald was pretty well pissed off. He had cavalry in the form of yeomanry. They carried sabres, and some of them might even have had lances. But you have to ask yourself, challenge yourself, why Chauvel chose the light horse, other than that they were Australian. Well, it may have been that he realised he would otherwise have a lot of problems in his headquarters afterwards with Grant and everybody else saying, "Hey, you let everybody else have a piece of the cake and we missed out", but I don't think so,' Kelvin says.

'My opinion is that I think Chauvel had a pretty good idea of the characters of both groups of men, the yeomanry and the light horse. And I think he knew that at that stage something radical was needed. And they were his boys. My view is that the cavalry had always been used to doing things in a set way. And if all of a sudden things just don't go according to plan, well, they wouldn't have had a fallback. Whereas with the Aussies, if things don't go according to plan on the spur of the moment, well, they can always improvise.'

Kelvin believes another factor might have been playing on Chauvel's mind that evening: if he didn't take the town from the south-east and quickly, Allenby might have decided to mount another infantry attack from the south and south-west. 'I'm sure that was a factor in Chauvel's thinking,' he says.

It's not something I have considered before. And it has not been canvassed in any military history that I've read about Beersheba, either. But it makes perfect sense. The charge was, perhaps, effectively the culmination of a race to take the town.

~

In 1993 Kelvin took a sabbatical and visited Australia and New Zealand, where he undertook more archival research. He also gave lectures on the Anzacs and the Middle East. He was stunned by how little Australians, particularly, knew about the conflict—especially the charge. He returned to Israel but after a couple of years decided to head back to Australia to write his book.

'I resigned and moved back to Australia for three years. I went back to the farm, worked in a shearing shed, and whenever it was raining, I'd be writing.

'Back then there were two groups who had an interest, who understood, what I was doing. You had Christians who were interested in Israel, and all those people were interested in what the Jewish people had done for Zionism. You had bodies that were interested in the light horse. And it was like they were in a world of their own. For them the idea of actually ever coming to visit Palestine/Israel—I mean, "Why do that when we've got our little Light Horse Club and a few little [historical] possessions?" But ... the number of groups, the number of Christians, coming from Australia to here, grew and grew and grew.'

There were, he volunteers, some fanatics and fantasists who contorted his teachings about the light-horsemen saying that the Holy Land was liberated by the Australian soldiers. 'What happened is that a lot of those groups rode off with the fairies, and they began to fantasise. And there were certain people who began to jump on this bandwagon, and I think they took it off in a slightly wrong direction. They began to embellish it a little bit. You know, they said the Holy Land was taken by the light horse and that if it wasn't for the Australians all of these things wouldn't have happened. There's a degree of truth in all of that. Where were the British? Where were the New Zealanders? This sort of stuff is just unhelpful. I have been out here with my books and my maps for twenty years now trying to work out what went on, so the off-with-the-fairies stuff is just a distraction.'

Kelvin doesn't believe the fairytales. But he does believe the hand of God was at work in Beersheba.

~

We stop as the bitumen road turns into a dusty track just next to the Be'er Sheva Zoo. We climb a gentle rise and stop on the crest. We look north-east back towards the city. The khamsin stings your eyes if you hold the view for too long from up here. But you don't need to look for more than a few seconds to appreciate the job Chetwode's infantry did here and further to the west, in the opening act of the Battle of Beersheba.

The British artillery began raining shrapnel into these hills at dawn. Unlike today, with its crying wind, the morning of the battle was deathly still, and the artillery raised a pall of dust and smoke that hung over the town's outskirts for most of the day. The dust was initially so thick that forward scouts were able to creep forward, undetected, and cut some of the barbed wire that the shrapnel hadn't destroyed.

The British foot soldiers then poured into the hills where we now stand. The landscape here is hostile to the invader; on each side of a series of deep gullies, Turkish trenches and dugouts have been hacked out of the stony ground. These steep embankments, protected by well-entrenched Turks, would have been difficult—and, given the poor visibility, frightening—for the infantrymen to rush.

Much of the fighting here was vicious and ugly. Casualties on both sides were very high. About twelve hundred British infantry troops were injured in the Battle of Beersheba, most of them in the hills to the south and south-west of the town. Turkish casualties have never been fully determined. But it seems a reasonable assumption, given that the Turks lost, that the figures were very high.

After the battle Allenby rightly emphasised the part played by the British infantry; there would have been no light horse charge had the foot soldiers not taken these hills early in the day. It's a fact too often forgotten by those who would argue that the charge of the 4th Brigade was the only act that mattered that day. The great charge of the light horse at Beersheba was undeniably the signature movement of the battle. But as the square metreage held in Be'er Sheva cemetery by infantry units from across the British Isles testifies, the PBI ('poor bloody infantry') did it harder than the light horsemen that day.

'You've got to remember, too, that these poor soldiers had to fight first thing in the morning after marching all night through the desert to get here.'

I walk down among the trenches and dugouts, still clearly defined—although filled with salt bush and loose rock—despite the years. I dig around with my fingers for a few minutes. It doesn't take long to unearth the detritus of war. Metal fragments and bullet casings and heads, detonators and other pieces of artillery shells are often found here. I pocket a small strip of heavy rusted metal; part of an armourer's kit or a haversack binding, or perhaps even part of a rifle.

~

It is still mid-morning, but the sun is high and even such brief periods out of the car dehydrate you. In just a couple of hours I've already drunk a litre of water. I can't help but think of Chauvel's horsemen who had to ride through the desert without the protection of air-conditioning. Each man was allowed one water bottle, holding only about a litre, per day.

We are heading across towards the Gaza border now. We are preparing to roughly trace the movements of Chauvel's men from the Second Battle of Gaza to Beersheba.

Kelvin explains that most of those interested in the Anzacs and Palestine in the 1990s were Christians; secular engagement with this part of Australian and Israeli history was scant.

'Well, there were a few groups that would occasionally come over here and would go down to the Anzac Memorial [on the Gaza border]. I got roped in by the Australian embassy and by the Australia-Israel Chamber of Commerce to talk to groups ... I noticed with the secular Aussies and the military ... well, they could only see the military side of things—they couldn't see the other dimension; they couldn't see the connection with the restoration of modern Israel. And in the last five or six years I've actually seen a change in that dimension, too.'

Crombie is rightly critical of those he believes have embellished the light horse story. But ask him how he sees the events of 1915–18 in the Middle East and Gallipoli, and he leaves you in no doubt about his belief in God's involvement.

'Oh, I see it as a sign of God's sovereignty, without doubt, definitely, because there were so many things happening, so many factors, somebody had to have written them up as part of a plan, a design, because you had so many of these things over a long period of time just culminating together,' he says. 'Even if I wasn't a Christian, if I had a secular take on it, I'd have to stand back and say our nation has been involved in the birthing of a new nation, and if that's not something positive to come out of the First World War then please tell me what is?'

Kelvin traces the re-establishment of Israel beyond the Palestine campaign and directly to the defeat of the British at Gallipoli.

'One of the things I've been trying to do over the years is to tell the Australians and New Zealanders that there was something positive that came out of these losses,' he says. 'Now if you look at Gallipoli it was a military failure. If you look at the Western Front ultimately it was a military victory, but at what cost? You'll see the importance of Gallipoli in the context of the restoration of Israel. The whole political program which ended up with the Balfour Declaration was triggered by the Gallipoli campaign ... I don't think that was ever brought out into the open until I did the research and wrote that down ... Militarily the defeat at Gallipoli meant they [British forces] went back to Egypt, some went to France, but the rest came back up here to defend the Suez Canal and slowly, slowly took over the Sinai and came into Israel, and it culminated at Be'er Sheva on 31 October 1917, which was exactly the same time as the Balfour Declaration was ratified in the British War Cabinet.'

~

We make two stops on the Gaza border. On the way we pass an old concrete military bunker or pillbox, a remnant of the 1948 war, which has long ago fallen off its plinth.

The first stop at the Black Arrow Monument, exactly 8 kilometres from Gaza City, offers yet another reminder of the ubiquity of battle in Israel. For the black arrow, with its commanding view of the ancient fort city over undulating golden crop fields, was the launching point for a daring reprisal raid by Israeli special forces on what was then the Egyptian-controlled Gaza Strip.

After constant attacks on Israeli border towns that killed five hundred Jews and wounded another thousand after it took control of Gaza in 1953, the Israeli Defence Force mounted the raid on 28 February 1953. The Israelis occupied and destroyed the main Egyptian army base and, according to the monument, 'attacked their soldiers and buildings while blocking their [escape] routes ... [Our] ambush wiped out their reinforcements.' Dozens of Egyptian troops were killed. Eight Israeli soldiers died, while all of the wounded were carried to safety back across the 8 kilometres of open ground, under heavy mortar and machine-gun fire, to Israel.

This place is usually teeming with Israeli visitors—especially during holiday times such as Passover—who like to picnic defiantly in the sight of Gaza. But not today; recent heated border clashes between Hamas fighters and the Israeli Defence Force have kept people away.

We take the old spice route to Gaza, these days a dusty, semi-sealed track, until we see the sign *ANZAC*

MEMORIAL 1¹/₂ →. This place, too, is usually crawling with predominantly Israeli visitors, attracted not so much by its commemoration of Australia's military link to this land as by the extraordinary close-up view of Gaza City afforded by the lookout turret that crowns the huge symbolic grey concrete A of the Anzac Memorial. We've been warned not to climb it for fear of snipers so we move on quickly, turning back on to the spice route and towards Tel Hareira.

Hareira, a strongly entrenched strategic high point with a commanding view across the open, wadi-creased plain to Beersheba was (together with an unforgiving set of trenches known as 'tank redoubt' that served its purpose well on the few occasions the British deployed tanks, and Atawineh) critical to the Turkish defence of the Beersheba–Gaza line. Trenches still snake their way across the top of Tel Hereira today. I fossick around with my hands and quickly find strands of barbed wire and shell casings. But the casings belong to another battle—probably the 1948 War of Independence.

~

'The tank, Atawineh and Hareira groups of earthwork overlooked a naked, low-lying triangle ... and across this triangle the British must advance in any attempt to break the enemy centre; it was also open to crossfire from ... the south east,' Gullett explained. 'From Hareira to Beersheba his line was not so strong and his flank was open. But there, as he believed, he was made quite safe by the difficulties of water supply on the British side.'[2]

But that is why Shellal, Tel el Jemmi and Tel el Fara, all of which, from about March 1917, served as forward posts for various mounted units, including cameleers. Shellal was particularly critical for the ultimate success at Beersheba. General Archibald Murray's failures at Gaza, and the rapid success attained by General Edmund Allenby when he assumed control of the war, eclipsed Murray's one critical contribution to ultimate victory: water. Shellal became the headquarters for Chauvel's Desert Mounted Corps after it was abandoned by the Turks before the Second Battle of Gaza in early 1917.

By August 1917 Murray had long departed the Palestine theatre of operations. But his pipeline had been pushed forward from Rafa to Shellal. Engineers constructed a dam to hold 50,000 gallons of water a day while natural springs in Wadi Guzze, in which Shellal effectively nestles, was also developed. They yielded about 300,000 gallons a day. The other side of Wadi Guzze was effectively no man's land and, in the countdown to Beersheba, no men or horses crossed the wadi.[3]

All the while, water was pumped out in an elaborate network of secret pipelines to the advanced trenches south of Gaza, and to watering points towards Beersheba. The plan was to move as much water as possible, by pipeline and by camel, on the heels of Chetwode's infantry so that when Beersheba was taken the troops would have enough water—when coupled with that in the wells at Beersheba—to march on to Tel Hareira and Gaza.

~

We drive into Shellal—Park Eshkoll today—which is packed with holidaying Israelis. The British dam is now an elaborate pool with concrete coping. Towering oak trees shade the picnicking families who are sprawled in the shade. Barbecue smoke hangs low over the park. It is a serene, laid-back scene as remote from the tension a few kilometres away on the Gaza border as it seems from the events of 1917.

'This', declares Kelvin Crombie, 'is about my favourite place in the Negev.'

We walk a short distance to a lookout on the site of an ancient Christian church, built in AD 622. I face north, away from the lake with its paddleboats and canoes, its splashing and screaming kids and its charred-meat aromas. I look out towards the horizon, shimmering in the midday heat. On my left stands Gaza City. To my right is Be'er Sheva. This is perhaps the best place to appreciate the very width of the Beersheba–Gaza line and the vastness of the trench-potted desert that held the key to British—and Australian—victory. Be'er Sheva is bigger and more discernible today. But the line is much as Chauvel might have viewed it from the same spot in the days before he ordered the attack on Beersheba.

In 1917, the now-famous Shellal Mosaic was found here when it was exposed by shellfire. In her much-loved

book *The ANZACs*, Patsy Adam-Smith tells the delight-
ful story of the mosaic as conveyed by the Oxford-
educated Padre Maitland Woods, senior chaplain to the
Australian Imperial Force in Egypt. Maitland Woods
oversaw the painstaking business of removing the
mosaic's tiles one by one and placing them in boxes for
transportation back to Egypt. In a letter to another
priest back home in Brisbane, Maitland Woods wrote
that he 'warned the watchmen to dig most carefully
with their trowels—what I expected happened—*We
found the bones of the Saint lying feet towards the
East*—These I reverently placed in a casket as they had
lain there 1,300 years you can easily imagine that some
of them were as delicate as the wings of a butterfly.'[4]

The generals, he said, were becoming 'exercised'
about what should happen to the mosaic and the saint's
remains. Maitland Woods had ideas of his own:

> What becomes of the pavement [the mosaic] I
> don't mind—I will willingly bear all the expenses
> of removal, and make no claim on the large col-
> oured portion—But I *do* want (1) the wonderful
> Greek inscription in black and white marble
> mosaic (a photo of which I intend to send to you);
> (2) the relics of the Saint (George of Shellal) and I
> want to place the inscription and the Relics in
> Brisbane Cathedral under the Alter there where
> they will be a fitting witness to the bravery of our
> Anzacs in Palestine and a link between our Holy
> Catholic and Apostolic Church in Queensland and

the Church (alas! now extinct, since it was destroyed by the Mohammedan invasion of the 8th century) in Southern Palestine.[5]

Palestine one day. Queensland the next. Alas, as Maitland Woods might have exclaimed, it was not to be for old Saint George of Shellal! The mosaic ultimately made its way to Cairo, along with George, whose whereabouts since have remained unknown.

The mosaic did, however, eventually make it to Australia. Measuring about nine metres by five metres, it remains behind a glass wall in the Australian War Memorial in Canberra. Verdant green grapevines and crosses encircle a holy chalice. It also features a tiger, peacocks, an elephant, a stag and flamingos of the type that still, occasionally, drink and fish at the watering holes of the light-horsemen.

For those who believe the hand of God was directing the Australian light-horsemen in Palestine, the Shellal Mosaic is the deal-maker—and the final link in the circle of serendipity that is Beersheba.

19

LAST DRINKS

Two nights before the Battle of Beersheba, Chauvel's Anzac and Australian mounted divisions left Shellal for their long journeys to their last watering stops at Bir Asluj and Khalasa. They rode south-east towards Beersheba while the big guns fired on Gaza from the ships in the Mediterranean—part of the ruse to make the Turks think the British were about to mount a third attack on the ancient fortress city.

As we leave Shellal and the barbecuing Israelis of Park Eshkoll, we follow a roughly sealed road across rolling fields of wheat. Before long it becomes windy, pot-holed and dusty as we trace Wadi Ghuzze. It's exactly the route taken by the horsemen to Asluj and Khalasa. In places the wadi is a cavernous valley, 30 or 40 metres deep. Smaller gullies branch out from the cavern.

Susan McMinn sits in the back of the vehicle swishing watercolour paint onto paper. She captures the colours of this place perfectly. With the dust and the vivid light they are washed-out yellows and greens. There is not a cloud in the sky. But all above is white with just a hint, perhaps, of crimson.

A herd of goats fights for the meagre shade of a lone acacia. They constantly mill around, gambolling on the spot, pushing and shoving one another, as the kids systematically pop out the back of the scrum and trot around to the shady front again. The shepherd, covered from head to toe in black robes, stands away from the tree in full sun holding a staff.

Suddenly the road departs the wadi. All around it is perfectly flat and open. The Australians would have been desperately exposed here. But they met no resistance on the clear, cold night of 29 October 1917, as the horses carried them to Beersheba.

Tel el Fara, a British forward command post, is suddenly visible as a gentle bump on the horizon. We continue west, past a camel ranch. There is a precarious surface of soft, fine sand under our wheels by the time we reach the Turkish well. Parts of the pump remain intact. So, too, is the concrete sluice at its mouth; the horsemen pumped water to the surface here, assembled one of their long canvas troughs and gave the animals a drink. It's deep; I drop a pebble and count to five before hearing its remote 'splish'.

The track edges along beside a vast orange orchard, testimony to drip irrigation and, of course, Israel's capacity—like that of the light-horsemen—to move water long distances across one of the world's most arid places.

A vast wall of cactus rises before us, indicating that the track is turning left. The ruins of Turkish military buildings hide among the prickly pear. Then we come upon a vast reservoir, fringed by towering bamboo and marshland. A flock of storks unfurl their vast wings, take off and head north on their migratory path towards Russia. A sign says the reservoir was funded by the Jewish National Fund of Australia.

As the road rises and winds into Khalasa, a herd of camels scatters. They bolt for the wadi as the car stops. 'On the 28th about 5PM we set out again getting to Khalara [Khalasa] about 10PM and there we camped for the night,' Trooper Jim Gallagher of the 1st Light Horse Regiment wrote in a letter home.[1] A picture of Gallagher taken at Khalasa two days before the final advance on Beersheba shows him sitting astride his heavily laden horse.[2] His left hand holds the reins, his rifle is slung and his right hand clutches what appears to be a piece of engineering equipment that was probably used to procure water. Two bandoliers hang around his horse's neck.

In 1917 a small Arab village stood among the ruins of Khalasa. The rubble of the ancient city is today much as it was back then. Two deep wells, repaired by the light-horsemen in the countdown to Beersheba, still hold water. Chauvel's men first surveyed the wells in May 1917 in the same operation when they blew up the railway line at Asluj. Gullett noted that the local Bedouin were, as always, a problem because they would tell the Turks what was going on. Although the Bedouin were forcibly kept out of the area during the May operation, Gullett did not elaborate how the locals were controlled in the weeks preceding the attack on Beersheba when the wells were being cleared and developed. He wrote simply, 'Khalasa, the Eleusa of the ancient Greek, had been a city of some sixty thousand people, and Asluj had also been a town of importance.'[3]

I am kicking at the ground, shifting small rocks, looking for shrapnel beside one of the wells. Kelvin approaches.

'Give us your hand, mate,' he says.

I put my hand out, and he drops a rusted bullet head into my palm.

'There you go—that's what you've been looking for. A keepsake, right, mate?'

'Yep.'

The sinking sun is lending a crimson hue to the previously white sky.

'It's a bushfire sky,' I say. 'If I was at home I'd be hosing the roof and turning the sprinklers on.'

~

Our next stop is Asluj. Idriess writes of a slightly surreal arrival in Asluj at 4 a.m. on 25 October 1917, after a hazardous night march:

This is a place unknown, giving the impression of quietly sleeping in a world that knows it not.

It is built on a tiny flat enclosing both banks of a wadi, hemmed in by sombre limestone hills. It has a snow white little mosque, and half a dozen Turkish barracks ... The queer place exists by its wells. Huge circular stone wells from which Moses and the Israelites drew water to fill their earthern jars. The Bedouins today draw water in the same way having a stone jar attached to one end of a rope, the other to the stern of a patient donkey ... the Turks ran a railway out to this place from Beersheba, the same that we blew up some months ago.[4]

Gullett wrote of the frenetic work that went into preparing the wells at Asluj before 'zero' day:

As the clearing and sinking continued, the men worked up to their waists in mud and water. At the outset it was found necessary to send back the horses of two regiments to Khalasa; but by the 29th, the wells were clear, with a strong and good flow; the necessary pumps had been installed; great lengths of canvas troughing and large canvas reservoirs had been established, and a limited supply of water was available for most of the men and horses of Anzac and Australian Mounted Divisions.[5]

The Bedouin village that Susan and I stumbled across a few days earlier is, it seems, not the same one that Idriess and the light-horsemen experienced. It was much closer to a small oasis, which included the wells and a natural spring that bubbled to the surface in the shadow of one of the distinctive limestone hills about which Idriess wrote.

Asluj is teeming with holidaying Israeli families when we arrive in the late afternoon. The barbecues sizzle and the kids mill around the billabong in what is now Park Golda, named in honour of the late Israeli prime minister, Golda Meir. Families are beginning to emerge from afternoon siestas under the date palms. One child casts a fishing line. Others sit on the edge and dangle their legs. A man plays guitar. This scene has all the serenity of a Seurat painting.

I look closely at the limestone hill. It seems familiar, as it did the other day when we passed through Asluj unaware, and found the Bedouin village and the fine desert sands instead. I recognise it because Trooper Ernest Pauls took a photograph here. The scene he captured is one of comparable calm: the dismounted men, clearly on the move, are watering their saddled horses beneath the limestone hill. The more things change ...

~

It is late afternoon, about the time of the charge, when we drive back into Be'er Sheva.

Kelvin wants us to see one more thing. So, due west of the town, we leave the main road and begin driving through the maze of hills that Chetwode's infantry also penetrated on the morning of the Battle of Beersheba. The surface is uncertain, gravelly. Underneath the fine gravel it is like concrete; pity, I think, the Turks who carved their myriad trenches and gun pits in here. The pits and redoubts are still discernible, and Kelvin tells us that shrapnel is still buried everywhere. I wonder aloud how it was that the British infantry didn't get lost in here—because we are. We traverse shallow, dry creek beds looking for a way out. Even here, so close to town, we come across two Bedouin women tending a flock of sheep. We eventually find a track that leads us to what appears to be a garbage tip. Old cars, fridges, mattresses and furniture are strewn everywhere. The road finds us and takes us back into town at sunset.

'You know, just a few years ago nobody except the Christian groups really wanted to know about all this stuff—about Beersheba. But now suddenly everyone is into it—everyone wants to know about Beersheba,' Kelvin says. 'And you know I honestly believe that I've had a calling from God to let people know what happened. I don't believe that God would want to hide and keep all of this information from others.'

He drops us in town. Tomorrow is Anzac Day and Kelvin is heading back to Jerusalem for the big ceremony at the Mount of Olives. I will be in Beersheba War Cemetery, waiting to see who visits the horsemen.

'Thanks for listening,' says Kelvin. 'God bless.'

~

I walked most of the few kilometres to the Beersheba War Cemetery. It was a calm, balmy pre-dawn with neither a breath of wind nor the dust from the khamsin that had stalked us across the desert yesterday. And as the sun rose on Anzac Day 2008, I stood alone among the tombstones, ghostly white in the half-light, as the residents of the surrounding high-rise apartment buildings began stirring from sleep. I could hear buses making their first trips into town from the central depot over near the landmark railway bridge.

In the inky half-light I wandered past tombstones of the men whose names—Cotter and Bradbury, Neirgard, Wickham, Beazley and Kilpatrick—were already so familiar. I wanted to see if someone else—anyone else—would turn up. It was well after daybreak and I left before another person, a young Jewish medical student from Melbourne, did so. Aaron Wagen and two mates—one British, the other French—had driven overnight from northern Israel so that they could be in Beersheba War Cemetery at dawn.

'We planned to have an hour's sleep but ... we slept late,' he explained. 'I knew about the Battle of Beersheba and the charge, and I wanted to be here on Anzac Day.

I had anticipated some sort of ceremony in the cemetery, and I was surprised to find that there wasn't.'

As I stood waiting for the dawn, I texted my friend and former fellow *Bulletin* writer, Tony Wright, who was at Anzac Cove on Gallipoli with his eldest daughter, Jessica: 'Mate, almost dawn at Beersheba; only one in cemetery. Not a soul. Hot and balmy. Very quiet. Unbelievable!'

Tony replied: 'Mate, hordes have descended as usual here at North Beach. 10,000 people, massive sound and light show, freezing bloody cold. Your lot should pay attention!'

Yes, they should, I thought. They really should.

20

WAITING FOR ROCKETS

Brigadier General Eran Dolev and Colonel Yigal Sheffy are former career soldiers. Throughout their lives, both have fought to defend their home, Israel. As those who have attained their seniority must be, both are keen students of war. They are also keen military historians; both have written books about World War I that are direct products of their respective expertise as soldiers, and they delight in traipsing around the battle-fields where the Australians and the Turks fought.

Sheffy, the younger of the two, is the author of *British Military Intelligence in the Palestine Campaign 1914–1918*. He is intense and strongly opinionated about the merits or otherwise of the 1917 charge and the strategic significance of the Battle of Beersheba for the outcome of operations in Palestine. He is a senior lecturer in security studies at Tel Aviv University. Sheffy believes that the myth surrounding the charge at Beersheba has overshadowed the fact that, as Gullett alludes to in his official history, the town could not supply enough water after it fell. This delayed the subsequent advance on Gaza, which should have fallen earlier.

'It is myth-making', he tells me even before we have left the hotel lobby where he and Dolev have come to collect me, 'to say that the charge or even the battle was the most critical part of the campaign.' Similarly, he believes the surprise element of the charge has also been exaggerated.

Dolev, a fit-looking 70-year-old who looks much younger than his years, is a former surgeon general of the Israeli Defence Force, a position he held during the 1982 war with Lebanon. He also served as chief medical officer for the famous raid in July 1976, when Israeli commandos flew into Entebbe Airport in Uganda at night to rescue hostages taken by Palestinian extremists. In 2007 Dolev, an associate professor of medicine at Tel Aviv University, published *Allenby's Military Medicine*, a history of British medical operations during World War I in Palestine.

'Are you familiar with General Rupert Downes—General Chauvel's surgeon general? Definitely one of my heroes,' he wrote to me before we met.

When we meet in Be'er Sheva, I explain that a fortnight or so previously I visited the general's now elderly daughter, Valerie Howse, at her Canberra home. She has strong views on Lawrence of Arabia, I say, and I think her father did, too.

'The circle of people in the world is small,' he says.

After a brief visit to the Beersheba cemetery I head out into the desert with these men. They take me to several places along the Beersheba–Gaza line to which I wouldn't otherwise have gone. Along the way their discussion about the light horse is infused with views about Israel today and concerns about the future of their country. As we drive north-west, Sheffy points out that many of the Turkish trenches that stretched from Beersheba to Gaza were dug into the wadies because their often deep crags and gullies afforded natural protection.

'There are trees everywhere today. When you are doing history ... you must do as I do and try to see the landscape as it was then. So no trees,' says Dolev.

We stop briefly at Ofaqim, the starting point of the British infantry attack on the morning of the Battle of Beersheba. Several giant wheat silos stand there today, testimony again to Israeli irrigation, which has filled the desert with fields of yellow grain, including barley and corn.

A few kilometres later we stop at an old Ottoman building in a lifeless high point called Patish. The building has a vast portico that looks down upon the dry wadi and across the undulating plain back to Be'er Sheva. It is about here, says Sheffy, that the famous 'lost haversack ruse' involving the mysterious Richard Meinertzhagen occurred.

~

Meinertzhagen first arrived in Palestine in late May 1917, briefly before Allenby replaced Murray as commander in chief.

According to the Australian historian Ian Jones: 'He showed some interest in the Savoy Hotel where General Murray had his headquarters, and in Shepheard's Hotel, where the overflow of officers shuffled papers and sipped drinks under the ceiling fans and palms. He also sought out Jewish refugees from Palestine; rode out into the desert, supposedly to study birds; was known to consort with Bedouin, whom he disliked ...'[1]

Meinertzhagen, Allenby's field intelligence chief, may have been instrumental in Murray's departure, given the timing of his visit just weeks before the much-maligned Murray received his marching orders. Certainly one of the first things Allenby did upon arrival was move his headquarters much closer to the front. As Banjo Paterson recorded in *Happy Dispatches*:

> Things began to move from the moment that 'The Bull' [Allenby] started to push against them. The Shepheard's Hotel generals were dispersed with scant ceremony. Army headquarters which had been located in Cairo (heavily surrounded by sentries) were moved a hundred and fifty miles or so nearer the enemy.
>
> 'We're a bit too far from our work here,' said the big man. 'I'd like to get up closer where I can have a look at the enemy occasionally.'[2]

The success of the attack on Beersheba relied on convincing the Turks that the main offensive was going to be made against Gaza, consistent with Chetwode's plan that was drawn up for Murray and later embraced by Allenby. But an intrinsic part of the deception— along with the continued bombardment of Gaza towards the end of October 1917—was a simple ruse planned and implemented by the spy chief Meinertzhagen. The ruse is compellingly re-enacted in *The Light Horsemen*, the film Jones wrote and co-produced. There has been ongoing debate among Beersheba aficionados about whether the story is apocryphal—much as there has been about the authenticity of the only purported photograph of the famous charge. But Jones's film and his book detail the ruse convincingly. Sheffy's scholarly account of British intelligence-gathering gives the story further credibility.

As the story goes, Meinertzhagen faked some British military documents showing that there would be a fake attack on Beersheba to distract the Turks from the true British target—Gaza. A British officer was dispatched to drop them in Turkish territory. When they weren't found a light-horseman was sent out into the desert with another lot of papers. The Turks missed them, too. Meinertzhagen then did it himself. Inside a haversack he put a combined notebook and wallet containing £20. The notebook included details of a conference about the attack on Gaza and the fake move against Beersheba.

As Jones makes clear, the ruse was made all the more convincing because it was left in the haversack with his lunch and a purported letter from another officer criticising the high command for not making the main attack against Beersheba. 'As a final touch of near genius,' Jones wrote, 'Meinertzhagen approached a "little hospital nurse at El Arish with girlish handwriting" and coached her to write a remarkably moving letter, supposedly from his wife, describing their recently born son. This was carefully folded and re-folded many times to appear much-read, then added to the collection in the haversack.'[3]

Meinertzhagen rode out into the desert to a point north-west of Beersheba, roughly where I'm standing with Dolev and Sheffy, where he enticed a Turkish patrol to chase him. When they desisted, he stopped and fired at them, drawing inaccurate return fire. Meinertzhagen stained his rifle with blood from his own horse, to give the appearance he'd been hit. He then dropped his rifle, binoculars and the haversack. 'These were found and accepted by the Ottomans as genuine,' Sheffy writes.

> Another technique was the briefing of unwitting Bedouin agents to collect information which ostensibly indicated special interest in the Gaza sector. According to Meinertzhagen, it was anticipated that the agents would be caught and betray the misleading material they had been fed ... But even

if the outcome turned out to be less dramatic and the agents completed their missions undisturbed, they would have still helped implement the deception, as details of many missions—real as well as fictitious—were frequently revealed to the Ottomans by the talkative Bedouin, especially as some of them were serving both masters.[4]

~

They take me to Tel el Jemmi, a mound of rock and earth that envelops an old town on Wadi Ghuzze about ten kilometres south-east of Gaza City. It was the headquarters for Chauvel's Desert Column at the Second Gaza Battle of April 1917. Like so many of Israel's ancient *tels*, El Jemmi is a treasure trove of relics from the past. With every heavy rain a thin layer of hard earth is exposed to reveal Roman coins, pieces of Byzantine pottery, trinkets dropped by the crusaders and ammunition used by light-horsemen.

It's a long, steep climb over a loose surface. But Sheffy and Dolev almost bound to the top. As we climb, pieces of white and ochre pottery crumble underfoot.

'Here, I have a present for you,' says Dolev, as he drops a small piece of elaborately carved pottery into my hand.

I pocket it and crouch down to pick through the gravel and pebbles, pulling out pieces of pottery and shrapnel. I could happily fossick away here for hours, just as I could whenever I come across a Turkish trench—or, for that matter, any old trench on any old battlefield the world over.

The two old Israeli soldiers seem bemused. A golden field of wheat, punctuated here and there with clumps of eucalypts, stretches before us and Gaza stands on the horizon.

First it is a low whirr. And then, before you know it, the noise from the two Israeli military helicopters all but swallows you as they scream low overhead en route to Gaza.

'Here it is always the same,' says Dolev, gesturing towards the city in the distance when the choppers have passed. 'They [Hamas militants] attack the [Israeli] terminal over here at Karni and two people are killed, then the Israelis go into Gaza and more people are killed. That's how it works. That's the cycle here.'

We clamber down the other side of the *tel* and walk back to the car.

'Now', says Dolev, 'let me take you to the most dangerous place in Israel.'

As we drive along the old front line, parts of which are in effect also the current front line between Gaza and Israel, there's a corrugated-iron shed in the middle of a field. Fresh bails stand neatly spaced across the freshly mowed paddock. Gum trees line the edges. It could be Australia, except that Gaza City is just beyond that rise.

As the car crawls into the outskirts of Sederot, a big town inhabited largely by Rusian Jews that is the target of daily Hamas rocket attacks from across the border, there is no other traffic. Bomb shelters are dotted along the street. An old woman drags a shopping trolley, and a couple of young guys, one with arms covered in tattoos, stand smoking by a shelter.

'It's too quiet. Only people with nowhere to go are still here,' says Sheffy, as we stop at the main square.

It's midday. For the first time while I've been in Israel, dark clouds, pregnant with rain, roll over. They are full of promise. But they deliver only an unbearable humidity that makes sweat pour down my arm and roll down my fingers in rivulets and on to the tip of my pen before they splosh, in little blue puddles, on to the pages of my notebook.

An outdoor snack stall, the only one we've seen open in this ghost town, is preparing to close. We buy drinks while a couple of women assiduously ignore one another while they pose—all leg and décolletage—on a nearby corner while simultaneously smoking and vacantly chewing gum.

As we sit, Dolev says: 'So now you are sitting in the most dangerous place in Israel. The rockets come in here from across the border about this time every day. There might be a rocket any moment.'

It is surreal and slightly edgy. Sheffy says he remains sceptical about whether the Charge of Beersheba had any great strategic significance. 'And I'm not sure that if the occupation of Beersheba had come later, in a day or two, it would have made any real difference to—not the planning but the execution of—the rest of the campaign. The plan was to encircle, to envelop, the Turkish troops there—not to gain territory there, but to annihilate the Turkish troops that day, to finish them off. Instead, many of the Turks actually escaped to fight another day,' he says. 'And the charge, well, I don't know if that made it easier. Because when they entered Beersheba they discovered to their horror that there was not enough water there. So they had to stop [in Beersheba] until all the horses could be watered. Some had to be even sent back to logistic centres to be watered.'

This, says Sheffy, slowed the offensive against Gaza, which was not taken until 8 November. Fierce fighting against many Turks who escaped Beersheba occurred in the days preceding the capture of Gaza that cost many Australian—and British—lives. Some of the fiercest fighting happened as British infantry, Australian and New Zealander—horsemen and cameleers—fought for strategic high points outside Gaza at Tel el Khuweilfe and Tel Hareira. A vast Commonwealth war cemetery in the middle of an industrial estate (literally in the shadows of the towering machinery from a cement processing plant), outside the modern Israeli city of Ramleh, is a testimony to the carnage that followed Beersheba.

'So this slowed the offensive. Not that they would not have conquered Beersheba eventually,' says Sheffy.

Dolev agrees.

A car backfires. A rocket? I jump. Neither of the old soldiers flinches.

'Now here, for example, the plan was wonderful ... Allenby wanted to go to the eastern side ... to take Be'er Sheva, and then Gaza would fall eventually. That's wonderful. And everything was concentrated on the timetable. Beersheba was taken. As Yigal said, eventually, nobody would care—neither the British nor the Turks—if it was taken in one night or two days, because they stopped anyway. They were stopped not because of the Turks but because of their own problems. They couldn't continue because they had to water the horses,' Dolev says. 'So, what would happen? ... Let's go to the Turkish side and see what their planning was. I would say—and I have said this before, based on documents— that they planned to withdraw that night, even if Beersheba would not have been taken, because ultimately it was indefensible.'

Meanwhile, says Sheffy, the charge—although a remarkable act of military courage and daring—should not necessarily be seen as a wholly unanticipated innovation. 'I think we have to look at it not as an innovative charge or an innovative tactic, but as something that they were always capable of doing, and something which Allenby's staff were very bright to introduce to the mounted infantry at that time,' he says.

The rockets are late today.

As we get up to leave, I ask whether the charge, leading as it did to victory at the Battle of Beersheba, could plausibly be said to be a critical moment in the re-establishment of modern Israel.

Sheffy speaks for both of them when he answers: 'The critical point was the 1948 War of Independence.' Dolev nods. For as sure as this country is a graveyard for thousands of Australians, New Zealanders, English,

Welsh and Scottish soldiers, it is also a vast cemetery for generations of Israeli soldiers who fought to gain their country as hard as they now battle to keep it.

On the way to Sederot we passed through Be'eri. It is a solemn place for most Israelis, for it has been the site for a temporary cemetery for Israeli combatants killed in conflict. The bodies were later retrieved and reinterred. We leave Sederot perhaps half an hour before three rockets lob in from Gaza and land close to where we had been sitting in the square.

'If a country has to go to war to protect itself, then it has to go to war,' says Dolev, apropos of nothing I have said. 'I have been in the army and I have been in the war. I have had children in combat units and it is a fact of being an Israeli. To do things on the battlefield for your country is one thing, but I believe we have to work to reach a settlement with the Palestinians. What do you think, Yigal?'

'I think that I do not want to spoil this very fine day when we have been speaking about the Australian light horse by talking about politics,' Sheffy says.

We drive past a Bedouin cemetery, its tombstones all facing Mecca, cross Wadi Saba and head back into town.

'I am very worried about this place. I was here before the [1948] war and I am still here. But I am very worried about this place. It's the best place on earth— great food, the best weather in the world. But I believe that we Israelis just can't continue to keep depriving ourselves of human values by the way we treat Palestinians,' Dolev says.

'How the Jews have forgotten so quickly what happened to them. I said it when I was a general, and I was very much criticised for it then, too. But I think the Jewish settlers are the plague of Israel—the cancer. Today we have 100,000 Jewish settlers in the neck of Palestinian territory. If there is one thing that is worse than killing someone it is humiliating them—and we humiliate them all the time. Every time a child sees his mother humiliated at a checkpoint he will remember that, and it plants the seeds of hatred. It continues the cycle of violence.'

He tells me I am lucky to live where I do, in peace and without having to ponder such delicate issues.

'I have known about Australia and Australians since I was a little boy ... if you ask anybody here who was the main actor in the [First World] war, they will say it was the Australians. Perhaps that is because some older people have an actual memory of them as being here during the Second World War. They were memorable then,' Dolev says. 'On a bus in Tel Aviv when I was a boy [during the Second World War], an Australian soldier gave me a piece of chocolate. It was the first time I have ever had chocolate. I'll never forget it. I can still taste it.'

21

COP THIS, DEAR JACKO

A single blood-red poppy, among the first of spring, blooms on the cusp of a ninety-year-old trench, cut deep into the crest of Tel el Khuweilfe. Khuweilfe is a dominating, bare, flat-topped mound the size and height of a small suburban shopping centre, about sixteen kilometres due north of Be'er Sheva. Standing at the northern apex of two rough sweeps of mountain, the *tel* offers a gun-barrel view of the clear, straight valley stretching out towards Be'er Sheva.[1]

Were Khuweilfe a person he or she would be labelled as experienced and battle-hardened; the nearby community of Kibbutz Lahav, an Arab target during the 1948 Independence and the 1967 Six Day wars, renders this a valuable strategic vantage point. There's still a concrete and corrugated-iron bomb shelter up here, its entrance obscured by rusting barbed wire. There's also the remains of a small, impromptu monument of bricks and stones; the family of an Australian light-horseman who died here constructed it a few days earlier.

In the days after Beersheba, an anxious Chauvel sent his troops north and north-west to steal this high ground from the retreating—although anything but defeated—Turks. Australian and New Zealand horsemen, British yeomanry and infantry, marched back and forth from Beersheba for six days, to attack Khuweilfe from the valley. It was a hazardous operation; men and horses had to march, fight and return to the limited water supplies at Beersheba. Some horses went forty hours without water in the process.

Brigadier William Grant, commander of the 4th Brigade, ordered members of his 11th and 12th Regiments to charge the trenches at the nearby strategic high point of Tel el Sheria. It was a virtual suicide mission. The men charged through a field of dozens of dead and dying British infantrymen. The fire was so intense that some Australians quickly dismounted and took cover in a wadi. But a single troop from the 11th Regiment persisted and breached the main enemy trench. The Australians were quickly isolated, as bullets cut down men and horses.

Hundreds of men were killed and injured at Khuweilfe and Sheria. Both fell on 7 November when British forces eventually conquered Gaza when the Turks succumbed after ten days of sustained bombing and several days of almost continuous infantry attack. When the Australians entered Gaza, it told a 'grim story of its occupation by a hard-pressed and filthy army, and of the effects of the British bombardment', Gullett wrote. He noted that the great mosque—originally a Christian church founded in the twelfth century—had been partially demolished by British gunfire in an 'act decided upon only when it was established beyond doubt that the Germans had used it as a large dump for munitions'.[2] Photographs taken by Trooper Ernest Pauls at Gaza elaborate on the official version; the mosque was effectively a crumbling shell by the time the British troops entered, and the detritus of the bombardment—huge pieces of shrapnel, rubble and even unexploded shells fired from the Mediterranean—was everywhere.

Next came the British advance on to Jerusalem, across the coastal plains north of Gaza and up the rocky and inhospitable spine of the Judaean hills—always on the heels of the retreating Turkish army. Pauls wrote on 6 December 1917:

> On the hills where our men now are it was where Christ was supposed, according to the Bible, to have arose again from the dead, and also to have fed the multitude from the 4 fish and three loaves of bread. From this mountain can plainly be seen Jerusalem and Bethlehem. The country all around is distinctly interesting. Large orange and almond groves everywhere, with fine Jewish colonies every few miles distance, the people being very friendly and showing how glad they were to be free of the Turk, who was a very undesirable master.[3]

Pauls was with his regiment's horses at Ramleh, close to the coast north-east of Jerusalem. Much of his regiment, meanwhile, was making its way on foot through the difficult Judaean Hills, towards Jerusalem.

~

Emboldened by Allenby's success at Beersheba, Lloyd George ordered the commander in chief to take 'Jerusalem before Christmas'. Together with the men of Britain's 53rd and 60th Divisions, who marched in light shorts—despite the rain and cold winds that heralded winter—Western Australia's 10th Light Horse Regiment rode into Jerusalem on the evening of 9 December 1917.

The Turks resisted until the very outskirts of the Holy City. Today when you move through the hills south of Jerusalem you can imagine the unstoppable momentum of Allenby's troops as they moved through the rocky crags and crevices, down the deep gullies and up and over the dangerous knolls that twisted through the towns—Latrun, Shilat, Nabi Shammuel, Kastel, Kolonia and Hebron—that preceded Lloyd George's prize.

The remnants of the Turkish defences can still be found in modern Jerusalem—if you know where to look. I am fortunate to have as my guide Rika Ishaki-Harel, an Israeli history teacher. Rika has searched the archives in Australia and Israel for details of the light horse in Palestine. She is knowledgeable and passionate in her belief that more Israelis should be aware of the trail of battles fought by the Australians across their land.

After bush-bashing in the heat through a conifer forest on a steep hillside on Jerusalem's western flank, we find an elaborate Turkish trench system cut into the rock. Today it is close to the centre of Jerusalem and runs across the back of the city's Yed Vashem Holocaust Museum. They are up to 1.5 metres deep in some places. Even today, despite the trees, the trenches would offer a sniper a commanding view of one of the city's main entrances. The same dogged British infantrymen who took the hills to the south, west and north of Beersheba managed to evict the Turks from these trenches.

~

A year to the day after the Charge of Beersheba an armistice with Turkey was signed.

Beersheba might have been the most colourful act of the British play for Palestine, but it was far from being the end of it. The Australian light-horsemen, like the British and, by late 1918, the Indian cavalry, did it tough as they chased the Turks north to a string of defeats at Jenin, Nazareth, Haifa, Amman, Damascus and finally Aleppo in Syria.

The Anzacs took tens of thousands of prisoners as the dispirited Turks surrendered in unthinkable numbers. Thousands who resisted were killed, many by Australian swords owing to the fact that by July 1918 the 3rd, 4th and 5th Australian Light Horse Brigades had been armed with cavalry sabres. The Turks, already fearful of the light-horsemen's ability with the bayonet, were terrified now that the Australians were wielding swords.

~

During and after World War I popular mythology— as reflected in Gullett's history and some of the correspondence and diaries of the light-horsemen—portrayed the Turk as something of a dear enemy. Despite the lost mates, the horrific memories many light-horsemen like Lionel Simpson and Ernest Pauls had of Gallipoli, and the fact that the Turks had by war's end taken to firing on Red Cross vans, a certain spirit of hearty competitiveness seemed to underscore—in spirit at least—relations between the Australian and the Turkish soldier. On the other hand, by almost every account the Bedouin was considered to be in another category, close to subhuman—a most inferior black fella, to be sure. But towards the end of the Palestine campaign three events involving Australian servicemen and Turks gave startlingly disturbing but contradictory impressions of how the Australians viewed the Turks—and the Bedouin.

The first happened in late September when Australian, New Zealand, British, Indian and French troops advanced north along the coast and through the hills, pushing the Turks towards the end-game at Damascus, taking fifty thousand prisoners along the way. A newly formed 14th Australian Light Horse Regiment, working with recently arrived Indian cavalry (whose harpoon-like abilities with the lance terrified the

Turks) and mounted Frenchmen, took nine hundred prisoners while riding into Nablus.

The French, it was said, had 'a desire for mounted action' that was difficult to suppress.[4] But most Turks had retreated from Nablus, and a huge column of about ten thousand enemy was spotted en route to Jenin. Chauvel ordered the 3rd Brigade to intercept them. The men of the 9th and the 10th Regiments were 'above themselves in their desire or action, and their keenness was sharpened by their eagerness to make play with their new swords'. A couple of charges on the way to Jenin prompted the frightened Turks to surrender quickly; eighteen hundred were taken in one camp alone when the Australians charged with their new sabres. The 3rd Brigade took up to eight thousand prisoners on the day they took Jenin, on 20 September 1918.

Predictably, the Bedouin then descended on the town to loot. 'If the natives of this old blood-drenched land have suffered by the wars of four thousand years, they have always been ready to seize all the compensation that offered,' Gullett wrote, in words that would become prescient—and ironic—from Australia's perspective.[5] The Bedouin men directed their wives to load material onto donkeys and take it from the town.

Many of the Turkish prisoners were sick with dysentery and thirst. Those who escaped were little better off.

On 21 September Australian airmen spotted a big column of fleeing Turkish soldiers and vehicles. After the word went out, the Allied planes hit the skies and found the Turkish column trapped in a gorge. Gullett wrote:

Down swooped the vanguard of the British and Australian bombers. Descending to within a few hundred feet of their helpless quarry, the airmen quickly smashed up the leading vehicles and choked the gorge. Then flying up and down the doomed, chaotic train of motors, guns, and horse-transport, through which surged thousands of distracted troops, the pilots and observers continued their terrible work with both bombs and machine-guns ... The fighting troops, scattered from the shambles on the road, were chased and machine-gunned as they sought cover across the hills.[6]

~

The second extraordinary and little-known incident happened a few days later at Ziza, about twenty-five kilometres south of Amman. A group of six thousand dispirited, thirsty and ill Turks en route to Amman was spotted from the air. A message was given to the Turks that if they did not proceed to Amman, which was held by the Anzac Mounted Division, they would be attacked from the air.

When the Turkish commander, Ali Bey Wahaby, didn't respond, two nearby squadrons of two hundred men from Queensland's 5th Light Horse Regiment were dispatched to determine the Turks' intentions. On meeting the Turkish commander, the 5th Regiment's commander, Lieutenant Colonel David Cameron, quickly came to understand why the Turks had stopped at Ziza and promptly fortified the village with trenches. A force of ten thousand Arab tribesmen was 'prowling like jackals' around the Turks, 'threatening each hapless straggler with pillage and murder'. Ali Bey Wahaby told Cameron he could not surrender to such a small group of light-horsemen because they could not guarantee the safety of his troops from the tribesmen if they gave up their arms. Cameron contacted Anzac Division commander Major General Sir Edward Chaytor, who cancelled the planned raid on the Turkish column, dispatched Ryrie and as much of his 2nd Brigade as he could muster and drove down to Ziza from Amman.

Chaytor arrived before Ryrie and his reinforcements. But the Turkish leader told the New Zealander to stand clear while the Turks attacked the milling Arabs. 'That suggestion', wrote Gullett, 'might in other circumstances have appealed to Chaytor, who was strong in his respect for the Turk and his scorn for the Arab, but it was impossible at the time, and the New Zealand leader, for once baffled, withdrew and left the situation to Ryrie.'[7]

Ryrie arrived with just one regiment, the 7th, to find Cameron and his men standing tensely by as the Turks stood in the trenches taking shots at the Arabs. The Arabs, apparently, were waiting for the light-horsemen to move in and do the fighting so they could do the looting. The Arab chiefs descended on Ryrie, urging him to attack the Turks and promising him support. But Ryrie took the only decision that he apparently considered open to him: to join forces with the Turks for the night to hold off the Arabs.

What followed was a scene reminiscent of that which occurred in Gallipoli years earlier when, during a brief ceasefire to enable the dead to be buried, the Turks and Australians swapped gifts and smoked cigarettes together when they met between the opposing trenches: 'The Turks and Australians proceeded, after years of bitter fighting, to bivouac together. They gathered about the same fires, exchanging their food, making chappaties together, and by many signs expressing reciprocal respect and admiration.'[8]

The Turks still feared an attack by the Arabs and maintained their sentries. The night was punctuated by constant machine-gun and rifle fire: 'The light horse-men, revelling in the strange situation, could be heard cheering on their activities. "Go on, Jacko," they would shout, "give it to the blighters"—and then indulge in shouts of laughter ... What was grim tragedy to the Turks was farce to the Australians.'[9]

The next morning, light horse reinforcements arrived, and the Turks surrendered and were escorted to Amman.

As the light horse moved towards Damascus, another column of ten thousand Turkish soldiers and machines poured out of the city towards the Baalbeck plain. They were fleeing the advancing combined British forces and making for Homs and Aleppo. Their escape route was a narrow road beside a swiftly flowing river at the bottom of the Barada Gorge.

Men of the 5th and 3rd Australian Light Horse Brigades, armed with machine-guns and rifles, looked down from the mountains on either side of the gorge with the Turks clearly in their sights. The Turks, and the German officers who led them, were exposed targets. German machine-gunners, who had mounted their guns on the tops of lorries in the gorge, rejected the order from the Australians to surrender. 'The result', said Gullett, 'was sheer slaughter. The light horsemen, firing with fearful accuracy, shot the column to a standstill and then to silence. For miles the bed of the gorge was a shambles of Turks and Germans, camels and horses and mules. Never in the campaign had the machine-gunners found such a target.'[10]

~

The massacre of the Turks at Barada had unforeseen consequences for the capture of Damascus, especially for Lawrence of Arabia who, it had been agreed by the British, would take the city.

Early on the morning of 1 October, the 10th regiment led the 3rd Light Horse Brigade south into Barada Gorge with the intention of skirting Damascus and stopping the Turks from fleeing the city. But the regiment became delayed while helping the wounded, taking prisoners and destroying suffering animals. A decision was made to cut through the middle of Damascus instead. The acting commander of the 10th, Major Arthur Olden, led his regiment into the city with swords drawn. Officials ushered him into the Hall of Government where the governor surrendered Damascus.

Lawrence, who had been delayed by Indian cavalry while driving into Damascus, arrived some time later.

The Turkish armies were in tatters. Those soldiers who had managed to flee towards Aleppo were dishevelled and sick with flu, which killed them by the hundreds. For the next twenty-five days, until the fall of Aleppo, the light-horsemen continued the chase. They killed countless more fleeing Turks and took thousands more captive.

Many of the Australians were themselves ill with malaria and dysentery. They arrived exhausted in Aleppo where dozens also contracted the flu. Despite the meagre rations, crippling thirst and the string of battles on the three-year track from the Suez Canal to Aleppo, a number died in hospital in Aleppo from flu.

The armistice with Turkey was signed on 30 October and enacted the next day. Eleven days later the war with Germany ended. The war was over for the light-horsemen.

III

A TERRIBLE THING

22

THE MASSACRE

Every country needs a place where its past is stored and tended, where the bare bones of its history, for all its chiaroscuro, are safeguarded under lock and key. In Australia, that place is Canberra. Canberra is much derided across Australia as being somehow unworthy of being this country's capital, perhaps because of its comparative youth, or maybe because it lacks Melbourne's European texture and Sydney's dazzling beauty. But when Federal Parliament moved to Canberra from Melbourne in 1927, the new city automatically became the custodian of many of this nation's memories. So, if you want to study Federal Cabinet's deliberations in 1918, you can go to the National Archives and see the original minutes of the meetings. If you want to know what your long-departed great-uncle did in the Great War, you can find out at the Australian War Memorial.

Here you can hold the past in your hands, be it in the form of official papers, personal correspondence and service records. Not all memories are good, of course. And it's a natural human trait to cling fast to the good ones and to deliberately try to erase the bad. But Canberra's memory is not discerning; it files the good with the bad, the flattering with the damaging, the ugly with the beautiful.

I went looking for light-horsemen's letters and diaries, and found in them soul-stirring poetry that showed the resilience of the human spirit when things are at their worst. But sometimes you discover dark secrets when you're not seeking them.

One winter's morning after returning from Israel I came across a voice recording made in Devonport, Tasmania, in 1988 with Private Edward 'Ted' Harold O'Brien from C Squadron of the 3rd Light Horse Regiment. A summary of the recording says that O'Brien talks about his job with the Post Master General after the war, and of the horses, his time working as a signals linesman in Palestine and visiting the pyramids. Interesting enough but, given all the material I'd seen and read, not exceptional. I was about to move on to the next item when a few words caught my eye: 'New Zealanders and Australians went to Bedouin village and killed the men with bayonet and broke up the buildings.'

~

Nobody except Chanan Reich, an Israeli academic working in Australia, had mentioned the massacre to me.

They didn't talk about it in 1918, and it remains an uncomfortable topic today. The reason is simple: it was as inconsistent with the growing light horse mythology back then as it is with the Anzac legend today. Nobody in Australia or Israel thought it was worthwhile telling me that the Australians and New Zealanders had massacred the able-bodied male inhabitants of an Arab village in December 1918, while they were camped on the Philistine Plain waiting to sail back to their former lives in the Antipodes. Reich was the first to do so— albeit in the most obtuse fashion—when I visited him in Melbourne just before I travelled to Israel. I was shocked by and completely unprepared for what he told me.

He is well positioned to know whether Beersheba has become an intrinsic part of the relationship between Tel Aviv and Canberra, just as Gallipoli has long been central to the dialogue and psychology of relations between Australia and New Zealand and, indeed, between Australia, New Zealand and Turkey.

'For the average Israeli, Be'er Sheva is a football team. And when was it liberated? When you ask people they will say '48 from the Arabs. First World War? Well, some would know—not necessarily—that the Australians actually took it. But most of them have never heard of it [the charge],' says Reich, an Israeli Defence Force veteran of the 1967 war.[1]

'They would not regard this as part of the history of establishing Israel—although in diplomatic documents it is often referred to. You know, diplomats, when they want to get on with each other, they suddenly remember all sorts of good things from the past. So they would say, "Oh yes, it was the Australians who liberated Be'er Sheva, and it was the Australians who fought together with us in the Second World War." Australians don't know it either. I remember I used to teach here in Australia at uni and some high schools, and I always used to make this joke that I had to come all the way from Jerusalem to teach you your own history.

'When I look at documents relating to the presentation of [diplomatic] credentials, when there is a new ambassador, it is always: "Oh yes, we fought together in Gallipoli, because there was a Jewish brigade there, and we fought together in France", and there was mention of Be'er Sheva also.'

The conversation turns to his country's Bedouin. He volunteers that his unit commander in the '67 war was a Bedouin—a cruel man who delighted in torturing the Palestinians.

'Oh, he used to beat them [the Palestinians] up very badly—any suspects in the occupied territories. I actually protected them a few times and he would say, "Oh, don't you be naïve." That's always been a theme that's recurring. "You Jews don't know anything about Arabs. You are naïve; they are very dangerous people"—that sort of thing,' Reich says. 'But they have a long tradition of retaliation. If you killed any person of an Arab tribe they would retaliate, sometimes hundreds of years later, because they didn't have a court system, a legal system, and so the only deterrent from violence was a fear of retaliation. And it still exists today. And it's not necessarily a personal retaliation. It can just be retaliation against the other tribe.'

Reich speaks slowly and deliberately as he explains how his archival research shows that the Australians forged much closer links with the Jews than they did with the local Arabs when serving in Palestine in both world wars. In World War II troops from the Second Australian Imperial Force fought the Germans and Italians in North Africa to stop them taking Egypt and then, inevitably, Palestine, where numerous Jewish communities had resettled under the post-Ottoman British Mandate. Throughout the early 1940s Palestine was a base for training and recuperation for Australian troops.

'I find in documents that Australians always felt more at home with the Jews than with the Arabs. What happened in World War II was that they really made themselves at home. They [the Australians] were in some circumstances in the kibbutz and in the Jewish homes, very quickly. It was like they were at home straight away,' he says. 'The description there is that within five minutes they started working on their farms, associating with the women and really having a great time. I can think of one occasion in 1940 or '41 when they even left weapons to the local settlements—weapons that they'd captured from the Italians, including machine-guns.

So the relationship then was very, very close. But not with the Arabs.

'Do you know about the massacre by the Australians? With the Arabs I think there was at least one incident in the First World War, when an Australian soldier was killed by the local Arabs and in retaliation the Australians demolished the whole village. There was at least one case.'

I ask: 'Do you know anything more about that?'

'No. No. But I remember that there was that one occasion ... I know of at least one incident, where you know they really wiped [killed] the whole village.'

'Are you sure this happened?' I ask. 'Surely there's no proof.'

Reich takes his time. He looks me in the eye. 'Yes,' he says. 'I think it actually happened. I remember it. I don't have the exact reference but I do remember it.'

We have coffee. Then he shows me out.

A blue heeler, a working animal with a thick trunk, alert ears and wiry coat, has been running around the perimeter of the yard while we talked inside, barking at imaginary intruders. It sits at the academic's feet as we stand in the front yard to say our farewells.

'It's a good Australian dog. It is a good dog for Israel also, I think. I'd like to take it home,' he says.

I bend down to pat the animal. It growls, then launches and snaps its jaws at my hand.

'It's very protective around strangers.' He smiles.

I sit in the car out front, thinking that this is not a story that I want to tell. But the journalist in me is compelled. Did the story of the light-horsemen, I wondered, have a dark cloud hanging over it? It was possible. They were, after all, men. They were in a war. And war brings out the worst in men as only war can.

~

Still aching with grief at my father's death, I now realise that the story I wanted to tell, the story in which I wanted to take solace, was the story of fraternalism and paternalism that had captivated me since my meeting with Lionel Simpson while a very young journalist. I was captivated by the myth and the legend. The purported massacre, even if it did happen, had no place in my story.

Soon I would go to Israel where I asked vaguely about a massacre by the Australians. While Kelvin Crombie's book mentions the massacre in passing, it somehow escaped my attention. Although he and a few others mention the Australian slaughter of the Turks in Barada Gorge to me, they do not bring up Surafend. Reich, I determined while in Israel, was surely mistaken. For months in Israel and Australia I shied away from his proposition, trying neither to prove nor disprove it. Nevertheless it hung in my consciousness like a malevolent shadow, stifling my narrative.

But the truth has a strange way of surfacing when you are seeking it least. After months of searching I finally found the newspaper interviews I had written about dear old Simpson. 'We were sitting ducks because we had to charge two miles over open ground to get to the Turks. It was an exhilarating feeling,' I reported him saying. In an earlier story he had told me that 'the big charge happened at seven in the morning on a beautiful bright sunny spring morning'. I should have known then that the old man was never in the Charge of Beersheba—it had happened during an autumnal dusk. He also served in the 3rd Brigade's 8th Light Horse Regiment. Only the 4th and the 12th Regiments of the 4th Brigade were in the charge. I didn't know that then.

I don't think for a moment, however, that old Lionel was lying to me. He was a very old man, and he had told the story to an inexperienced journalist such as myself and amateur historians so many times that he had, perhaps, become a greater part of it than he actually was. Throughout Simpson's life he had always been careful not to claim participation in the charge. He was modest about his achievements in developing the wells at both Beersheba and Khalasa, which earned him a Distinguished Conduct Medal for 'devotion to duty'. His earlier experiences at Gallipoli, where he cheated death at the Nek, were always accurately relayed. But Simpson taught me that different people, especially with time's passage, could have wildly varying recollections of the same events. I found this helpful when the truth about the massacre finally started to seek me out.

Gullett's official history, written closer to the time, dealt with the massacre briefly and uncomfortably—although just how uncomfortably is not immediately apparent in the text. I was relieved to find that journalism some years later dealt with the terrible incident more objectively, albeit with a literary flourish that I think represented a search for a way to diminish its gravity.

Paterson, a literary hero to my father and a great writer whose spirit could occasionally still be felt about the *Bulletin* in its twilight years when I worked there, confronted the massacre openly. My father grew up reading the best of Paterson while at school in the 1930s. As a frail old man with worsening dementia and little time left, my father was satisfied that his son had succeeded—if only because he worked, metaphorically, with the legacy of Paterson—in a game that he little understood. In middle age, I still experienced boyish embarrassment at his pride. The magazine closed a month to the day before my father died. He was still lucid enough to understand. But I couldn't tell him.

~

Paterson persuaded me, through the final words of a long, eloquent and colourful piece about Allenby in his 1934 book *Happy Dispatches*, that Surafend must become part of my narrative:

> A New Zealand trooper was fatally knifed by an Arab thief who was robbing his tent; and the New Zealanders and their blood brothers, the Highlanders, organized a revenge party. They were sick and tired of being robbed and murdered

by an allegedly friendly population, and they knew that nothing would be done unless they did it themselves [Paterson wrote]. A few Australians went along with them—there couldn't be any trouble on any front without an Australian being in it—and the revenge party followed the thief to his village, recovered the stolen goods, and killed every able-bodied man in the village. Then they threw the bodies down a well; filled the well up; burnt the village, and retired in good order to their camp which was within half a mile of Allenby's headquarters.[2]

Paterson's account, with its journalistic economy, is brutal. He goes on to explore the impact of the crime on Allenby, who as a consequence churlishly turned his back on the Australian light-horsemen of the Anzac Mounted Division, whose fighting courage and sacrifice had largely carried his Palestine campaign. But Paterson gives no assessment of the premeditated nature of the crime or of the apparent lingering cover-up that followed.

~

Few in Australia will have heard of Leslie Lowry, a 21-year-old New Zealand trooper who died in Palestine more than ninety years ago, yet the events that followed his murder on a wintry night in northern Palestine in late 1918 cast an enduring cloud over the otherwise extraordinary wartime achievements of the Australian light horse.

After the armistice, Australians and New Zealanders from the three brigades of the Anzac Mounted Division were camped near the Jewish settlement of Richon le Zion, close to the Mediterranean, not far from the Israeli seaside city and capital, Tel Aviv. Ninety years ago, however, it was a bucolic playground for the light-horsemen after the hardships and illnesses of the long ride through the deserts, the Jordan Valley and Syria.

The Australians were well known and liked in the Jewish villages. By war's end in late 1918, some of the Anzacs who camped at Wadi Hanein near Richon met. up with old friends, having stayed there around Christmas 1917. The Australians made the most of Richon's fine food and wines. After the fall of Jerusalem, the Jews had welcomed the Australians with open arms. 'The world wide dream of having a Jewish nation established once more in Palestine, which had for nearly 2000 years sustained their scattered race, seemed already a reality; and in their joy they showered hospitality upon the staff officers billeted in their houses and upon the troops encamped on the surrounding sands hills,' wrote Gullett.[3]

Despite the comparative ease of life after what had been, for many, years of battle, the men were eager to return home. The brigade diaries at the time outline a life of relative ease, albeit with constant drills, shooting practice, football games, races and socialising.

The small Arab village of Surafend stood close to Richon. The local Arabs quickly began stealing from the Anzacs once their camps were established, and the soldiers, who had tolerated the Bedouin for the past four years, had exhausted their patience. They saw no difference between the town and village Arabs and the Bedouin. To the Anzacs, they were all trouble. The burning resentment against the Arabs was fuelled by the fact that the mostly British commanders of the Anzacs had an informal policy of effectively turning a blind eye to the misdeeds of the natives. It was part of a strategy to engender Arab support for British rule of Palestine and, of course, because TE Lawrence had helped to foment Arab unrest on behalf of the British.

There was a sense, especially among the Australians, that the British tended to punish Australians for any minor misdemeanour or affront to the local Arabs. By the end of 1918 relations between the Anzacs and the Arabs was a matter for delicate military management. But there is no evidence that the British command tried to solve the problem or to avert what seems, in retrospect, to have been a predictable—although, from the Australians' and New Zealanders' perspective, absolutely unforgivable—clash with the Arabs. But what happened at Surafend was more than just a showdown with the Arabs. After the horrific ineptitude of English command at Gallipoli and a tendency—especially under Allenby's predecessor, Murray—to credit the British disproportionately with battle victories and subsequent decorations, it was seen by some, unjustifiably, as much a show of defiance against British command as it was against the natives.

Trooper Robert Ellwood of the 2nd Light Horse Regiment, who was camped near Surafend, later recounted that 'we had to treat the natives or the desert Arabs or the Bedouins, or whatever you like to call them, with kid gloves'.[4] He wrote somewhat obliquely of a unit—'not our unit, but I'm not mentioning any names'— that was camped beside a village 'where the Arab ... wasn't altogether antagonistic to us but he was a thief':

> And if you happened to wake up—you were unfortunate enough to wake up while he's doing it—the next thing you knew he'd have a knife in you. So this went on for quite a while despite orders that we were to treat them with kid gloves ... Anyhow to cut a long story short, we complained to headquarters about it and word came back that they had to be treated with respect and all this sort of business on account of the delicate position and the people took it, some of us took in our own hands at the finish, to teach the Arab a lesson. They got together and went through the village one night and chastised those who they found owning rifles belonging to, you know, our people, with the result that the results didn't please Allenby.[5]

On the most generous assessment, Ellwood's reference to what happened at Surafend village on the night of 10 December 1918 skirts the truth.

~

Late on the chilly winter's night of 9 December 1918, 21-year-old Trooper Leslie Lowry, a machine-gunner from the New Zealand Mounted Rifles Brigade, slept in his tent. The local Arabs had been thieving from the Anzac camp night after night of late and, like many of the Anzacs, Lowry used his kitbag as a pillow so that he'd wake if the barefoot robbers tried to pinch his valuables. Sure enough, the young New Zealander stirred just as someone was tugging his kitbag. The robber bolted, and Lowry sprang out of bed and chased him through the picquets around the camp and into the nearby dunes.

Lowry overtook and grabbed the robber, who turned and, using a revolver, shot the trooper through the chest. Lowry died about half an hour later, 'in agony', according to one witness. Nobody actually saw Lowry's attacker. But the picquets who raced to find Lowry lying in the sand apparently found his kitbag close by. An Arab skullcap was also found.

According to Trooper Ambrose Stephen Mulhall of the 3rd Australian Light Horse Regiment, Lowry 'told his comrades before he died the thief and his murderer was a Bedouin and that he had gone to the Bedouin village'.[6] True to Lowry's word, the attacker's footprints were tracked to a hole in the fence near Surafend.

The New Zealanders threw a cordon around the village. Nobody, including the women and children, was allowed to enter or leave. The next morning the New Zealanders entered Surafend, found the village chiefs and ordered them to surrender the murderer.

Predictably the chiefs, accustomed to complaints about their residents from the Anzacs, pleaded ignorance and did nothing.

That morning, Lowry was buried in the nearby cemetery. It was the same cemetery where the graves of other New Zealanders had been dug up by the Bedouin—their customary practice right across the Palestinian battle trail.

Meanwhile, the divisional commander, Chaytor, dispatched an officer to the nearby command headquarters at Bar Salem. Perhaps fearing exactly that which eventually happened, he sent another officer to ensure that the cordon was conducted with appropriate military order. But to everyone's amazement, word came back from headquarters that the cordon was to be abandoned. After Chaytor tried to get British command to reverse this decision, the cordon was reluctantly abandoned in the afternoon. Up to twenty Arab men hastily fled Surafend.

The crime against Lowry, and the emotion and anger it sparked among his Kiwi colleagues and their Australian and Scottish mates, is undisputed. They wanted revenge, and they took it. How many people they killed and exactly who was involved has, however, always been hotly contested.

By most Australian accounts, the New Zealanders led the attack on the village while the Australians at best stood by and watched or at worst participated, albeit in vastly smaller numbers. Patsy Adam-Smith deals with it briefly, but doesn't absolve the Australians:

The troops, a mixed bunch of Australians, New Zealanders and Scots, raided the village in their anger and undoubtedly killed men there. One report states that they threw villagers down a well and rolled a large grindstone down on top of them. Their excuse was that they were sick of the natives stealing; for five years they'd put up with their small private possessions from home being stolen as well as their uniforms and gear, were weary of their men being ambushed and killed while the authorities 'did nothing'.[7]

Henry Gullett deals with the Surafend massacre in four pages of his 844-page history. It should be remembered that Gullett was in a difficult position. Before the publication of his history in 1923, numerous others—including Chauvel—would pore over it for inaccuracies of fact and, perhaps just as importantly, matters of tone that displeased them. That he managed to address the massacre at all, no matter how perfunctorily, is a credit to him.

Gullett establishes a scene that, while sympathetic to the Anzacs, does not excuse their response:

In fairness to the New Zealanders, who were the chief actors, and to the Australians who gave them hearty support, the spirit of the men at that time must be considered. They were the pioneers and the leaders in a long campaign. Theirs had been the heaviest sacrifice. The three brigades of Anzac Mounted Division had been for almost three years comrades in arms, and rarely had a body of men been bound together by such ties of common heroic endeavour and affection ... The war task was now completed and they, a band of sworn brothers tested in a hundred fights, were going home. To them the loss of a veteran comrade by foul murder, at the hands of a race they despised, was a crime which called for instant justice. They were in no mood for delay. In their movement against Surafend, therefore, they felt that, while wreaking vengeance on the Arabs, they would at the same time work off their old feeling against the bias of the disciplinary branch of General Headquarters, and its studied omission to punish Arabs for crime. They were angry and bitter beyond sound reasoning. All day the New Zealanders quietly organised for their work in Surafend, and early in the night marched out many hundreds strong and surrounded the village. In close support and full sympathy were large bodies of Australians. Good or bad, the cause of the New Zealanders was theirs. Entering the village, the New Zealanders grimly passed out all the women and children and then, armed chiefly with heavy sticks, fell upon the men and at the same time fired the houses. Many Arabs were killed, few escaped without injury; the village was demolished. The flames from the wretched houses lit up the countryside, and Allenby and his staff could not fail to see the conflagration and hear the shouts of the troops and the cries of their victims.

The Anzacs, having finished with Surafend, raided and burned the neighbouring nomad camp, and then went quietly back to their lines.[8]

In his account of the New Zealand Mounted Rifles in Palestine, *Devils on Horses*, Terry Kinloch says that while estimates of the size of the raiding party varied from fifty to about two hundred men, the latter number was probably correct because 'a large force would have been necessary to isolate the village and to carry out the killings and the destruction so quickly, and without any casualties being suffered by the attackers'.[9] The accepted number of Arabs killed is between twenty and forty. But one Australian, who blamed the New Zealanders entirely, says he counted 137 dead in Surafend the next morning. This witness, Trooper Ambrose Stephen Mulhall—a former policeman—would try in vain for decades to come to clear the name of the light-horsemen.

~

While both the New Zealanders and the Australians were quick to mount official inquiries into the killings, the inquiries were a farce. The Australians blamed the New Zealanders or claimed they were unaware of what had happened. The Kiwis blamed the Australians or feigned ignorance. There was a good reason for that, at least among those of the 1st, 2nd and 3rd Light Horse Regiments. It seems that members of the 1st Australian Light Horse Brigade kept their mouths shut because that is exactly what they were ordered to do by their beloved commander, Brigadier General 'Fighting Charlie' Cox. All but one would respect this order, as we shall see.

The war diary and intelligence summary of the 2nd Light Horse Brigade, commanded by Ryrie, is an exemplar of military obfuscation. It can be interpreted as the point at which the Surafend cover-up began. The diary records that, at 8.10 p.m., 'A disturbance was observed in the village of Kh. Surafend. A & NZ Mtd Div. was notified immediately by telephone, the Brigade was stood to and a picquet was sent to patrol the ground between the village and the brigade area.' Another entry for 11 p.m. reads: '2nd LH Field Ambulance supplied ambulances to remove injured natives.'[10]

Four days later Ryrie, who had been in Cairo, returned after ordering an inquiry—held in his absence on 13 December—into 'the part played by this Brigade in the recent raid on the village of Surafend on the night of the tenth of December 1918'.[11] Ryrie left the next day, 15 December 1918, to take up his new command of the Australian Mounted Division.

On 16 December the diary says obliquely: 'C-in-C addressed Division dismounted. Owing to C-in-C inspection rations were not drawn till 1600.'[12] The

'C-in-C' is, of course, Allenby. The diary neglects to mention that when Allenby stood the entire Anzac Mounted Division to attention that day while astride his black stallion Hindenburg, he told them they were a bunch of 'murderers' and, with that, he wiped his hands of the Australian light-horsemen.

23

ALLENBY AND THE ANZACS

Allenby was an aloof, hot-headed, proud—and perhaps conceited—man. He was also a strict disciplinarian. Throughout the war in Egypt and Palestine the Australian contempt for British command grew exponentially. It began with the botched landings at Gallipoli and the subsequent needless sacrifice of thousands of Australian lives in the hills above the peninsula, in such senseless British-commanded battles as that at the Nek.

The first battles against the Turks in Egypt were instrumental to Australian perceptions that the British yeomanry—with their luxurious camps, fine rations and sporting perspective of the war—were useless. The yeomanry's tragic early failures against the Turks only confirm this perception.

What little respect Murray had managed to garner from the Australians evaporated at the two battles for Gaza in early 1917. By the time Allenby took command in mid-1917, contempt for the British among Australians was all but complete:

> They suspected softness, gross negligence and cowardice, and were made more bitter by what they regarded as the disproportionate awards given to British troops and staff officers after the incident. Their anger at British incompetence in medical care and provision of fodder for horses was only increased by the British withdrawal from the first battle of Gaza and the airs and graces the British high command gave themselves.
>
> So the Light Horse not only failed to salute Chetwode and his orderlies as they rode through their ranks, but laughed aloud at their stiff and formal way of sitting on their horses.[1]

Allenby was, however, a popular replacement for the comparatively inept Murray, whose mutual contempt for the Australians was never far from the surface. Allenby's decision to base himself close to battle, unlike Murray, won him immediate respect. While there were moments of tension between Allenby and Chauvel, most of which stemmed from misunderstandings created by technical communications problems during the Palestine campaign, Allenby was immediately accessible and came to know many of the Australians by name.

Paterson describes Allenby's 'second coming' as an event that instilled new discipline into the Australian ranks and frightened hell out of the generals—whether from the Antipodes or Britain: 'By some sort of mass psychology they felt that such capers as running riots, disobeying orders, and burning motor vehicles were definitely off ... "They'll never give it to Chauvel," said one brass-bound brigadier. "Fancy giving the command of the biggest mounted force in the world's history to an Australian. Chauvel's sound, but he's such a sticky old frog."'[2]

All the generals, including Chauvel, were effectively on trial for their jobs when Allenby arrived. Allenby's decision, therefore, to leave Chauvel in command of the Desert Mounted Corps was seen as vindication of his good tactical judgment and a tacit acknowledgement of the importance of the Australian troops to winning the campaign. It showed that he did not instinctively favour the British. As Paterson correctly observed: 'Allenby did not care whether a man were an Australian or a Kick-a-poo Indian; he wanted to win the war.'[3]

After relying so heavily on the Australians and New Zealanders in the final phase of the war, the massacre at Surafend came to represent a complete betrayal of the trust and affection Allenby had invested in the Australian light-horsemen. His outraged response to the massacre was justified given the gravity of the crime.

But the disproportionate blame he levelled at the Australians was not.

~

Gullett noted that Allenby and his staff could not have failed to see the flames and hear the shouts of the troops from nearby command headquarters. The next morning, he says, 'all the disciplinary machinery of the army was active as hitherto it had been tardy'.[4] But Allenby, it seems, was, like Ryrie, absent at the time. Regimental and brigade commanders had been attending a conference in Cairo, and it seems probable that Allenby was there, too. There can be little other plausible explanation for the six-day delay between the torching of the village and his dressing-down of the troops.

At 10.35 on the morning of 16 December the Australian and New Zealand men of the Anzac Mounted Division were ordered to assemble without their horses in a square, about midway between their camp at Wadi Hanein and Richon. Allenby, followed by his staff, galloped up on Hindenburg. He ignored the salute of Chaytor, the divisional commander. He did not dismount. Rather he stood in his stirrups and looked down on the men as he addressed them. There are varying accounts of what he said. Gullett describes the confrontation thus:

> The Commander-in-Chief addressed them in
> strong, and even, one might say, ill-considered

language. He used terms which became his high position as little as the business at Surafend had been worthy of the great soldiers before him. The division fully expected strong disciplinary action for Surafend, and would have accepted it without resentment. But the independent manhood of the Anzacs could not accept personal abuse from the Commander-in-Chief. Allenby's outburst left the division sore but unpunished.[5]

Precisely what Allenby said next remains unclear. But its tone is indisputable. Private Mulhall wrote that Allenby said: 'You who were not there know who were and know all about it but you are not game to come forward and say so. You are a lot of cold-blooded murderers and cowards.'[6] According to other accounts, Allenby said that he had been proud of the men once but was proud no longer and that they were nothing but a bunch of murderers whose crimes overshadowed any evil deed committed by the Turks during the war. Towards the end of his life, Trooper Ted O'Brien of the 3rd Regiment recalled the incident: 'We were all lined up ... [Allenby] stood up in the stirrups and he said, "I was proud of you once but I'm proud of you no longer." Then off he went again at a gallop, and that was that. But afterwards he apologised. But he did say that and it was a dreadful thing.'[7]

Paterson, meanwhile, describing Allenby as a 'hot-headed potentate', said 'he fell them in and harangued them'. 'I was proud to command you,' Paterson quotes

Allenby as barking. 'But now I'll have no more to do with you. You are cowards and murderers.' Paterson lends the impression that the Australians were not overly fussed by Allenby's outburst. 'Did the Australians rise up to a man and protest? Not a bit of it! All they said was: "The old Bull has got things wrong somehow."'[8]

But Paterson is demonstrably wrong on this count, as evidenced by the anger articulated in Gullett's official version and in numerous diary notes and letters written by the men he castigated as murderers. Trooper Ellwood recalled:

> He galloped into the middle of the square and before his staff had put up their horses, he started on us, and he started to abuse us and tell us what a lot of this and that and all the rest of its we were on account the way we had behaved. Well, the sound, and if you can imagine millions of hives of angry bees, the hum, that come [sic] from it, anyhow he read the message and he simply turned on his heel, he thrashed his horse around and jabbed his spurs in, scattered his staff and the last we saw of him was going over a sand hill.[9]

By some accounts the Australians and New Zealanders responded with immediate anger and a deliberate, provocative absence of respect for the commander in chief. There were suggestions that Allenby was counted out by the division, which involves soldiers counting slowly from one to ten; if the subject of the count had not departed by the time the men reached ten, he would be physically removed. While the men were agitated, it seems Allenby was wise enough to depart before they reached ten. Perhaps that's why he chose not to dismount.

'As he bellowed out that he no longer felt any pride in them, there was laughter in the ranks and, probably sensing that his audience was un-cowed and on the verge of grosser insubordination, he prudently rode away,' Allenby's biographer, Lawrence James writes. 'Afterwards rumours buzzed about to the effect that he had been jeered and barracked, but these were denied by eyewitnesses.'[10]

Warrant Officer Nick Curtain, a Tasmanian from the 3rd Regiment's C Squadron—some of whose members participated in the massacre—recalled in June 1989:

> He said, 'Since I've been with you you've done some wonderful things. You overran the Turks in Beersheba and you did this and you took so many thousand prisoners and you did that.' He said, 'That was good, but ah! You put the blotch on yourself when you killed some innocent Arabs.' And didn't he go crook. He said they were innocent. So he ended up by saying, 'I thank you for what you've done … but I hate what you did to the Arabs.' He said, 'I thought a lot of you once, but I think it of you no more.' And he galloped off.

And then the colonel in charge—he was a New Zealander [Chaytor] I think—he told us before the parade broke up, he said, 'He is a great man and a great soldier, but,' he said, 'I want a great apology from him.' And it wasn't long before he came out in orders, signed by Allenby ... that he was angry at the time and he didn't mean it, you know, doing the harm and all that ... I can see him galloping away and some of us singing out, 'Out, you b ...'. Not everyone, but quite a few sang out, 'You so-and-so.'

So he got a bit of Aussie while he was there.[11]

Curtain, it seems, was correct on all but one matter. While Allenby did send a message, under considerable Australian pressure, praising the light-horsemen, it did not amount to anything like an apology. He never publicly withdrew his criticism of the Australians as murderers who had let him down.

Allenby's biographer, Lawrence James, writes that a 'furious' Allenby said the men 'were murderers and cowards and by killing the Bedouin had taken away the good name of Anzac—in fact it was a worse atrocity than any the Turks had committed'.[12] He immediately withdrew all leave passes and recalled any men who were already on leave. The division was also ordered to pack up and move to Rafah. This, in itself, was a punishment because it denied the men such small comforts as Richon had afforded them, not least wine and fresh food. Allenby also took the vindictive measure of ensuring that early recommendations for gallantry decorations for some light-horsemen—regardless of whether they were suspected of involvement in the mass murders—be indiscriminately withdrawn.[13]

Although New Zealanders and Australians were confined to their camps immediately after the attack on Surafend, there is no evidence that any genuine attempt was made for a day or two to find those responsible. When an effort was finally made, it seems that the inquiries were being directed at the wrong place. Ryrie, the 2nd Brigade's commander, ordered an inquiry into the part played by his brigade's 6th Regiment (the only regiment of his at Wadi Hanein) in the massacre. It seems that most of the Australian killers belonged to Fighting Charlie Cox's 1st Brigade and, more precisely, to Colonel Bell's 3rd Regiment of Tasmanians and South Australians. The 3rd Regiment's war diary makes it plain that Bell oversaw an inquiry for two days—12 and 13 December 1918—into his regiment's participation in the killings. But it appears his inquiry was separate from, or at least parallel to, Ryrie's investigation.

Ryrie's original records of the inquiry seem to be intact. The whereabouts of the records of Bell's inquiry are less certain. The absence of documents makes it unclear whether they are part of the same inquiry or separate inquiries. While Ryrie's intent was no doubt genuine, it now seems obvious that he was never going to flush out the truth.

Given that up to two hundred New Zealand, Australian and Scottish troops were involved, it is likely that members of other regiments camped with them—the 1st and the 6th—also participated. If they didn't, then such was the intimacy of life in camp that they would have known who did. But, as Gullett points out, the Anzacs 'stood firm' so that 'not a single individual could definitely be charged'.[14] This shoulder-to-shoulder approach is evidenced by the war diaries that cover both the massacre and Allenby's subsequent dressing-down of the troops. The diary of the 6th Regiment for the night of the killings records benignly: 'Disturbance in the village of Surafend at 2000 about $\frac{1}{4}$ mile north of camp. At 2215 the regiment was ordered to stand to ...' Of Allenby's excoriating attack on the horsemen, the diary records simply that 'the C-in-C delivered a short lecture in reference to the disturbance that occurred on 10th instant'.[15]

The diary of the 3rd Regiment, meanwhile, approached the attack on the village even more distantly, passively noting on the morning of 11 December: 'Lieut Treloar ... with one troop proceeded at 0700 to the village of Surafend on picquet duty, the village having been burned and some of the inhabitants killed and wounded during the night.' The diary noted that Bell returned from Cairo on 11 December and the next day presided over a board of inquiry 'into the burning of the village of Surafend and the killing and wounding of several of its inhabitants ... [The] court sat all day and adjourned till tomorrow.'[16]

The diary shows that Bell 'was again engaged all day on [the] court of inquiry at DHQ [Divisional

Headquarters]' on 13 December and that he left again for Cairo the next day. Of what surely would have been Allenby's unforgettable visit on 16 December, meanwhile, the 3rd Regiment diary notes simply and with dramatic understatement that the 'C in C addressed the division'.[17]

~

The loyalty and deception with which the Australians covered for one another and comprehensively blamed the New Zealanders is breath-taking and farcical. This is evidenced by the original transcripts of the proceedings—such as they were—of Ryrie's inquiry, which are held at the Australian War Memorial.

Beginning with Major Claude Easterbrook of 2nd Brigade, and ending with the dozen or so other members of the brigade who testified, the inquiry reeks of cover-up, so uniformly consistent are the statements. Easterbrook testified that, about 8.10 on the night of the massacre, 'a whistle blast was heard from the direction of ... Surafend and a few minutes later several small fires were noticed in the village and a few shouts were heard'.[18] He said that the acting brigade commander instructed him to report the disturbance to divisional headquarters and to order all of his units to stand to in their tent lines:

> This order was given verbally to the 6th Light
> Horse and by telephone to the other units ...

an officer (Lieut. Allman) and 24 other ranks mounted were sent to patrol ground between brigade and the village, with orders to prevent men moving into the village.

A picture show was being held in the YMCA in the brigade area and the majority of the men of this brigade were present. I heard Major White [the acting brigadier] give orders to the effect that these men would return to their lines and stand to. At about 2030 DHQ gave instructions by telephone ... that the brigade would stand by ready to turn out, and stated that two squadrons of another brigade had been ordered to clear the situation. At about 2045 the whistle signal for 'Rally' was heard and the noise in the village practically ceased. By this time the whole village was in flames.

About 2200 Lieut. Allman reported back and stated that no men of this Brigade had attempted to pass through his cordon, either going towards or coming from the village. After giving order for 'stand to' Major White visited the lines and assured himself that all ranks were ready to move.

About 2200 2nd LH Field Ambulance were asked to supply ambulances and remove injured natives, three of whom died in Field Ambulance during the night.

I know nothing of the burning of the Bedouin encampment.[19]

The premeditated nature of the attack and the clinical planning of the massacre were made plain in evidence from the 6th Regiment's Corporal Barton as well as being borne out in the evidence of numerous others. Barton told the enquiry:

> On the morning of December 10th about 1000, I was with other men marking out a football ground near 6th LH Camp when a New Zealand soldier rode up and told us that the New Zealanders were going to raid the village of KH. SURAFEND that night and said if any of us cared to join in, we would be welcome. He then rode away ... At about 1900 two New Zealand soldiers walked to the door of my tent and one said he was a friend of the New Zealander lad who had been murdered and told us the New Zealanders intended to raid the village that night and that a meeting was to be held at about 1930 to decide plan [sic] of the raid and he invited any of us to attend the meeting.[20]

Sergeant Henry Fotheringham of the 6th Regiment told the board what would, after two days of evidence from a number of other soldiers, become a familiar story. According to a transcript of his evidence, about three o'clock on the afternoon of 10 December 1918, he saw a New Zealand soldier nearby.

> The New Zealander said to me, 'We are going to raid the village at daylight tomorrow—let any of

the men know it's on and if they care to join us they can'. Fotheringham says he walked away and then, between about six and six-thirty that evening, he said he saw another New Zealand soldier in the lines of C Troop, A Squadron.

He was mounted and speaking to some men … I overheard him say, 'We've altered the time of the raid and it's going to take place in about an hour's time'.

I did not hear any reply from any man. I went to the latrine and he was still there when I returned. I then went to my bivvy and did not see him again. The next thing I knew of the matter was when the raid started. I heard a number of men in the lines talking about it and apparently watching the raid.[21]

Trooper HS Spaven, also of the 6th Regiment went into more detail. He expressed reservations about joining the New Zealanders on the raid because of the anticipated consequences. He said that a New Zealander approached him at about seven o'clock on the night of the raid, and they had the following conversation:

New Zealander: 'Do you know the New Zealanders are going to raid the village over here tonight?'

Spaven: 'No, I was not aware that any raid was taking place.'

New Zealander: 'Well, we are going to raid it, of course you have heard of one of our chaps being shot.'

Spaven: 'I have heard different rumours about a man being shot.'

New Zealander: 'I can tell you the right story as I'm one of his mates. We feel very badly about it. These people have given us a very bad spin and we intend to make an example of them this time.'

Spaven: 'I could not go over ... if any raid was made we would almost certainly be stood to.'[22]

Spaven said the New Zealander then called the men out of a number of nearby tents and told them what was about to take place.[23] According to the official transcript forwarded to divisional headquarters in February 1919, Spaven testified that his New Zealand counterpart said:

'Don't bring any ammunition or we will be shooting each other in the dark, but bring a pickhandle or some such weapon or a bayonet will be as good as anything, as we may be attacked ourselves.' He then said, 'If you go back down and wait at the lower side of the village, I will come back later and lead you round to the opposite side where the attack is going to take place ... as of course the raid is organised and the plan will be explained to you when you get round there. I have been to B and C Squadrons, are there any other regiments about here?' He then said, 'I will go over to the YMCA—there is a good crowd there.'[24]

The official transcript also records him as saying:

> About half an hour later he came back through the squadron lines but there was no one with him. I heard the men say 'A man does not want to be going over there' and I know that none of the men he spoke to when I was present took part in the raid and I do not know of a single man who did. I remarked, 'You never know where these things are going to end—especially if there is a rum ration', and one of the men said, 'No, when things get started they will probably end up raping the women.'[25]

But the official transcript differs markedly from the handwritten court transcript in which Spaven makes no mention of the men's fears that the combination of the rum ration and the raid might lead to rape. Similarly, the official record quotes Spaven thus: 'When we got the order to "Stand to" I believe nearly all the men of my troop were there and they kept coming in from the pictures. I spoke to a good number of the men the following day and they all expressed themselves as disgusted with the raid.'[26] This sentiment—which would reflect extremely well on the men under the circumstances—is not included in the handwritten transcript of the inquiry's proceedings.

Meanwhile, Trooper Bodinnar of the same regiment testified that after the order was made to stand to, at least twenty men were in the lines, from a usual troop of about twenty-five.[27] He does not discuss the whereabouts of the absent men. Captain Thompson of the 2nd Brigade Field Ambulance swore that to the best of his knowledge none of his men were absent while the attack on Surafend was taking place.[28] Lieutenant RB Stocks testified that as soon as the fires started he and the commanding officer assured themselves that all the men were in camp.[29] Lieutenant ER Mayes of the 2nd Brigade's machine-gun squadron, however, left open the possibility that some of his men had been involved. He testified: 'I found a number of men on the top of the hill watching the fire and I asked if any machine-gun men were there. I found that all machine-gun men who had been there had returned to their bivvies.'[30] Troop Sergeant Saunders, meanwhile, testified that he found two men missing when he called the roll.[31] But they returned a few minutes later.

A string of other troop sergeants testified to pretty much the same story, which gave the overall impression that when the fire in the village was seen, the vast majority of men answered the roll call and those who were unable to do so could adequately explain their actions. As to the general attitude of the men who had been asked to go on the raid, most considered it 'not their affair' and that they were best 'out of it'.

But one member of Allenby's staff, perhaps unwilling—or unable—to psychologically distinguish between Australians and New Zealanders, suggested that members of the General Headquarters (GHQ) assisted the Antipodean killers. In notes, Lieutenant

Colonel Richard Andrew, Allenby's nephew and a member of his staff, wrote:

> After the Armistice the Chief [Allenby] was in Cairo a good deal, and on one of these occasions the Australians, who were in camp near Surafend, had one of their men shot by a Bedouin trying to steal a rifle. A party of them (said to have been assisted by a number of men from the GHQ Camp) set fire to the village and a good many of the Bedouin inhabitants were killed.
>
> We could see the village on fire from the chief's house at GHQ and [an officer] Walter Campbell asked [a senior officer] Western what he meant to do about it. I think Western decided to let well alone, but when the Chief came back a few days later there was a great to-do. He had the whole Australian Division paraded ... The Australians were very sore and almost mutinied I believe. The actual slaughter of the Bedouins was said to be mostly the work of the bad hats from the GHQ Camp ... such incidents were not helpful to the Chief or his policy.[32]

24

A REAL BAD THING

The voice is soft and slightly gravelly. He is an old, old man, and he has been very sick. It is seventy years since the war ended. But his mind is alive with memories of Egypt and Palestine, of the many 'stunts' he participated in, of the frustrating business of running telephone lines across the desert and of the ever-present water problem. He is talking to Doug Wyatt, a since retired lieutenant colonel and army historian, who was conducting research into the Tasmanian Light Horse.

Trooper Harold 'Ted' O'Brien of the 3rd Light Horse Regiment's C Squadron—which comprised mainly men from Tasmania—had called Wyatt out of the blue when he'd heard about his research. The old man did not know he was being tape-recorded. But he recalled, with obvious affection, the bravery of his regimental commander, Colonel George Bell—a man later knighted who went on to achieve great heights in federal politics. He also talked of getting malaria during the great ride through the Jordan Valley, and of football matches against the South Australians in his regiment.

When Wyatt asks O'Brien whether he and his mates had to carry their own feed and water, the question, for some reason, prompts the old man to talk about Surafend.

'That was where that big stink happened over there where a New Zealand sergeant was killed, a Bedouin, pinching. And he chokes this fella and apparently there was some other people and they turned on him and they killed him ... So they got their heads together and ... the New Zealanders and the Australians, they went out to this village and they went through it with a bayonet.'[1]

Did they? Wyatt asks.

'Yeah. Broke the village up and everything. Oh, men and that, they'd string them up. That was that. When Allenby, he came to see it ... For days after you could hear these people, women and kids, trekking over the horizon. But, oh dear, it was awful. For a sergeant to be killed like that. And everyone was a bit het up with that sort of thing.'

There is a brief pause before he continues to muse about Surafend and more generally about the horrors of war and its impact on seemingly normal men. He uses himself as an example, talking about stabbing a dying Turkish soldier in the stomach and stealing from the dead.

'You know, you do things you wouldn't normally do in this [sic]. But they did, they went in there ... Yes, a lot of dirty work. War, it's, you know, there's no beg your pardons about that. If you can get a fella dirtier, you get him ... war is a shocking thing, Doug, no doubt about that. No doubt. I never want to talk about it. I've had some dirty scrapes with that. It's shocking just what men'll do. Crikey,' he says.

'Do you know, I could tell you something that I've never told anybody. When we got ambushed and there was ... before that, we went down in the north, a few of us and had a scrap and everything. There was one bloke standing up, dying on his feet, and we used to go through them—you know. We used dead coins and ... we was going to rob the dead sort of business. And I pulled my jackknife and ... I would pull his belt off like that and I let his guts come out, you know. He was gone as far as I was concerned ... Those sorts of things, you'd do them and you wouldn't think anything. In your own private life you never want to speak of it again.'

He then talks in detail about how he and his mates stole coins from the dead. They also used the Turkish dead for target practice. 'They were in the barbed wire, you know, and everything. And then, afterwards, in the daylight, bodies lying everywhere like that. We used to pot-shot them and you would see them up like that and they'd bounce. Oh, dear, it was a bit of sport—but the wind changed. Crikey, the stink! I'll never forget it. Oh, it was a horrible stink that, no doubt about it.'

Wyatt steers to conversation to other matters, including the affection felt by the men for their horses. O'Brien then mentions that he and his wife have just celebrated their sixtieth wedding anniversary. He laments that only four men from the 3rd Regiment are still alive.

Before long, however, O'Brien's bad memories dominate the conversation again, steering it back to 'this time when I opened the fellow's guts with a jackknife' and Surafend. O'Brien said he thought that only the 3rd Light Horse Regiment was involved in the massacre.

'Oh yes. And some New Zealanders. Well, I think perhaps the New Zealanders were the main ones, because a New Zealand sergeant it was,' he says. 'And these Bedouins. They were wicked. The Bedouins, you see, you didn't know whether they were for you or not … and they had to be treated as enemies, to finish up, you know … You'd shoot them on sight.'

Wyatt then asks O'Brien, slowly and deliberately, 'Were there any Tasmanians involved in that little incident?'

O'Brien does not hesitate. 'Oh yes. Our squadron was there. I was down there. I don't know what I did with it, I was cranky and that. But they had a good issue of rum and they did their blocks. But I don't know.'

Was the entire squadron involved?

'Oh no. I think it would be only the sergeants, from the sergeants down. I can't think how it was organised or anything like that, it just happened. And everyone did their block. This sergeant was a very popular man, you know. It was really these New Zealanders came round our lines and tell them about it—they decided they'd go in and clean it up. And they did, I think.'

'And you went yourself?'

'Yeah, I was there, but I don't know if I did anything like that.'

Wyatt lists a number of names of other men from C Squadron, and asks O'Brien whether they were involved.

'We were all pretty well ... because it was our crowd that did it.'

Asked whether there were any repercussions apart from Allenby's general admonition, O'Brien says: 'No. Not from our personal crowd. They sort of wiped it off. It was one of those things. I think it got back to Australia and then I think Allenby sort of part apologised or something like that. But it was a wrong thing— it was bad, that's all. But there were these things that went on all the time.'

'What did you actually do? Did you go in and wreck the village?'

'Oh, absolutely. Yes. It didn't matter. There was cows and ducks and geese. There were kids. But men. They all went for the men with the bayonet and they got it.'

'The women then moved out, I suppose?'

'There were some left. And they trekked out. They left their village and they went away. It was a bad thing. It was a real bad thing.'

The interview finishes when Wyatt suggests to O'Brien that he should go and see Ian Jones' movie, *The Light Horsemen*, which had been recently released.

'I don't know,' the old man replies. 'I was there long enough to get disgusted with the whole bloody thing. And I thought to myself when I come back I don't want to see anything like that again. It was ungodly.'

Ted O'Brien's account would appear to place beyond doubt the fact that Australians were actively involved in the massacre and were not merely lending moral support or cheering on the Kiwis.

~

Wyatt passed his tape-recording of O'Brien to the Australian War Memorial in 1990. Its existence has never really been remarked upon publicly. Now, just after the passing of the ninetieth anniversary of the massacre, its significance seems profound.

O'Brien was apparently unaware that he was being taped. But it appears that he deliberately confided his haunting experience to Wyatt. Why? Maybe it was just an impulse triggered by his reflections on the war, or perhaps because he could no longer hold true to the regiment's vow of silence with Cox until his death. Perhaps he just couldn't take this filthy secret to his grave.

Wyatt told me: 'I'd never heard about the incident at Surafend that he was referring to, but I've since found out that it's been mentioned elsewhere. I thought about it and it is really a part of the regiment's history. I decided that you can't just ignore it. They tried to cover it up. So I gave the tape-recording to the War Memorial because I thought it should really be on the public record—people should know about it.'[2]

Wyatt bases the assertion of a cover-up on a conversation he had after driving to Fingal in Tasmania where he visited old Cyril Newitt, another survivor of the 3rd Regiment's C Company. 'They tried to cover it up. Major General Cox told his soldiers never to speak of it again. I went to see another old fellow, Cyril Newitt, and I asked him about it. He said to me, "General Cox told me never to speak of it again and I'm not going to."'[3]

In 2006 a history of Tasmania's light-horsemen—C Squadron of the 3rd Regiment—was published. Wyatt, who wrote the section on Surafend, concluded: 'Brigadier General Cox is reported to have addressed the members of the 3rd Light Horse Regiment in 1919 and said: "We will speak of this incident no more."'

This order was obeyed by at least one C Squadron soldier present, Trooper Ted O'Brien of Tunnack, 'until this day'.[4] In the C Squadron history, Wyatt wrote:

> It was suggested to me that I should perhaps consider not including the Surafend incident, but I do not believe in revisionist history. The Surafend incident did occur, and the interests of history are best served by recording as much detail, and factual evidence as can be obtained. As an ex-serviceman and great admirer of my predecessors, I do

not believe that this incident in any ways tarnishes their great achievements, but rather adds a human dimension to the times through which they lived and died.[5]

These are noble and courageous sentiments.

~

Kelvin Crombie and I catch up briefly in Canberra a few months after my story took such an unanticipated—and unwelcome—turn, courtesy of O'Brien. I confide that Surafend has influenced my book and that I am struggling to reconcile the light-horsemen who fought in and around Beersheba with the actions of those who participated in the massacre.

I am half expecting—and perhaps hoping—he'll talk the incident down. But he does not.

'It's really important, I think, to be honest about something like this—difficult as it may be,' he says. He points out to me that he had mentioned the incident in his book, albeit fleetingly, because he was chronicling a history of Palestine and Israel from 1798 to 1948. 'But I am of the view that history has not dealt with this episode, Surafend, adequately at all. You have to take the good with the bad ... you can't just eulogise the Light Horse for the many wonderful things they achieved, without looking at the bad things that a few of them also did. It's time to get it all out there, mate.'

Kelvin says that a few years ago a group of Christians visiting Israel asked him to take them to the place where the light-horsemen had massacred the Bedouin, so they could conduct an intercessory prayer meeting. Intercessory prayer involves praying on behalf of others, he explains. And the Christians wanted to pray on behalf of the light-horsemen.

'So we looked around and found roughly where the village, Surafend, used to be,' Kelvin explains. 'This group of people were very definite—they wanted not only to go to the sites of the great light horse battles, but they also wanted to pray at the place where this terrible event had taken place. They wanted the light and the dark. And so they prayed at Surafend for the light-horsemen.'

25

INCONVENIENT TRUTH

oug Wyatt did not let the matter rest. Around the
time of Trooper O'Brien's death he wrote to
William Bell, the son of Colonel George Bell, the much-
respected commander of the 3rd Regiment. He wanted
to know what, if anything, the father might have passed
on to the son about what happened at Surafend and
what, if any, disciplinary action was taken against
those involved.

Bell's response to Wyatt in July 1990 included a
copy of a letter from Mulhall, the former policeman
turned light-horseman who purported to have seen 137
dead Bedouin in the village, the morning after the massacre. Mulhall was a taxi driver at the time he wrote to
Bell senior in 1936.

Mulhall, it seems, was hell-bent on clearing the
name of the light-horsemen. It is clear from his letter to

George Bell, written on 12 September 1936, that he was running a campaign against Allenby and, to an extent, Gullett, whom he believed had criticised the light-horsemen without foundation.

It is worth recounting the letter in full for two reasons. First, because it represents a purported eyewitness account of what happened that night and the next morning that, like Ted O'Brien's, has not previously been on the public record. Second, because it is similar in tone to at least one other letter Mulhall wrote to the government of the day—correspondence that the government assiduously ignored because the facts did not fit Mulhall's theory.

Dear Sir,

I desire to inquire from you relative to certain facts concerning the Bedouin massacre Palestine Dec. 1918. In communications recently Sir Henry Gullett said that you Colonel Bell presided over a Court Martial concerning the Bedouin massacre. I know of no such inquiry of any kind ever held into this affair. If such were the case would you be good enough to inform me (1) What was the nature of the inquiry. (2) When were the persons tried next.

I fail to see how you could possibly be connected in the trial of them seeing that you were one of us whom Allenby charged with being a lot of cold blooded murderers and cowards.

You were there on parade that Sunday morning when Allenby made that criminal attack on us.

I saw you there, you were standing in front of the 3rd ... Regiment and this is what Allenby said: 'You who were not there know who were and know all about it but you are not game to come forward and say so. You are a lot of cold-blooded murderers and cowards.'

Are you aware that I had full particulars of the Bedouin massacre at that time but neither myself or anyone else had an opportunity to bring them forward. I was at the village at 7AM the morning following the massacre and I was astounded to see the numbers who had their heads bashed in by the use of blunt instruments. Being an experienced man in the detection of crime, I might say I resigned from the NSW Mounted Police to go to the war. I counted 137 dead within the village. It was a most gruesome sight the manner in which their heads were bashed and battered. The first thing I asked, why should soldiers use blunt instruments to do to death their victims when each soldier had rifle and ammunition. At this stage I was under the impression it was the New Zealanders who did the diabolical crime. However, I decided there and then to go right into the matter and find out the full facts, and this is it briefly.

On the Sunday night at midnight Sgt Lawry [sic] attached to the New Zealand Mounted Rifles was asleep in his bivy. He was suddenly awakened by his kit bag which he was using as a pillow being pulled from under his head. Upon opening his eyes he saw the form of a man disappearing through the doorway of the bivy. He jumped, chased and caught the thief within the lines. Sgt Lawry was bringing him back when the thief fired point blank and shot Sgt Lawry through the stomach and escaped. Attracted by the sound of the shot and his groans the pickets found Lawry in a bad way. They quickly aroused the whole camp. Sgt Lawry lived half an hour and died in terrible agony. But he told his comrades before he died the thief and his murderer was a Bedouin and that he had gone down to the Bedouin village.

On the following morning, Monday, Sgt Lawry was buried in the New Zealand Cemetery. They passed your camp on the way to the cemetery. That same evening at 10 minutes to six a meeting was held near the Bedouin village. It was decided at this meeting that evening (1) To raid the village and capture the murderer of Sgt Lawry. (2) To send a dispatch rider to the various camps for assistance.

The dispatch rider was duly sent off whilst preparations were carried out for the raid. As you know in December at 6 P.M. it is dark. The despatch rider had not gone far when he got confused with the lights of the camps and lost his way. But he reached the Tommy Artillery camp. As you know artillery men are not armed with rifles. The Tommys decided to go there that night in full force and having no rifles decided to take bludgeons with them.

Later all assembled at the village. 10 minutes were given the Bedouins to hand over the murderer of Sgt Lawry. They refused. Time up, all women and children under the age of sixteen years were removed from the village. Then the slaughter commenced, the New Zealanders using their rifles and the Tommy artillerymen using bludgeons. The Australians were not there, they did not know any trouble was on. The despatch rider did not visit their camps. None of your regiment the 3rd ALH took any part in the massacre, the dispatch rider never reached your camp. I concentrated on this, I wanted to ascertain if any of our men, the 1st ALH Regiment, took any part in this stupid senseless slaughter, and the dispatch rider would have had to come through your camp to reach our camp.

Allenby later went to England and in a speech at Dover he said among other things, the Australian Light Horse are no other than a lot of murderers and cowards. This part of the speech was cabled to Australia and published in the Sydney Sun newspaper and has never been refuted.

We are going to clean up this slander against Australians and sheet home to Allenby's own Tommy countrymen their guilt. Allenby hated us Australians and he used this for spite against us and [to] throw a smokescreen over his own countrymen.

When I completed my inquiry I was fully convinced the New Zealanders had done a foolish act in taking the Tommys in with them that night. As I said at the time, the New Zealanders must not take the full blame for cowardly uncalled for slaughter by the Tommys. But what a shock when Allenby threw the full blame on us Australians. He left out the New Zealanders and the Tommys.

In his book *Official History of the Palestine Campaign*, which is to be seen in the Sydney Public Library, Sir Henry Gullett says the Australians were there that night in large numbers. Sir Henry's writings are only hearsay, you have only to read the portion of this book dealing with the massacre to find he was never there. He says the soldier chased the Bedouin through the sandhills. As you know, there were no sandhills within 3 miles. He also says guards were placed around the village that night and all the next day. No such thing ever happened.

The attack will shortly be launched to clear our name from that frightful stigma. You, Bourne, Cox will then have full opportunity to test your metal [*sic*] as dinkum Australians.

Yours

A. S. Mulhall[1]

~

Today Mulhall would be regarded as a conspiracy theorist and a vexatious correspondent. Perhaps he was then, too. Parts of his letter to George Bell might be true. Certainly, it seems large portions are not. Too many other men had been contacted by the New Zealand dispatch riders to believe Mulhall's assertion that the Australians hadn't been told about the planned massacre. Indeed, one NCO, Boorman of the 6th Regiment, told the board of inquiry it was 'current rumour through the lines that a raid was to take place'.[2]

And what of the assertion that 137 were killed? Certainly the regimental war diaries played down the number of dead and injured. The 3rd Regiment's diary, for example, referred to 'the killing and wounding of several' Surafend inhabitants.

Paterson says the revenge party killed 'every able-bodied man in the village' while Gullett said that 'many Arabs were killed'. Lawrence James, Allenby's biographer, said the violence 'left at least thirty dead or wounded'. Meanwhile, *The Official War History of the Wellington Mounted Rifles Regiment 1914–1919* says simply that 'the able bodied men were dealt with'.[3] Ted O'Brien also gives the impression that many men died. We can safely conclude that more than 'several'—in fact, many—men died at Surafend and the adjoining Bedouin camp.

But Mulhall is demonstrably wrong when he assures Bell that nobody from Bell's 3rd Regiment was involved. We know from O'Brien, himself a member of the 3rd, that this is untrue. It is clear from Mulhall's letter that he contacted Gullett and asked him to justify his assertion in the official history that 'large bodies of Australians' were among the 'many hundreds strong' who attacked the village. Gullett, of course, knew the truth as well as Bell, Cox, Ryrie and, indeed, Allenby. For Gullett had dared to published the truth, or the closest thing to a version thereof, in his official history, despite the fact that nobody had admitted complicity before Ryrie's inquiry or any more secret inquiry that Bell may have convened.

Certainly the 3rd Regiment's diary makes it clear that Bell was involved in an inquiry. But none of its records have been publicly retained, and it was not, as Mulhall says Gullett indicated to him, a court martial. It seems likely Gullett, knowing that regrettably he could not uphold Mulhall's belief that the light-horsemen were innocent, fobbed him off to Bell.

Gullett's view of the situation had never been in doubt. He believed that some Australians were guilty. And he also believed Allenby had behaved appallingly by blaming all light-horsemen for the crime of a comparative few. 'Without making excuses for the Anzacs, it may be said that the affair arose out of the simple fact that British regular officers entrusted with Australian commands in Egypt and Palestine ... too often failed to grasp the vital fact that the narrow traditional methods of handling the soldiers of England, Scotland, Ireland and Wales are not by any absolute law also the way to handle young men of the dominions.'[4] More specifically, perhaps, the Australians and New Zealanders resented the fact that the British disciplined them for often minor offences against the local Arabs while the natives were effectively free to do as they chose.

Gullett, unlike some of the others involved, was never of a mind to whitewash the ugly incident. He explains how a strained situation continued until mid-1919 when the Australians of the 2nd Light Horse Brigade were about to depart for Australia, yet Allenby had not in any way acknowledged the light-horsemen since his attack on them over Surafend: 'Allenby was then in control of the affairs in Egypt; he was visited by an Australian, who pointed out to him the unsatisfactory position which existed.'[5]

Allenby expressed surprise that the Australians were so hurt, while insisting that the actions of the Australians at Surafend had warranted everything he said about them at the time. He then wrote a glowing farewell order and reference for the Australians, which ended:

> The Australian light horseman combines with a splendid physique a restless activity of mind. This mental quality renders him somewhat impatient of rigid and formal discipline, but it confers upon him the gift of adaptability, and this is the secret of much of his success mounted or on foot. In this dual role, on every variety of ground—mountain, plain, desert, swamp, or jungle—the Australian light horseman has proved himself equal to the best.
>
> He has earned the gratitude of the Empire and the admiration of the world.[6]

It seems that modesty prevented Gullett from publicly declaring his own part in extracting what was, it seems, little more than a minor concession from Allenby. For Gullett was the nameless 'Australian' who—as recorded in Gullett's book—visited 'the Bull' in Egypt in mid-1919. 'Allenby sulked,' writes James.

> His fury did not subside ... Allenby was genuinely distressed by an act of monstrous indiscipline which could have damaged relations with the Arabs. He was also inwardly discomposed by his inability to overawe the Anzacs, who had publicly humiliated him. Hurt pride as much as a concern for military law probably contributed to his vindictive treatment of them. It did, however, have an ironic appropriateness, since they too had punished indiscriminately.[7]

~

In February 1936 Mulhall wrote to Robert Menzies, the future prime minister who was then federal Attorney General. There is no record of Mulhall's letter, but it is fair to assume it was similar in tone to those later sent to Bell and others. Menzies' private secretary wrote back to Mulhall simply to acknowledge that his letter had been 'noted'.

The commanders, Cox, Ryrie and Bell, had never paid more than lip-service to military justice over the Surafend massacre. In fairness, however, it should be remembered that there was little they could do at the time given that the men involved had so comprehensively closed ranks.

There is no evidence to suggest that Sir George Bell, as he was by then, had ever responded to Mulhall's cantankerous and misguided letter. But in 1990 Bell's son William wrote to Doug Wyatt, the Tasmanian army historian who was picking at this nasty historical scab. Bell junior included a copy of Mulhall's letter to his father. William Bell's letter is curious because it does not directly address Mulhall's principal assertion, namely that the light-horsemen had been blamed for something they did not do.

In the last paragraph of the letter Mulhall is critical of Sir Henry Gullett, yet Sir Henry's opinion of Allenby is very close to his own and I have a press cutting bearing this out [William Bell writes].

Referring to a speech by Allenby, which was cabled to a Sydney newspaper, about the composition of the Middle East armies in which he made no mention of the Australian Light Horse, Gullett had this to say in a letter to the newspaper concerned: '"The Sun" apologises for the absence of the reference to the Australian Light Horse and generously puts it down to an "unintentional slip" on Allenby's part, or to the British papers that reported the speech.'

Possibly 'The Sun' is right, but I doubt it. The omission is characteristic of Allenby's attitude towards the Light Horse.[8]

The letter ends curiously with what appears to be a direct quote about the seething resentment towards the Arabs and the enduring British policy of appeasement, at almost any cost, to them. It seems to reflect the sentiments of Gullett—and all of the commanders—involved. It also confirms Australian participation in the massacre. It reads:

> The British policy towards the Moslem during the war was carried to stupid extremes. The Arab of Palestine could do as he pleased and in consequence we had a number of Australians murdered and could obtain no redress. The natural spirit of resentment culminated within a mile of Allenby's own headquarters when after the foul murder of New Zealander by an Arab, who was robbing his tent at night, and after GHQ had refused justice, the Anzac Mounted Division burned the village which sheltered the murderer and took a terrible vengeance. Allenby never forgave that audacious affront to his immediate presence.[9]

~

The commanders went on to resume successful lives, unsullied by a stigma that might ordinarily, if justice took its course, attach to a crime such as that committed at Surafend. Ryrie went back to Federal Parliament and later became High Commissioner to London. For a short time he was assistant Defence minister. Cox, who ordered his men never to speak of Surafend again, had a long, if not distinguished, career as a senator. He was a popular and enormously colourful public figure in New South Wales. Gullett himself entered Federal Parliament in 1925; at the time Mulhall was harassing him, he was a senior minister in the Lyons government. George Bell, meanwhile, had entered Federal Parliament in 1922. At the time Mulhall was pressing him to disclose what he knew about Surafend, he was the Speaker of the House of Representatives.

The Australian War Memorial holds a biography of Bell's military career.[10] It is neatly typed on crisp white paper and recounts his service in the Boer War and later as a Tasmanian farming pioneer. It records his service in Gallipoli and his participation, later, in some of the great battles across Palestine, including at Tel el Saba on the day of the great fight for Beersheba. It was prepared with great pride and obvious affection by William Bell, the son of the great soldier and parliamentarian, who presented it to the War Memorial in 1969. It makes no mention of Surafend.

How uncomfortably the secrets of precisely what happened at Surafend must have rested among the senior law-makers of our land. Like most obsessive types, Mulhall did not stop with Bell. But he received no comfort from Bell's parliamentary colleagues, who did their best, it seems, to ignore or give him the run-around.

26

BURYING THE PAST

Doug Wyatt urged me to go to the National Archives of Australia and ask for a file from 1936. He thought it would shed more light on Surafend—or, at least, the Federal Government's attitude towards it.

By now, I was dreaming about the massacre. Because I had come to equate the rough location of the massacre with an Israeli army base, the Anzac crime had irrationally morphed, in my imagination, into a suicide bombing of young Israeli soldiers in 2003. And I was absorbed—no, obsessed. I wondered if Mulhall might actually have been right. Had there been a conspiracy to stitch up the Australians from the inside— to blame them for a horrible crime they had not committed? Bell, commander of the 3rd Regiment, had never apparently made the findings of his court of enquiry public, and he had not, as far as I could determine, directly responded to Mulhall.

Acting on Wyatt's recommendation, I bolted down to the archives. It was mid-Friday afternoon. The archivist told me it would take three, maybe four hours to retrieve the file. That would mean next week. I begged her. Please, I said, I *must* have it today. She took pity.

My hands were shaking when the file—a manila folder containing a brown envelope and bound with a ribbon—was passed to me. At first I thought it was a mistake and that I'd been handed the wrong papers because, when I pulled the contents out and put them on the desk, the first papers were House of Representatives Hansard from 22 October 1936. The Hansard recorded, over eight pages, speeches in support of a constitutional amendment regarding the international marketing of primary products. I tossed the Hansard aside to find a letter written in black fountain pen in a spidery hand: 'No. 8 Mawson Street, Punchbowl, 17th July 1936'.

It was Mulhall! This time he was writing to Senator Sir George Pearce, the External Affairs minister. Pearce had been Defence minister for all of World War I, under five successive governments of Andrew Fisher and Billy Hughes. Mulhall's letter to Pearce begins: 'I desire to ask if you would be good enough to furnish me with a copy of the report which was made to you at that time as responsible Minister [Minister for Defence] relative to the Bedouin massacres in Palestine in December, 1918.'[1]

Most of the letter was similar to that which he wrote Bell, less than two months later. But it becomes

clear towards the end of the letter (apparently transcribed into typed-print and described by someone on
Pearce's staff as 'almost illegible') that Bell has already
communicated with Mulhall and told him what he did
not want to hear.

> Now Mr George [Bell] says he presided over a
> Court of Inquiry and that ample proofs were given
> that the Australians were there in large numbers. At
> the same time Mr Bell strictly avoids mentioning
> what units they belonged to. But he can not escape
> this. He must speak in the near future. Australia
> and the Australians name has been tarnished in the
> foulest crime and we are innocent men. And it is
> only the likes of me who realize the terrible reality
> of it all. It was the most gruesome sight it would be
> possible to describe to see these corpses lying their
> heads bashed and battered and the huts smoulder-
> ing ruins. And after completing my inquiries I said
> then that these New Zealanders were foolish taking
> these Pommys ... in with them for the New
> Zealanders must now take the full blame for the
> stupid senseless destruction of life.[2]

Although Mulhall had not, at this stage, officially
corresponded with Bell, Mulhal's letter to Pearce makes
it clear that Bell had at some point apparently told him
that the Australians were involved in the massacre. But
he would not, it seems, tell him which units they
belonged to, perhaps because Bell knew there was no

record anywhere that members of his own 3rd Regiment—men like Ted O'Brien—participated in the massacre. The only official record seems to be the transcript of evidence by members of the 6th Regiment. And they had closed ranks so comprehensively that it was impossible to apportion blame.

But Pearce's response seems to have been to treat Mulhall like the unstable serial pest he had clearly become. He might have used some initiative by referring Mulhall's letter to the old regimental commander, Bell, by then Speaker of the House of Representatives, for some clarification. Someone determined to find truth might also have walked a few metres towards the back of the Senate to ask Senator 'Fighting Charlie' Cox what he knew. Maybe he did. Clearly he gave the matters raised by Mulhall considerable thought because it took his secretary more than three months to reply to him.

22nd October, 1936.

Dear Sir,

On behalf of the Minister for External Affairs, Sir George Pearce, I desire to acknowledge receipt of your letter requesting a copy of the report on the Surafend incident, Palestine, 1918.

Your letter will be submitted for the consideration of the Minister on his return from Western Australia in a fortnight's time.

Yours faithfully,

Secretary.[3]

The date is significant because it is after Mulhall wrote to Bell on 12 September 1936. And that letter to Bell followed some sort of early communication with both Gullett and Bell during which both had apparently told Mulhall that Australians had indeed been involved in the killing at Surafend. By writing to Pearce, Mulhall was clearly trying to let each man know he had spoken to the other. Mulhall was a threat to them all because, his good—although utterly misguided—intentions aside, he was threatening to publicly air an extremely ugly incident in Australia's past that had already been comprehensively buried. All the men Mulhall was stalking, not least Pearce, were to a degree complicit.

Pearce eventually asked Sir Archdale Parkhill, Defence minister at the time, to deal with Mulhall. Parkhill wrote to Pearce on 26 November 1936, saying he had received Pearce's letter about 'the Bedouin massacre in Palestine in 1918' and that he 'shall have inquiries made into this matter, and as requested by you, will communicate direct with Mr Mulhall'.[4] Pearce could have saved Parkhill the trouble. After all, he knew exactly what had happened and how Australia ultimately responded. There is no record of Parkhill ever dealing with Mulhall, and the file dies with Pearce trying to sidestep Mulhall by flicking him to Parkhill. Or does it?

I was initially convinced that the Hansard debate about primary industries had been mistakenly filed with Mulhall's correspondence at the National Archives—until I realised the date of the Hansard—22 October

1936—was the same date as that on the tardy response from Pearce's secretary to Mulhall. The Hansard had not been filed with the Mulhall correspondence accidentally. The debate covered by the Hansard is totally unrelated to Surafend, but the opening remarks by the then Prime Minister Joseph Lyons might just as well be a direct reference to how the Australian Government had attempted to deal with the massacre and redress the wrong that occurred at Surafend on 10 December 1918. 'Many times in the past', says Lyons, 'it has been our experience that, when a proposal was made to remedy some evil, if we may call it so, opposition arose because something else was not being done.'[5]

What was the 'something else' in relation to Surafend, I wondered, that 'was not being done'? It was of course volunteering the names of the guilty Australians. And what, then, was the proposal that had been 'made to remedy some evil'? It was money. Blood money. But you won't find mention of that in our archives. For that you have to go to New Zealand.

BLOOD MONEY

Allenby's fury after the massacre knew no bounds. As well as ordering the division to move immediately to Rafah, he cancelled all leave and ordered those who had already departed for leave to return. But it was his next move that would earn him the lasting opprobrium of the light-horsemen. Allenby maliciously withdrew recommendations for all gallantry awards for the light-horsemen and studiously avoided mentioning them at any significant public occasion over coming years.

This policy began when Allenby arrived at the English port of Dover to a hero's welcome after the war. 'The Recorder has referred to my cosmopolitan army,' Allenby told the crowd, according to the *Times* of 17 September 1919.

There were 11 or 12 nationalities represented, but every one of them was actuated by the same spirit. Jerusalem is the Holy Place of three great religions—Christians, Jews and Mahomedans. All three of those religions were represented in my army—in fact, during the last year two thirds of my forces were Moslems. Every one of them fought valiantly and, whatever their nationality or religion, they were actuated by one spirit—loyalty to the cause and the Empire and determination to do their best in any circumstances.[1]

As the aggrieved former light-horseman Ambrose Mulhall of Punchbowl would indicate to Bell, Gullett, Menzies, Pearce and presumably others many years later, there was indeed an angry reaction to Allenby's omission of the Australians at Dover.

On 18 September 1918 the *Times* carried a piece from its Sydney correspondent, reading: 'The telegraphed account of the speech made by Field Marshal Allenby on his arrival at Dover in which he described his Army in Palestine as cosmopolitan but made no mention of the Australians, has given great offence to the Light Horse.' Allenby, apparently asked to respond to the Australians' anger, reportedly 'stated that his troops consisted of many nationalities, including British, Australian, New Zealand, French, Italian, Indian, West Indian, Egyptian, Arab, Jewish, Algerian and Armenian. The omission of the Australians from the report of his speech must have been due to a verbal error. The good work of the Australian Light Horse was such they could never be forgotten by him.'[2]

But within three weeks Allenby compounded his insult to the light horse when making a speech at a grand reception in his honour at London's Guild Hall. Allenby did not omit them from this speech; rather, he referred to them almost disparagingly as mere assistants to the actions of the British infantry—especially the 60th Division—at both Beersheba and later in the Jordan Valley. While the onerous contribution of the 60th at Beersheba is undeniable, it should not be forgotten that the 4th Light Horse Brigade performed the critical act that stole the town from the Turks on 31 October 1917.[3]

Of Beersheba, Allenby said: 'That Division [the 60th] took a very leading part in the capture of Beersheba.' Of the bitter fighting in the Jordan Valley, which occupied the Australians and New Zealanders for *all* of the summer and beyond in 1918, Allenby said: 'Subsequently the 60th Division fought in the Jordan Valley … They fought there the whole of the early part of the summer and took part or practically carried out, with the help of the [British] Cavalry, the Australian Light Horse and the New Zealand Mounted troops, two great raids on the Hedjaz Railway.'[4] He then omitted the Australians altogether when finally listing the nationalities who had served him so well. He did not fail to mention the British, French, Italians, New Zealanders, the West Indies, Jewish and even a unit from New York.

Special mention was also made of the Arab army, even though it had failed to materialise—as anticipated—in one of the attacks on Amman. Together with the infamous incident at Ziza when Ryrie had to protect Turkish prisoners from the Arab tribesmen, the failure of the Arabs to show up for battle at Amman heightened the anti-Bedouin sentiment that preceded Surafend.

There could be little doubt that Allenby, in his speech to the Guild Hall, was deliberately snubbing the light-horsemen again.

~

Despite the fact that Henry Gullett had managed to extract a glowing reference for the light-horsemen before they went home, Allenby would not budge on the question of awards. According to some accounts, his relationship with Chauvel became extremely strained.

In his 1974 book *The Desert Hath Pearls*, Chauvel's former aide-de-camp Colonel Rex Hall recounts how he was in a 'box position' to view Allenby's actions:

> General Chauvel became ill and was in hospital. He told me of General Allenby's action, which had disturbed him greatly. At his dictation I wrote several letters on the subject to the War Office, to authorities in Cairo and to certain senior officers. One, I remember, was a plea for a knighthood for Brigadier-General Granville Ryrie ... This was

successful, but the other Commanders and Staff Officers of the Desert Mounted Corps (perhaps with one other exception), many of whom had been submitted ... missed their awards.[5]

Chauvel's recommendations, Hall mused, 'got lost between Cairo and the War Office, while those who deserved battle honours 'remain "unhonoured" and "unsung"'. Hall described the Surafend massacre as 'tragic'. But of Allenby's response, he wrote: 'History should, in my opinion, record this drastic action as being to Allenby's lasting shame.'[6]

What exactly Chauvel—who died in 1945—made of the massacre at Surafend has never been established, although his biographer Alec Hill said, probably correctly, that it 'may easily be imagined'. Chauvel the disciplinarian, he said, would have been outraged that the regimental officers allowed their men to put themselves in such a position.[7] As Hall points out, Chauvel pushed Allenby on the question of awards. Allenby softened in 1921. But it was too late because, in January 1921, the War Office declared that no further awards would be considered.

Gullett, meanwhile, was apparently struggling with how exactly to deal with Surafend in his forthcoming official history of the Palestine operations. He clearly believed that Chauvel was trying to stop him from criticising Allenby. In an exchange with his mentor, CEW Bean, he wrote:

> I have been held up by Chauvel ... he made a hid-
> eous lot of trouble. His aim is to trim everything
> critical of the British out of the book. Most of it
> is, I think, vanity. He sees in it a good deal of self-
> advertisement and he is therefore anxious not to
> jeopardise it by criticism of British weakness. I
> fear there will be a very hot fight indeed about
> the Surafend stuff. Chauvel is outraged at the
> thought of it.

Bean responded by saying that Gullett should 'stand
pat' on what he'd written, otherwise he would be 'con-
cealing from Australians a truth'.[8]

~

A letter from Chauvel to Allenby's biographer, Archibald
Percival Wavell, dated 13 October 1936, corroborates
Gullett's assertion that Chauvel had wanted to effectively sanitise the official historian's version of the conflict. Chauvel wrote: 'I don't know of anything of much
interest that has been written about him in Australia.
There are a few "incidents" in the Australian Official
History. I would miss out anything about the Surafend
affair. It should never have been mentioned in the
Australian Official History and has been long forgotten
in Australia.'[9]

Although Chauvel was angry with Allenby for effectively withholding awards from Australian light-horsemen and their commanders because of Surafend, all, it

seems, was forgiven when Allenby visited South Australia, Melbourne and Sydney in 1926. Both Allenby and Chauvel were effusive in their respective praise. Chauvel even described Allenby as the greatest soldier Britain had produced since Wellington. Allenby, for his part, also praised the Australian light horse, saying: 'They carried through their work, difficult and dangerous thought it was, in a gallant manner that was a great credit to Australia and of inestimable service to the Empire.'[10]

There is no record of Surafend having been officially raised while Allenby was in Australia, and the great soldier was feted at official functions—and greeted warmly by veterans—at numerous public events in Melbourne, Adelaide and Sydney. 'As an example of what Australians thought of him: [I] was speaking at the Melbourne Town Hall at his civic reception and said that I thought he was the greatest soldier Great Britain had produced since Wellington and when I was interrupted by an Australian ex-soldier who said he would go further and say he was the greatest soldier since Hannibal!' Chauvel wrote.[11]

Given the pressure Gullett faced from Chauvel, he ultimately deserved commendation for including the Surafend massacre and Allenby's response to it in the official history. Although he deals with it perfunctorily, given the enormity of the crime, he does so judgmentally, describing the actions of the Anzacs as 'inexcusable'. But neither does he not spare Allenby for his punitive overreaction in effectively punishing all of the light-horsemen.

Allenby would have better served the situation if he reconvened—and perhaps even oversaw—the Australian and New Zealand inquiries that seemed destined from the start to fail.

There is no evidence that the Australian Government was overtly or diplomatically taking up the cause of the light horse while Allenby denied them decorations. Perhaps that is because it was involved in behind-the-scenes manoeuvrings to absolve Australia of the stain of Surafend by making New Zealand admit to a greater share of the blame.

~

No soldier—Australian, New Zealander or Scot—was ever held responsible for either the destruction of the village or the murder of the the inhabitants of either the village or the Bedouin camp. Palestine's new occupiers, the British, quickly set about rebuilding Surafend and making it a military base.

But the British Government was most unwilling to let the matter rest there. And so, in late 1920 or early 1921, the War Office began pushing New Zealand and Australia to compensate the British, if not for the actual massacre, then for the destruction of the village itself. The pressure on Australia and New Zealand was applied in London, primarily on the dominion military representatives at their respective high commissions on the Strand.

New Zealand has meticulous records of what transpired at the time, and the archives in Wellington make it absolutely clear that the British contacted Australia ahead of New Zealand to push the compensation issue, presumably because they initially held the light-horsemen primarily responsible for what happened at Surafend. A letter, 'Burning of Surafend Village, Palestine', to New Zealand Military Headquarters in Wellington from the country's military representative in London, Lieutenant Colonel HV Avery, dated 19 February 1921, makes this clear:

> On the night of 10th December 1918, the Arab village of Surafend, Palestine, was the object of a raid by troops quartered in the neighbourhood. The place was burnt out and there were several casualties among the natives. The NZMR Brigade was implicated but a Court of Enquiry failed to fix any responsibility and there the matter stood.
>
> The village of Surafend has been rebuilt by the British Government at a cost of £2060.11.3, and the War Office has now written to the Australian authorities suggesting that the cost should be borne in equal shares by the Australian and New Zealand Governments. No communication has yet reached me to this effect. The file has however been shown to me by the Australian representative, and I have told him that NZ will not recognize the claim.[12]

New Zealand continued to hold out, but only until May 1921, when it received another letter—this one remarkably strident in apportioning blame to the Kiwis—from the War Office, urging it to 'admit liability to the extent of one third of the total damage':

> I am commanded to add, that having regard to the fact that the Dominion Troops stationed in the neighbourhood of the Village of Surafend largely predominated in numbers over the Imperial Contingent (which consisted of only three batteries) that ... the Army Council do not feel justified in admitting more than one third liability as a strict maximum in regard to the occurrence, and feel bound to suggest that the remaining two thirds of the total cost (£2,060.11.3d) be borne by Dominion Funds i.e. £1373.14.2d.
>
> As the Army Council have accepted the offer of £515.2.9 from Australian Funds, I am to request you to admit the claim to the extent of £858.11.5d.[13]

Suddenly Lieutenant Colonel Avery was on side. In a memo to his High Commissioner, Avery—who just three months earlier would not recognise the claim against his countrymen—now wrote: 'I recommend that we accept liability for the amount named £858.11.5. The court failed to fix responsibility but there is little doubt that New Zealanders were largely responsible.'[14]

Australia, unlike New Zealand, had not contested its liability and promptly offered to pay. Australia had quickly, if not unquestioningly, coughed up its £515.2.9. Given the fact that New Zealand had initially been reluctant to pay anything, Australia did well to inadvertently pressure the Kiwis to, in effect, formally acknowledge that their soldiers played a greater part in the massacre than the Australians. Australia's decision to make the payment cannot be seen as anything but an acceptance of—and an attempt to right—the wrong committed by its soldiers. But there must have been a cathartic element to making the payment as well, for the British Government clearly saw payment as a discharge of financial and perhaps moral liability for what had happened. In accepting New Zealand's cheque on 26 May 1921, the War Office wrote that it did so 'in full discharge of New Zealand liability in regard to the incident at Surafend'.

Presumably the same applied to Australia. It was a small price to pay for such a heinous act. All that remained was to erase it from Australia's official memory.

~

The Surafend incident fitted awkwardly, uncomfortably, with an illustrious Anzac legend that began with Bean's dispatches from Gallipoli and became mythologised in the minds of later Australians by the movies and books that focused on the diggers' egalitarianism and their great and undeniable sacrifice. Surafend played no part in Australia's national conversation.

There was, however, a brief flurry of interest in 1964 when a British infantryman, Captain Cyril Falls, published *Armageddon, 1918*, a book about the British campaign in Palestine.[15] Falls' book was significant because it picked at the scab of Surafend; it revisited the forgotten incident, largely, it seems, on the basis of Gullett's account.

News of the book quickly reached New Zealand where an ex-servicemen's organisation, the Auckland Mounted Rifles Association, announced it would hold an inquiry to get to the bottom of what happened, once and for all, while some of the men involved were still with the world.[16] In a 'reaction' story from New Zealand, the *Times* of London quoted the association's secretary, MR Reed, as saying, 'Ours is a story of intolerable provocation and murders of our own troops.' The story continued:

> He denied that Australian troops had applauded as the New Zealanders massacred the Arab villagers, after an Arab thief had shot a New Zealand trooper. 'It happened that the New Zealand bivouacs were nearest to Surafend, and when the row started a large number of them were drawn into it,' Mr Reed said.
>
> 'British and Australian troops were involved, the British being represented by men of the Royal Horse Artillery of the Anzac Mounted Division. It is not in the character of the Australians to stand aside while exciting events are occurring.'

Mr A. M. Davidson of Dunedin, who said he was on duty in Surafend the day after the massacre, tonight said it was 'a lie' that New Zealand troops were responsible. In the camp there were not only New Zealanders but also Australians and Scots. Because nothing was done to bring the murderer of the New Zealand trooper to trial, a meeting was called which decided to avenge the trooper's murder.

'The Australians organised the raid and an Australian trooper led it. It was only a small party, but though soldiers from all three countries were involved, there were only a couple of New Zealanders,' Mr Davidson said. 'There was not a woman or child touched and not all the men were murdered. Some of them were badly injured and some, admittedly, were killed.'[17]

The New Zealanders were at last trying to settle the score with their Antipodean brethren, who had been blaming the New Zealanders since 1918. The Kiwis were now blaming the Australians. The British continued to blame both.

The elderly former governor of Be'er Sheva, AF Nayton, heard about Falls' book and wrote that he was forced to spend a good deal of his time 'trying to convince indignant Bedu shaikhs that the half-naked horsemen who chased them, beat them up, stole the "sacred mares they were riding—each one descended by Allah from the prophet Muhammad's own strain and worth untold gold"—as well as taking from them their silver embossed heirloom swords, were really their allies. Then trying, hopelessly, to trace the stolen animals and swords and/or endeavouring to obtain some sort of compensation for them ... the Surafend incident was much discussed.'[18]

Nayton experienced a good deal else in Beersheba after the war while governor from 1918 until 1946, just before the restoration of Israel. The mysterious Joseph Hokeidonian—grandfather of Joe Hockey—would surely have heard the stories about the wild, shirtless Australians, too, for he was hired in the 1920s as the deputy clerk of Beersheba. Seventy years later his grandson, Joe Hockey, would eulogise those Australians and their actions at Beersheba in his maiden speech.

28

A BASTARD OF A PLACE

Passover has almost finished, and the crowd at the big hotel in Be'er Sheva is thinning out. But the soccer game in my hallway continues daily—first thing in the morning and again, for the second half, roundabout kids' dinner time at 5.30 each evening. That's usually my cue to hit the bar for a kosher shiraz.

'Only a few more days and we can all drink beer again,' the barmaid says. 'Passover sucks towards the end.'

For gentiles in a Jewish city such as this, Passover's enforced culinary deprivations are constantly trying. At the end of another day, Anzac Day as it happens, most of which I've spent in the cemetery again, I head to Jerusalem.

I am over Be'er Sheva. And I am over Beersheba.

I stay with friends and go to dinner in the city's Arab east with a group of international journalists. The talk turns to work, as it inevitably must when journalists gather. They criticise the Israeli Government's fuel blockade of Gaza, and they criticise Hamas. All are despondent about the future of Israel and dismissive of the possibility of short-term solutions to the intractable violence. Things, they all predict, will get dramatically worse. And they do within the year when, understandably impatient with the relentless Hamas rocket attacks on Israeli towns such as Sederot, Israel launches a major offensive against Gaza.

But this is Israel, where the talk inevitably focuses on the perpetual cycle of violence and of possible new ways to fix it. The talk turns to my interest in Beersheba and the light-horsemen—especially the Evangelical Christian interpretation that they were fulfilling a biblical prophecy by helping to return Israel to the Jews.

'I wonder whether your light-horsemen really thought they were latter-day crusaders and what they would think about Israel today,' one of them says.

I think, but don't say, that such was the affinity many of the light-horsemen had with the Jews they encountered in Palestine—so warmly were they embraced in 1917 and 1918—that they might well have no regrets. And as for being part of another crusade—no, I don't think so. They traversed a land that most of them had known about only from the Bible. The names—the Nile and the Dead Sea, Jericho, Jerusalem, Bethlehem and Jordan—certainly had a biblical resonance for them. But there is no genuine sense that the men or their commanders saw themselves as doing God's work.

The historian Dr Richard 'Harry' Chauvel was born a year too late to meet his grandfather, the great general Sir Harry. But he has studied his grandfather's papers and letters, and he recalls that the home of his late grandmother was filled with his grandfather's presence by way of memorabilia and photographs. When he was a child, therefore, the story of his acclaimed grandfather was 'taken up in part by osmosis'.

'He died the year before I was born, but my grandmother lived for many years after that, so I received the family stories via her, rather than directly from him. She was very active, in that sense,' says Chauvel, a thoughtful and quietly spoken man whose voice is all but drowned out by the noise in the hotel lobby where we sit.

'I don't remember when it was exactly, but I gave a talk on an occasion related to Beersheba—perhaps around the ninetieth anniversary—and a guy later rang me up, introducing himself as associated with the Australian Light Horse Association,' Richard says.

'And he asked whether it was true that my grandfather had a Bible in his saddlebag. My response was that, well, I guess he went to school when things like reading the Bible were perhaps taken a bit more seriously ... but I do not get any sense of him being or seeing himself as a crusader or some such. I would say that perhaps because he knew the Bible he had a sense of history of what had gone before him in this place, if you like. He was one of my heroes ... but not quite a crusader.'

There was no sense in his family, he says, that his grandfather's achievements in Palestine were not given due acknowledgement or that they were somehow overshadowed by Gallipoli and the Western Front. Similarly, he says there was never a sense that the military act for which his grandfather is perhaps best known, the October 1917 Charge of Beersheba, was *the* most important event involving him.

'No ... the charge was important. I'm not saying that it wasn't. But I think in the family history Beersheba was just a part of a greater story in which many significant things, with considerable political implications flowing from them, happened.'[1]

Beginning with his grandmother, who lovingly preserved in a series of scrapbooks the letters and photographs charting her husband's life, Richard Chauvel's family have contributed enormously to the cultural promotion of the light-horsemen.

Sir Harry's daughter Elyne Mitchell penned the much-loved 'Silver Brumby' books—the product of an imagination sparked by her father's exploits and her own accomplishment as a horsewoman, as both a child riding with Sir Harry and later on her vast property in north-eastern Victoria. Elyne, who married Tom Mitchell, a son of the squattocracy, also more directly charted her father's achievement in the Middle East in another children's novel, *Light Horse to Damascus*.[2]

Meanwhile Elyne's cousin, Charles Chauvel, produced and directed *Forty Thousand Horsemen*. Shot in and around Sydney, including in the dunes around

Cronulla, and starring Chips Rafferty, this movie eulo-
gised the horsemen and recreated the famous charge.
The horsemen were portrayed as the penultimate good
guys, the Turks as singularly evil and the everyday Arab
as something of a comic foil to both.

~

I leave Chauvel's grandson and go across town to East
Jerusalem to meet friends. I bump into my real-life
Palestinian comic foil, Rasheed.

'Hey, Mr Paul—how do you like your long time in
Be'er Sheva?' he asks.

I tell him it felt, as he'd predicted, like a long time.
But what I don't tell him is that I also felt an intense
connection with a place that is dormant in Australia's
national consciousness.

Be'er Sheva, the desert capital, is not beautiful. It
is not especially welcoming or friendly. Its climate is
oppressive and, stuck out there in the Negev just a
stone's throw from Gaza, it is highly susceptible to
Hamas rocket attacks. But Be'er Sheva nonetheless
represents the future of Israel's settlement of the
Negev—a future that began when the daring charge of
the light-horsemen helped steal Beersheba, the town
within it, from the Turks on 31 October 1917. Be'er
Sheva lacks Tel Aviv's exciting cosmopolitanism, its hip
Mediterranean vibe and its party atmosphere. And it
has nothing of Jerusalem's enchanting history and
constant edginess.

As if to mimic what he considered to be an Australian insult, the driver had described Be'er Sheva to me as a 'bastard of a place'. Perhaps that's what the Australian light-horsemen first thought of Beersheba, too, when they first saw it across the dusty plains on the day of the great battle. But it should be remembered that to Australians, 'bastard' is both a pejorative and a term of endearment. And you can't help but feel, when you spend time in Be'er Sheva, that you are stumbling through a piece of 'bastard' Australian history, too—a unique place that links Australia to Israel and Palestine, but one that—unlike Gallipoli and Kokoda, Long Tan and the Western Front—we have yet to truly embrace.

I know now why I was continually drawn to that peaceful British War Cemetery at Be'er Sheva, with its lush lawn, its gum trees and its grevilleas, its gentle Bedouin gardeners and its towering date palms. Quite simply, I felt as if I was with my kind there, among the young Australian dead, with their immaculately kept graves and stories half-told.

The next morning I am heading back to Israel's desert capital in a car with Peter Corlett, an acclaimed Melbourne sculptor. He has been back and forth to Be'er Sheva for weeks installing his life-size bronze sculpture of a light-horseman breaching the trenches during the famous charge. The sculpture, commissioned by Richard Pratt for whom he has completed commissions previously, is the key feature of the philanthropist's Park of the Australian Soldier, due to be opened the next day.

Corlett has spent thousands of hours creating the statue to Pratt's very precise specifications. The opening of the park will be a big deal; the Australian and Israeli heads of state and numerous ministers will be there. Corlett's sculpture will be the focal point—the symbol, as Pratt wanted us to view it, of the part Australia played in Israel's genesis.

As we drive, the sculptor looks out the window at the straw-coloured fields and the washed-out sky. 'I want you to look at this landscape and tell me if we're not in New South Wales. We could be driving on the Hume,' he says.

We are not, of course. I am heading for Beersheba. Again.

EPILOGUE

Passover has finally passed, and the bar at the big hotel in Be'er Sheva is jumping. Australian soldiers and members of the Light Horse Association are swarming around the bar, lured as much by the two swarthy young barmaids as by the cold beers and the Bundy and Cokes. It'll be the making of blazing hangovers for some of the men who, the next afternoon, must stare into the sun while holding the regimental pennants of the Australian light horse aloft during the ceremony to open Richard Pratt's park.

It's a hot afternoon. But the park is a shady oasis in modern Be'er Sheva's dusty outer metropolis. The Pratt Foundation has thought of everything and spared little expense. Special showbags, containing broad-brimmed hats and bottles of water, are given to each invitee. Throughout the vast park comfortable lounges and bars have been set up for the guests. Some people with a special link to the Beersheba story have been flown in.

As the beginning of the ceremony approaches Richard Pratt and his wife arrive, having flown to Israel on their private jet. He is a big man, towering and broad. Dressed in a dark suit and with his hands folded behind his back, he walks funereally—appearing to almost glide—down the main path of his park, inspecting the play equipment for disabled children and the plaques that tell the story of the light horse. He is escorted by Sam Lipski. Pratt looks tentative, unwell, detached and nervous—little wonder, perhaps, given the significant turn-out by the Australian media to what is one of his first major public appearances since the initial court action involving his company was settled. Not too many people know how desperately ill he is. He will die of cancer a year later to the day.

There is a long and moving ceremony. Australia's Governor General Michael Jeffery speaks like the former soldier he is, of muscle and grit. As he prepares to speak, an Israeli fighter jet leaves its mark in the form of a sonic boom overhead. Guests jump.

'The sounds of thousands of hoof beats on the desert sand, the sweat, the leather, men and animals being hit and then into the trench line. Close up, hand-to-hand stuff, rifle butt or bayonet doing its grisly work.'

But the Israeli President Shimon Peres, also a former soldier, seeks and finds a more spiritually rousing tone. He speaks so softly, so barely audibly, that the crowd must strain to hear. The Australians among us are left wanting national leaders who have a capacity to similarly stir our emotions.

'The terrorists who lost the war gained a future,' he says of the Ottoman Turks who went on to construct, from the ashes of humiliating defeat, the modern secular state of Turkey. 'I cannot think of a more courageous confrontation than a man on a horse with a bayonet in his hand fighting face to face,' he said, describing the charge as 'the most courageous, most romantic battle of times'.

'I don't think anyone here remembers the First World War, but we remember the Second World War, and your troops came again to help fight the Nazis— another danger—and I think the Israelis fell in love with your boys. We loved [them] from the first sight—and we didn't change our minds the next day. They are soldiers but they are most perfect soldiers. Men of decision and men of care. The feeling in this country for them is deep, permanent and sincere. Today we don't fight other soldiers, we fight the desert … it is either that we shall overcome the desert or the desert shall overcome us.'

Then the words of Ion Idriess are appropriately invoked to remind guests of the 'berserk gallop' of the light-horsemen and how their 'mad shouts' as they feverishly attacked the Turkish trenches that day, echoed through the hills around Beersheba: 'Then came a whirlwind of movement from all over the field, galloping batteries—dense dust from mounting regiments— a rush as troops poured for the opening in the gathering dark—mad, mad excitement—terrific explosions from down in the town. Beersheba had fallen.'[1]

Many guests are, by now, close to tears as Corlett's statue is unveiled.

Those moved to the emotional precipice by Peres and Idriess are pushed over by a Turkish diplomat who lays a wreath at the base of Corlett's statue. Turkey's dead, unlike Australia's, are not resting in the immaculately kept cemetery at Be'er Sheva. Rather, the bones of thousands of Turkish soldiers are scattered randomly in the earth and under acres of concrete across this vast desert city. Many are in mass graves—perhaps, it is said, on the flat, dusty earth over which the Australians charged.

As the diplomat stands and turns to walk back to his seat, he stops before Australia's head of state, Jeffery, and nods. Both men smile. What was left unsaid here could never be said.

Spontaneous applause—hesitant at first, then deafening—fills the place.

Then there is a call for those in uniform to salute. Barry Rodgers and his men from the Light Horse Association, dressed in their World War I uniforms replete with slouch hats and emu plumes, stand in their places. They hold their salutes with the same rigour as the serving military men and women.

As the official guests depart, Pratt lingers with his coterie of minders and friends. He seems reticent and nervous as he explains that the park was built because his oldest mate, Digger James 'wanted to do something to commemorate a battle'. 'The battle of the Light Brigade seemed to me to be an appropriate battle. It includes Israel, it includes Australia. I'm an Australian first, but I have affection for Israel and I sympathise with their problems,' he says.

~

John Cox is milling in the crowd nearby, close to Richard Chauvel and his wife Janet. John, the son of

Jack Cox—a born adventurer and Beersheba hero who foiled the Turkish machine-gunners during the charge—stands with his wife Nancy.

He is beaming. His eyes moisten as he talks again about a long-dead father whom he helped nurse when he was dying; a father who was recommended for, but never received, a Victoria Cross; a father who, only when close to death, finally confided in his son all the stories he'd kept to himself while full of life.

'You know, he and I were so totally different,' John says. 'He was this adventurer type—you know, he even tried to join up—lied about his age—for the Second World War. He did all these things and I spent my working life in a bank. He had an amazing life—amazing.' He shrugs his shoulders. 'I've never quite worked it out just how we could be so different.'

It's part of the great mystery that binds us to our fathers. And our sons. And our sons to us.

John's wife Nancy says to me: 'He died fifty years ago. But he still misses him, you know?'

Yes.

~

There are Australian accents everywhere. Young Australians appear to have come straight from that fixture on the backpackers' map—Anzac Day at Gallipoli. I find them a curiously confronting sight, dressed in thongs, boardies and Victoria Bitter singlets, and shrouded in Australian flags.

Flag-wearing makes me and many other Australians uncomfortable. I challenge myself: 'What's wrong with wearing the Australian flag like this?' In Israel, after all, the flag is both a proud sign of hard-won nationhood and a defiant symbol of land ownership or occupation, military presence and protection. We do not fly our Australian flag with the same purpose or intent at home, and in recent years wearing it has became synonymous with gauche forms of nationalism imbued with racial overtones. I tell myself that young Australians wearing the flag that day represents, surely, little more than a proud acknowledgement of Australia's place in Israel's history. The discomfort lingers, regardless.

The young flag-wearers flock to Joe Hockey, a huge bear of a man who exudes an easygoing, blokey charm. He signs autographs. It is ninety-one years since his fellow conservative politician and predecessor as the member for North Sydney, Sir Granville Ryrie, helped take Beersheba, a small Ottoman town where Hockey's grandfather, Joseph Hokeidonian, would soon live and work. Joseph Hokeidonian's Beersheba is long gone, swallowed by the vast metropolis of Be'er Sheva—the place where his grandson stands today.

The deep emotional resonance of all this is not lost on the Armenian–Palestinian–Australian Hockey when he quips: 'I reckon I'm ready to charge the trenches ... It'd need to be a bloody big horse, though, wouldn't it?'

No bigger than any horse ridden by Ryrie, who was, after all, the second-biggest bloke to take to an Australian saddle in Palestine.

On the way out of the park I stop to take a closer look at Peter Corlett's magnificent statue. The horse is in full flight while the soldier leans forward into the trench, the bayonet in his right hand poised to strike home. The face of the light-horseman is frozen as it contorts to utter one of Idriess's mad shouts. It is the face of a young Digger James. It is Pratt's gift to James—a better mate than most men could hope for. And so, their friendship from boyhood will be immortalised not in Australia, but here, in this dusty Israeli city on the edge of the desert just down the road from Gaza.

Beersheba.

ACKNOWLEDGEMENTS

Sometimes it takes somebody else to recognise a good idea. So it was with this book.

My fascination with the subject of the Australian light horse began more than two decades ago when, as a greener than green cadet journalist, I interviewed an old soldier, Lionel Simpson. Like all the light-horsemen, he died many years ago now—but not without inadvertently planting the seeds of the following story. If I could thank him today I would. So, too, would I thank the men of the Australian light horse whose letters, diaries and memories helped to drive this book.

In the years after my meetings with Lionel Simpson, I often talked to my friends and family about this old man and his descriptions of the momentous military event he had witnessed: the 1917 charge of the Australian light horse at Beersheba. But it was nothing more than a conversation piece. It took somebody else to identify within my patchy nostalgic memories the first threads of a complex narrative tapestry about courage and war, about fathers and sons, about history and integrity, about memory and truth. My wife, Lenore Taylor, a journalist of exceptional talent and dedication, and an endlessly supportive partner, must take credit for this.

It's not easy for the children of people whose lives involve long absences from home. Eugenia, Joe and Claudia have always lamented (if not entirely patiently) my departures and embraced my returns. Their unconditional love makes my world.

Louise Adler, chief executive of Melbourne University Publishing, was quick to see the potential of this story. She has been endlessly enthusiastic and encouraging. So, too, has MUP's executive publisher, Foong Ling Kong. She patiently steered me onto a narrative track when I was, at times, dispirited and struggling for voice. Thanks also to Cathryn Game for applying a critical eye and sound perspective to this work, and to Phil Campbell for the cover design.

Thanks also to Sam Lipski of the Pratt Foundation. Sam was an enthusiastic supporter of this project from the start, without ever attempting to be censorious or interfering.

Thanks, also, to Joe Hockey and his father Richard for letting me into their family's story, with all its rich connections to Beersheba.

Robert Unicomb and his mother, Patricia Unicomb, generously granted me access to the diaries, maps and treasured photographs of Ernest Pauls, their light horse grandfather and father. Thank you.

I'd also like to extend my appreciation to Kelvin Crombie, who so generously imparted to me his knowledge and time on the trail of the light horse in Israel. Thanks also to Barry Rodgers and Phil Chalker, Richard Chauvel and Valerie Howse. I'd like to especially acknowledge Rika Ashahi Harel for helping me to appreciate the movements of the horsemen in and around Jerusalem and for pointing me in the right direction for

Abraham's Well. Thanks, too, Matt Brown and Toni O'Loughlin, for your generous hospitality and sage perspectives on Israeli and Palestinian issues while I was in Jerusalem, and to Susan McMinn, whose sense of humour and eye for detail helped my story enormously. I would also like to express my appreciation to the Israeli academic Chanan Reich, to Lt Col. Doug Wyatt and to Terry Kinloch.

This is a book about mates. So I'd like to thank the best of mine—Peter Fray, Mick Collopy, Michael Bowers, Ian McPhedran, Paul Cleary, Michael Brissenden, Tony Wright and Chris Hammer—for supporting this idea from the start. Thanks also to Bruce Haigh, John Cox, Yigal Sheffy, Eran Dolev, Gabi Chan and Eugenie Baulch from MUP.

My mother Margaret, my sister Cathie and her husband Mick have never wavered in supporting me along the path I have chosen. The same must be said of my father, Patrick. He would, I now feel sure, have understood.

~

I read widely while preparing this book, but I would like to give special acknowledgement and thanks to the following authors and their work: Ian Jones, *A Thousand Miles of Battles: The Saga of the Australian Light Horse in World War I* (Anzac Day Commemoration Committee, 2007); Terry Kinloch, *Devils on Horses: In the Words of the Anzacs in the Middle East 1916–19* (Exisle Publishing,

2007); Ion Idriess, *The Desert Column: Leaves from the Diary of an Australian Trooper in Gallipoli, Sinai and Palestine* (Angus & Robertson, Sydney, 1932); Kelvin Crombie, *Anzacs, Empires and Israel's Restoration* (Nicolayson's, Jerusalem, 1998); AB 'Banjo' Paterson, *Happy Dispatches* (Angus & Robertson, Sydney, 1934); Alec Hill, *Chauvel of the Light Horse: A Biography of Sir Harry Chauvel* (Melbourne University Press, Melbourne, 1978); Lieutenant Colonel Neil C Smith, *Men of Beersheba: A History of the 4th Light Horse Regiment* (Mostly Unsung Military History Research and Publications, Melbourne, 1993); Lindsay Baly, *Horseman, Pass By: The Australian Light Horse in World War I* (Simon & Schuster, Sydney, 2003); Doug Wyatt, 'The Surafend Incident, 10 December 1918' in PJ Pickering, *Tasmania's AIF Lighthorsemen C Squadron 3rd Light Horse Regiment* (self-published, Ridgeway, Tas., 2006); Patsy Adam-Smith, *The ANZACs* (Thomas Nelson, Melbourne, 1978); Rex Hall, *The Desert Hath Pearls* (The Hawthorn Press, Melbourne, 1975); Lawrence James, *Imperial Warrior: The Life and Times of Field Marshal Viscount Allenby 1861–1936* (Weidenfeld and Nicholson, London, 1993); EM Andrews, *The Anzac Illusion: Anglo-Australian Relations during World War I* (Cambridge University Press, 1994) and Yigal Sheffy, *British Military Intelligence in the Palestine Campaign 1914–1918* (Frank Cass, London, 1998).

I would also like to thank the staff in the Research Centre at the Australian War Memorial for their courtesy and diligence in finding elusive files. Thanks also to the Liddell Hart Centre for Military Archives at King's College, London, and also to the researchers at New Zealand Archives in Wellington.

Paul Daley
Canberra

NOTES

Prologue

1   Henry Gullett, *Official History of Australia in the War of 1914–1918*, Vol. 7: *The Australian Imperial Force in Sinai and Palestine 1914–1918*, Angus & Robertson, Sydney, 3rd edn, 1937, p. 249 (hereafter Gullett, *Sinai and Palestine*).

1 Hebron Road

1   Gullett, *Sinai and Palestine*, p. 249.

2 Bushmen of the Empire

1   AB Paterson, *Happy Dispatches*, Angus & Robertson, Sydney, 1934, chapter 16, at http://setis.library.usyd.edu.au/ozlit/pdf/p00055.pdf.
2   Ian Jones, *A Thousand Miles of Battles: The Saga of the Australian Light Horse in WWI*, Anzac Day Commemoration Committee, Aspley, Queensland, 2007, p. 4.
3   Gullett, *Sinai and Palestine*, p. 30.
4   ibid., p. 31.
5   Lionel Simpson, interview with author, *Mail Express* (Melton), 9 September 1987, p. 2.
6   Ion Idriess, *The Desert Column: Leaves from the Diary of an Australian Trooper in Gallipoli, Sinai and Palestine*, Angus & Robertson, Sydney, 1932, p. 62.
7   ibid., foreword.
8   Idriess, diary, 12 July 1916, AWM 1DRL/0373.

9   Barry Rodgers, interview with author, Canberra, March 2008.

10   Gullett, *Sinai and Palestine*, p. 39.

11   Jones, *A Thousand Miles of Battles*, p. 4.

3 Sideshow in Sinai

1   *Australian Light Horse*, Department of Veterans' Affairs, 2007, p. 21.

2   Gullett, *Sinai and Palestine*, p. 47.

3   ibid., p. 71.

4   RJ Dunk, typescript, AWM PR00469.

5   Gullett, *Sinai and Palestine*, pp. 60–1.

6   ibid., pp. 60–1.

7   ibid., p. 81.

8   Idriess, *Desert Column*, p. 60.

9   Gullett, *Sinai and Palestine*, pp. 59–60.

10   ibid., pp. 185, 103.

11   Jones, *A Thousand Miles of Battles*, p. 70.

12   Lindsay Baly, *Horseman, Pass By: The Australian Light Horse in World War I*, Simon & Schuster, Sydney, 2003, p. 101.

4 Mystery Joe

1   Gullett, *Sinai and Palestine*, pp. 384–5.

2   Richard Hokeidonian, interview with author, 2 April 2008.

5 Legends of Romani

1   Jones, *A Thousand Miles of Battles*, p. 42.

2   Gullett, *Sinai and Palestine*, p. 88.

3   ibid.

4   ibid., p. 89.
5   ibid., p. 90.
6   ibid.
7   ibid., pp. 60–1.
8   Tony Wright, 'The Woman from Snowy River', *Bulletin*, 12 December 2001.
9   Richard Chauvel, interview with author, Jerusalem, 26 April 2008.
10 Gullett, *Sinai and Palestine*, p. 144.
11 Idriess, *Desert Column*, p. 101.
12 Gullett, *Sinai and Palestine*, p. 157.
13 ibid., p. 150.
14 Idriess, *Desert Column*, p. 102.
15 ibid., p. 103.
16 ibid., p. 106.
17 Jones, *A Thousand Miles of Battles*, p. 54.
18 Idriess, diary, undated but describing events of 5–6 August 1916, AWM 1DRL/0373.
19 Idriess, *Desert Column*, p. 144.
20 Gullett, *Sinai and Palestine*, p. 192.
21 ibid.

6 Ghosts of the desert

1   Simpson, interview, 9 September 1987.
2   Ernest Pauls, Diary of a Lighthorseman: Trooper Ernest Pauls 1891–1969, 30 August 1916, copy in author's possession (hereafter Pauls, Diary).
3   Pauls, *Diary*, 8 and 10 September 1916.
4   Gullett, *Sinai and Palestine*, p. 206.
5   Idriess, diary, November 1916.
6   Gullett, *Sinai and Palestine*, p. 207.
7   Idriess, *Desert Column*, p. 162.
8   Gullett, *Sinai and Palestine*, p. 208.

9   Idriess, *Desert Column*, p. 165.
10   Gullett, *Sinai and Palestine*, p. 226.
11   Idriess, *Desert Column*, p. 164.
12   Chauvel, letter, 7 February 1917, Papers of General Sir Henry George Chauvel, AWM PR00535, Series 4: Family correspondence, 1887–1937 (hereafter Chauvel Papers).
13   ibid.
14   Gullett, *Sinai and Palestine*, p. 228.

7 Badlands

1   Idriess, *Desert Column*, p. 185.
2   Gullett, *Sinai and Palestine*, pp. 252–3.
3   Jones, *A Thousand Miles of Battles*, p. 68.
4   Idriess, *Desert Column*, p. 190.
5   Gullett, *Sinai and Palestine*, p. 279.
6   Idriess, *Desert Column*, pp. 193–4.
7   ibid., pp. 197–201.
8   Gullett, *Sinai and Palestine*, pp. 284, 287.
9   ibid., p. 295.
10   Quoted in ibid., p. 296.
11   Pauls, Diary, 19 April 1917.
12   ibid.
13   Gullett, *Sinai and Palestine*, p. 327.
14   Idriess, diary, undated section headed 'Gaza', referring to April battle, AWM 1DRL/0373.

8 The Bull arrives

1   Gullett, *Sinai and Palestine*, p. 335.
2   Paterson, *Happy Dispatches*, p. 81.
3   Sergeant Charles Doherty, 12th Light Horse Regiment, unpublished MS, AWM PR01376.
4   Sir Harry Chauvel, letter to Lady Chauvel, 3 May 1917, Chauvel Papers.

9 Beersheba

1 Gullett, *Sinai and Palestine*, p. 379.
2 ibid., p. 380.
3 ibid.
4 Jones, *A Thousand Miles of Battles*, p. 98.
5 Pauls, Diary, 29, 30 and 31 October 1917.
6 Lance Sergeant Patrick Hamilton, 4th Light Horse Field Ambulance, manuscript account of Battle of Beersheba, AWM 3DRL/3826 (hereafter Hamilton, manuscript).
7 Doherty, unpublished MS, AWM PR01376.
8 Idriess, *Desert Column*, pp. 248–9.
9 ibid., p. 249.
10 Gullett, *Sinai and Palestine*, p. 390.
11 Edward Harold O'Brien, C Squadron, 3rd Light Horse Regiment, interviewed by Major Douglas Wyatt, 1988, AWM S00681 (hereafter O'Brien, interview).
12 Gullett, *Sinai and Palestine*, p. 393.
13 ibid.
14 Doherty, unpublished MS, AWM PR01376.
15 Pauls, Diary, 1 November 1917.

10 Neck or nothing

1 Doherty, unpublished MS, AWM PR01376.
2 Lieutenant Colonel Neil C Smith, *Men of Beersheba: A History of the 4th Light Horse Regiment*, Mostly Unsung Military History Research and Publications, Melbourne, 1993, p. 122.
3 Major James Lawson, letter to sister of Trooper Edward Randolph Cleaver, 14 January 1918, in Cleaver papers, AWM 3DRL/4114.
4 Jones, *A Thousand Miles of Battles*, p. 113.

5 Trooper Phil Moon, quoted in Jones, *A Thousand Miles of Battles*, p. 113.
6 Hamilton, manuscript.
7 Gullett, *Sinai and Palestine*, p. 398.
8 ibid.
9 Pauls, Diary, 1 November 1917.
10 Gullett, *Sinai and Palestine*, p. 400.
11 Trooper Edward Dengate, 12th Regiment, letter, 17 January 1918, AWM 3DRL/7678.
12 War diary, 4th Regiment, 31 October 1917, AWM4, 10/9/34.
13 Lieutenant Colonel Murray Bourchier, letter, 5 November 1917, AWM 2DRL/0444.
14 Chauvel, letter to wife, 1 November 1917, Chauvel Papers.
15 Gullett, *Sinai and Palestine*, p. 404.
16 Pauls, Diary, 2 November 1917.
17 Lionel Simpson, interviews with author, *Sunday Observer* (Melbourne), *Mail Express* (Melton), 1987, 1988.
18 Gullett, *Sinai and Palestine*, p. 412.
19 Hamilton, manuscript.
20 Idriess, *Desert Column*, p. 252.

11 Oasis for the dead

1 Pauls, Diary, 1 November 1917.
2 Jim Gallagher, State Library Victoria, MS Box 2564/6.
3 GP Walsh, 'Cotter, Albert (Tibby) (1883–1917)', *Australian Dictionary of Biography*, www.adb.online.anu.edu.au/biogs/A080131b.htm.
4 Gullett, *Sinai and Palestine*, p. 327.
5 Ian Jones, 'Beersheba: The Light Horse Charges and the Making of Myths', *Journal of the Australian War Memorial*, no. 3, October 1983, pp. 26–37.

6 Hamilton, manuscript.

7 ibid.

8 ibid.

9 Trooper Edward Randolph Cleaver, letter, 10 June 1917, Cleaver papers, AWM 3DRL/4114 (hereafter Cleaver papers).

10 Cleaver, letter, 27 August 1917, Cleaver papers.

11 Cleaver, letter, 9 October 1917, Cleaver papers.

12 Cleaver, letter, 10 October 1917, Cleaver papers.

13 Cleaver, letter, 26 October 1917, Cleaver papers.

14 Lawson, letter, Cleaver papers.

15 Lieutenant Edward Ralston, 12th Australian Light Horse Regiment, letter, papers of Trooper Ernest J Craggs, AWM 3DRL/7812.

13 Serendipity

1 Joe Hockey, *Hansard*, at http://joehockey.com/mediahub/speechDetail.aspx?prID=50.

2 Allenby, quoted in *Argus*, 15 November 1917.

3 Joe Hockey, quoted here and below, interviews with author, Canberra, 17 March and 22 September 2008.

14 Cobbers

1 O'Brien, interview.

2 Digger James, here and all subsequent quotes, from interview with author, Brisbane, 10 April 2008.

3 Cameron Stewart, *Australian*, 6 October 2007.

4 See 'Who's who in Australian military history: Air Vice Marshal Francis Hubert (Frank) McNamara, VC, CB, CBE', Australian War Memorial, www.awm.gov.au/people/258.asp.

5   David Flint, 'Beersheba and Philanthopy', On Line
    Opinion, 9 April 2008, www.onlineopinion.com.au/
    view.asp?article=7215.

15 Hoarding the legend

1   Susan McMinn, interview with author, Canberra,
    24 July 2008.
2   Gullett, *Sinai and Palestine*, pp. 60–1.
3   Phil Chalker, interview with author, Queanbeyan,
    NSW, 19 March 2008.
4   Valerie Howse, interview with author, Canberra, 4 April
    2008.
5   Rupert Downes, diaries, 3rd Series, DRL No. 0518,
    AWM 12/11/5484.
6   Alec Hill, *Chauvel of the Light Horse: A Biography of
    Sir Harry Chauvel*, Melbourne University Press,
    Melbourne, 1978, pp. 182–3.
7   Liddell Hart Centre for Military Archives (hereafter
    Liddell Hart Centre), King's College, London, Allenby
    2/5/7.
8   Liddell Hart Centre, Allenby 7/4/1.
9   ibid.
10 Chalker, interview with author, Be'er Sheva, 27 April
    2008.
11 Sam Lipski, interview with author, Canberra, 3 April
    2008.

16 Inside Jaffa Gate

1   Balfour Declaration, 2 November 1917, Israel Ministry
    of Foreign Affairs, www.mfa.gov.il/MFA/Peace+Process/
    Guide+to+the+Peace+Process/The+Balfour+Declaration.
    htm.

2   Kelvin Crombie, quotes here and below, interview with
    author, Jerusalem, 16 April 2008.
3   Kelvin Crombie, *Anzacs, Empires and Israel's
    Restoration 1788–1948*, Nicolayson's Ltd, Jerusalem,
    Israel, 1998.
4   ibid., p. 181.

17 Desert dogs

1   Gullett, *Sinai and Palestine*, p. 344.

18 The hand of God

1   Gullett, *Sinai and Palestine*, p. 436.
2   ibid., p. 341.
3   ibid., p. 365.
4   Patsy Adam-Smith, *The ANZACS*, Thomas Nelson,
    Melbourne, 1978, pp. 316–18.
5   ibid.

19 Last drinks

1   Jim Gallagher, letter, February 1918, State Library of
    Victoria (SLV), MS Box 2564/6.
2   SLV, MS Box 2564/6.
3   Gullett, *Sinai and Palestine*, p. 376.
4   Idriess, *Desert Column*, p. 244.
5   Gullett, *Sinai and Palestine*, pp. 378–9.

20 Waiting for rockets

1   Jones, *A Thousand Miles of Battles*, pp. 91–3.
2   Paterson, *Happy Dispatches*, p. 83.
3   Jones, *A Thousand Miles of Battles*, p. 93.
4   Yigal Sheffy, *British Military Intelligence in the
    Palestine Campaign 1914–1918*, Frank Cass, London,
    England, 1998, p. 273.

21 Cop this, dear Jacko

1 Gullett, *Sinai and Palestine*, p. 414.
2 ibid., p. 429.
3 Pauls, Diary, 6 December 1917.
4 Gullett, *Sinai and Palestine*, p. 704.
5 ibid., p. 708.
6 ibid., p. 710.
7 ibid., p. 725.
8 ibid., p. 726.
9 ibid., p. 727.
10 ibid., p. 755.

22 The massacre

1 Chanan Reich, interview with author, Melbourne, 28 March 2008.
2 Paterson, *Happy Dispatches*, p. 88.
3 Gullett, *Sinai and Palestine*, p. 529.
4 Robert Ellwood, 'Relations with the Local Population', War Memories of Robert Ellwood, www.jcu.edu.au/aff/history/net_resources/ellwood/ellwood09.htm.
5 ibid.
6 Trooper Ambrose Stephen Mulhall, 3rd Light Horse Regiment, letter to GJ Bell, 12 September 1936, in possession of Douglas Wyatt, Tasmania.
7 Adam-Smith, *The ANZACS*, p. 313.
8 Gullett, *Sinai and Palestine*, pp. 788–9.
9 Terry Kinloch, *Devils on Horses: In the Words of the Anzacs in the Middle East 1916–19*, Exisle Publishing, Waitakere, NZ, 2007, p. 332.
10 War diary, 2nd Light Horse Brigade, AWM4, 10/2/48, p. 3.
11 Covering note, 'Proceedings of a Court of Inquiry assembled at Wadi Hanein to enquire into the part

played by the 2nd Light Horse Brigade in a raid on
Surafend on 10 December 1918', AWM 27 357/11
(hereafter 'Proceedings').

12 War diary, 2nd Light Horse Brigade, p. 3.

23 Allenby and the Anzacs

1 Eric Montgomery Andrews, *The Anzac Illusion:
Anglo-Australian Relations during World War I*,
Cambridge University Press, Melbourne, 1993,
p. 165.

2 Paterson, *Happy Dispatches*, p. 83.

3 ibid.

4 Gullett, *Sinai and Palestine*, p. 332.

5 ibid., p. 790.

6 Mulhall, letter to GJ Bell, 12 September 1936.

7 O'Brien, interview.

8 Paterson, *Happy Dispatches*, chapter 16.

9 Ellwood, 'Relations with the Local Population'.

10 Lawrence James, *Imperial Warrior: The Life and Times
of Field Marshal Viscount Allenby: 1861–1936*,
Weidenfeld & Nicolson, London, England 1993,
p. 184.

11 Warrant Officer Nick Curtain, interview, June 1989,
AWM S00682.

12 James, *Imperial Warrior*, p. 183.

13 ibid.

14 Gullett, *Sinai and Palestine*, p. 789.

15 War diary, 6th Light Horse Regiment, December 1918,
AWM4 10/11/49.

16 War diary, 3rd Light Horse Regiment, December 1918,
AWM4 10/8/49.

17 ibid.

18   Major Claude Easterbrook, 2nd Brigade, 'Proceedings'.
19   ibid.
20   Corporal Barton, 6th Regiment, 'Proceedings'.
21   Sergeant Henry Fotheringham, 6th Regiment,
       'Proceedings'.
22   Trooper H. S. Spaven, 6th Regiment, 'Proceedings'.
23   ibid.
24   ibid.
25   ibid.
26   ibid.
27   Trooper Bodinnar, 6th Regiment, 'Proceedings'.
28   Captain Thompson, 2nd Brigade Field Ambulance,
       'Proceedings'.
29   Lieutenant RB Stocks, 'Proceedings'.
30   Lieutenant ER Mayes, 2nd Brigade, 'Proceedings'.
31   Troop Sergeant Saunders, 'Proceedings'.
32   Lieutenant Colonel Richard Andrew, undated notes
       (January 1918–October 1919), Liddell Hart Centre,
       Allenby 6/9.

24 A real bad thing

 1   This and all subsequent quotes from O'Brien come
       from his interview with Douglas Wyatt, 1988, AWM
       S00681.
 2   Douglas Wyatt, telephone interview with author,
       20 August 2008.
 3   ibid.
 4   DM Wyatt, 'The Surafend Incident, 10 December
       1918', in PJ Pickering, *Tasmania's AIF Lighthorsemen
       C Squadron 3rd Light Horse Regiment*, self-published,
       Ridgeway, Tasmania, 2006.
 5   ibid.

25 Inconvenient truth

1 Ambrose Stephen Mulhall, letter to George Bell, 12 September 1936, in possession of Douglas Wyatt, Tasmania.

2 Corporal Herbert James Boorman, 6th Regiment, 'Proceedings'.

3 Paterson, *Happy Dispatches*, chapter 17, p. 88; Gullett, *Sinai and Palestine*, p. 789; James, *Imperial Warrior*, p. 183; *Official War History of the Wellington Mounted Rifles Regiment 1914–1919*, www.nzetc.org/ tm/scholarly/tei-WH1-Moun.html.

4 Gullett, *Sinai and Palestine*, p. 791.

5 ibid., p. 790.

6 ibid., p. 791.

7 James, *Imperial Warrior*, p. 184.

8 William Bell, letter to Douglas Wyatt, 20 July 1990.

9 ibid.

10 William Bell, 'Bell, Sir George KCMG DSO VD (Colonel)', biographical notes, AWM, 3DRL/3601.

26 Burying the past

1 Mulhall, letter to George Pearce, 17 July 1936, National Archives, series A981/Item: PERS 237.

2 ibid.

3 Pearce secretary, letter to Mulhall, 22 October 1936.

4 Sir Archdale Parkhill, letter to George Pearce, 26 November 1936.

5 Lyons, Hansard, 22 October 1936.

27 Blood money

1 *Times*, 17 September 1919, available at http://archive. timesonline.co.uk/tol/archive.

2   *Times*, 25 September 1919.

3   *Times*, 8 October 1919.

4   ibid.

5   Rex Hall, *The Desert Hath Pearls*, Hawthorn Press, Melbourne, 1975, p. 108.

6   ibid., pp. 110, 108.

7   Hill, *Chauvel of the Light Horse*, pp. 192–3.

8   Lachlan Coleman, 'The Surafend Incident', *Wartime*, issue 39, 2007, http://www.awm.gov.au/wartime/39/index.asp.

9   Harry Chauvel, letter to Archibald Percival Wavell, 13 October 1936, Liddell Hart Centre, Allenby 6/9.

10 *Sydney Morning Herald*, 18 January 1926, available at National Archives of Australia.

11 Harry Chauvel, letter to Wavell, to assist with Wavell's biography of Allenby, 13 October 1936, Liddell Hart Centre, Allenby 6/9.

12 Lieutenant Colonel HV Avery, letter, 19 February 1921, 'Burning of Surafend Village, Palestine', Archives New Zealand/Te Rua Mahara o te Kā wanatanga Wellington Office, AD 10/1 2/10.B (hereafter ANZ).

13 Major White, War Office, letter to Lieutenant Colonel Avery, 7 May 1921, ANZ.

14 Avery to NZ High Commissoner, 'Burning of Surafend Village, Palestine', ANZ.

15 Cyril Falls, *Armageddon, 1918: The Final Palestinian Campaign of World War I*, Weidenfeld & Nicholson, London, England, 1964.

16 *Times*, 19 May 1964.

17 ibid.

18 *Times*, 29 May 1964.

28 A bastard of a place

1   Richard Chauvel, interview with author, Jerusalem, Israel, 26 April 2008.
2   Elyne Mitchell, *Light Horse to Damascus*, Hutchinson, Melbourne, 1971.

Epilogue

1   Idriess, *Desert Column*, p. 252.

INDEX